TRULY
OURSELVES
TRULY THE
SPIRIT'S

Reflections on Life in the Spirit

TRULY
OURSELVES

TRULY THE
SPIRIT'S

Reflections on Life in the Spirit

LAURENCE W. WOOD
Foreword by Dennis F. Kinlaw

FRANCIS ASBURY PRESS
of Zondervan Publishing House

Grand Rapids. Michigan

Truly Ourselves, Truly the Spirit's
Copyright © 1989 by Laurence W. Wood

Francis Asbury Press is an imprint of Zondervan Publishing House,
1415 Lake Drive, S.E., Grand Rapids, Michigan 49506.

Library of Congress Cataloging in Publication Data

Wood, Laurence W.
    Truly ourselves, truly the Spirit's : reflections on life in the spirit /
Laurence W. Wood.
       p. cm.
    Bibliography: p.
    ISBN 0-310-75051-2
    1. Holy Spirit—Meditations. 2. Spiritual life—Methodist authors. I.
Title.
    BT121.2.W63 1989
    231'.3—dc20   89-31919
                                                 CIP

Edited by Robert D. Wood

Printed in the United States of America

89 90 91 92 93 94 95 96 / AK / 10 9 8 7 6 5 4 3 2 1

To
Mary, my wife
and our children
Laura, Daniel, Christy, and Andrew

CONTENTS

FOREWORD

The Wesleyan Revival in the eighteenth century prepared the way for rediscovery of the relevance and power of the Holy Spirit which is so evident in the life of believers throughout the church today. The early Methodist preachers proclaimed across the frontiers of America the sanctifying grace of the Spirit. The camp meeting movement of the nineteenth and early twentieth centuries promoted a Spirit-filled message that offered believers a power for successful Christian living. Gradually, almost imperceptibly, the dynamic of a Spirit-filled life has become an aspiration throughout the Christian church and has penetrated a wide range of communions.

Dr. Laurence W. Wood is himself the product of the Wesleyan movement with its message of the deeper life of the Spirit. He is the Frank Paul Morris Professor of Christian theology at Asbury Theological Seminary and an ordained minister of the United Methodist Church. He writes as a scholar who believes that faith is best understood as one practices the Christian life in devotion and worship. Here in these reflections on the ministry of the Holy Spirit, Dr. Wood combines theology and devotion. Often a book is either practical or academic; it is written either for lay people or scholars. Dr. Wood brings the two approaches together as he speaks about the personal dimensions of a Spirit-filled life.

Truly Ourselves, Truly the Spirit's is an invitation to think seriously about God's self-revelation as Father, Son, and Holy Spirit. For those who have difficultly in relating modern thought to their spiritual life, here is a helpful guide for sorting through the maze of conflictng notions concerning the implications of life in the Spirit. For those who have difficulty understanding the biblical meaning of the Spirit-filled life, here in nontechnical terms is an explanation from which Christians across all denominations can profit. If we accept this invitation, we will find ourselves enjoying a more personal friendship with God as we come to know him in his Trinitarian fullness in our innermost being.

Dennis F. Kinlaw, President
Asbury College
Wilmore, Kentucky

1

WAITING FOR
THE HOLY SPIRIT

He charged them . . . to wait for the promise of the Father.

Acts 1:4

"Wait, Daddy, till I catch up with you! You're walking too fast!" So cried out my eight-year-old daughter as we rushed to get in line for a big event at Disney World. A visit to an amusement park always teaches our family an important lesson of life—how to wait for each other. Long lines, hot days, empty stomachs, hurting feet, and throbbing headaches make waiting difficult.

These little trials are important for building meaningful relationships with family members. Learning to be patient with inconveniences created by our children helps to contribute to the feelings of self-esteem which they will carry with them for the rest of their lives. Early childhood experiences set the stage for a resourceful life ahead. Happy occasions spent together as a family give children their feelings of significance and enhance their capacity to relate to their peers.

One of the joys of Christmas and Thanksgiving is the opportunity for families to get together and relive their childhood experiences. Families that laugh and cry together on such occasions are those who had time for each other during the formative years of childhood.

To have time for each other means to be willing to wait for each other. To wait means to relate to others as persons of significance who deserve our attention. Often in our impatience and insensitivity, we rush about without waiting for other family members to be a part of our activity. We too easily forget that our children are part of the story of our lives and have their part to play in shaping family life.

Most of us parents are guilty in this regard. We see a task needing attention, and find it more efficient not to be bothered with waiting for the children to do it. Mom can't be bothered with asking Susie to clean up her own room. So Mom does it. Dad can't wait for Bill to come home from school to wash the car. After all, he'll gripe about it. So Dad takes it down to the station. And so on and on it goes.

We become permissive rather than confront our children with the need for responsible behavior. Patience is a virtue which requires much time, but most of us have the motto, "Ask me to do anything but wait!" When family members share little together in work and play, boredom sets in and they experience an increasing loss of mutual respect and love for each other. Fortunate indeed are those who were brought up in homes where family members did things together—worked, played, and worshiped together. These persons have roots that are deep and a life story that is worth telling.

I attended a get-acquainted party one evening with a group of students where we played a word-association game. A single woman was given the word *sad,* and she replied, "My childhood." On another occasion I was sitting in a fast-food restaurant in Amsterdam when an American high school student sat in front of me. She had hitchhiked through Europe. As she lifted her arm to drink her cup of coffee, I noticed the word *lost* tattooed under her forearm.

These two women did not feel like "persons." They had no story to their lives except meaningless and unrelated happenings. Both were pawned off onto foster homes where they took up space but experienced no meaningful time with others. They had no family members to make them feel a part of someone else's life and they got little positive attention from others. They had no story because they had experienced few happy events. They shared space with others but nobody had time for them. Sadness is the feeling of loneliness; it is the sense of those who have no continuity in their life story because no one gives them attention or needs their affection.

I was waiting for my daughter in the orthodontist's office last week. On the wall hung a painting of a little boy lying in green grass; he was holding colorful balloons in his hands as they reached toward the sky. Engraved in the painting were these words: "Talk with children and see that each day each child enjoys some small success and some recognition as a person." I was moved to pray silently that my daughter would feel that she is a person deserving of recognition.

God has waited for us! He waited patiently for the human race for thousands of years (2 Peter 3:8) until the time was ready for him to appear in Jesus of Nazareth. He waited because he wanted us to know that he recognizes us as children who deserve his attention. The Bible is the record of that wait.

Jesus Christ is God's time for us. God waited to come to us as a fellow human being until we were capable of fully recognizing him as our Father and he could adopt us as his children (Gal. 4:4). He came in the history of salvation as recorded in the Bible, but this history continues today. We should not think of God's saving acts in the past as merely past, for he waits for us and invites us to become a part of his saving story. We can share in this same drama. Though the Bible contains the completed revelation about God, the history of salvation continues through the existence of the church until Jesus comes again.

Jesus Christ is God's way of recognizing us as persons deserving of his attention, but God also wants us to recognize him as the person of ultimate significance in our lives. One of the saddest events in the life of Jesus occurred when friends from his hometown rejected him by refusing to recognize his true worth (Mark 6:1–6). Jesus was stunned by their shunning of him. What patience on the part of God that he reaches out to us even though we have repeatedly ignored him!

God did not get in a hurry with the human race when we were slow catching on to his design and plan for us. Unlike parents who rush ahead without waiting to involve their children in all the events that form their family life, God waited for us so that we could get involved in the events of his history. Only in this way can our lives be shaped and our spiritual identity be formed.

We now see why God did not rush out impulsively in the history of salvation to build a relationship with us. It was not because he lacked interest but because we are limited in our capacity to understand and slow in our ability to appreciate the meaning of this relationship. Our self-centeredness causes us to be insensitive to his feelings and thoughts, and our insensitivities have tried his patience (Gen. 6:5–7). But God did not give up on us.

Jesus called the disciples "foolish men" as he appeared to them incognito on the way to Emmaus. He explained that his death, tragic as it might have seemed, was necessary for them. The irony in this situation was that God's design in history for our salvation was almost completed and still the disciples did not understand what was happening. Only when Jesus later sent his Spirit to them did their understanding of his personhood become truly available to them. The Holy Spirit is like Jesus' alter ego whose possession of them unlocked their understanding and gave them insight into God's purpose in history for the human race. It was not enough for God to reveal something about himself through the events of history; it was not enough for God to become a human being in Jesus of Nazareth. The indwelling of the Spirit of the risen Christ was essential for their spiritual formation, their growth in grace. Only as God's saving events in history are internalized within our emotional and spiritual makeup can feelings of authenticity and personal ownership of who we are "in Christ" be real. The Holy Spirit is God's guarantee in our hearts that we have experienced his redemption history (Eph. 1:13).

We can be eternally grateful that God has waited for us and not forged ahead with a selfish and impatient agenda. Think how different this world would have been had there been no divine encounter with Abraham, Isaac, and Jacob. What would it have been like if no Moses had lived to lead the Israelites through the Red Sea and from the release of bondage? What if no thundering had roared from Sinai? What if God had given no tablets of law? No commandments to obey? What would it have been like had Joshua not led God's people into the Promised Land? If there had been no David to unite the nation of Israel and make it great? If Solomon had never built the temple of the Lord in Jerusalem? If there had been no consequences of Israel's disobedience and if God had simply become permissive and overlooked sin? There would have been no law, no prophets, no Israelites to bear witness to the reality of the living God. No Mary, no Joseph, no Jesus, and no disciples. No Easter and no Pentecost. In short, no divine history and no spiritual life. And we would be individuals without hope, without God, and without any significance.

But God has waited for us! His waiting forms the history of our salvation as recorded in the Bible. It has been an active waiting! He has been seeking us and desiring to be our friend, for he recognizes us as persons of worth. Jesus said that he regarded his disciples not as slaves and servants but as friends. Because we are his friends he laid his life on the line for us (John 15:12–15). The psalmist recognized that the whole point of God's covenant in history was to make us friends. "The friendship of the LORD is for those who fear him, and he makes known to them his covenant" (Ps. 25:14). God desires our friendship. In his presence our loneliness is transformed into a bond of friendship which inspires faith, hope, and love.

God's waiting for us is an active soliciting of our attention. Friendships require effort. Relationships are not instantly achieved. They take a great deal of time, hard work, personal sacrifice, and determination. John Wesley's sermon "The Means of Grace" shows that waiting on the Lord is not merely being quiet before the Lord as if we were to put our minds in neutral and just be still.[1] To wait on the Lord is an active participation in God's presence. It is an attitude of seeking the Lord with the whole heart.

Some well-meaning persons in Wesley's day taught that believers should just be "still" and do nothing, not even read the Bible or pray or attend public worship. They supposed that these activities were attempts to earn one's own righteousness by doing good deeds. So they said, "Faith means being inactive and doing absolutely nothing since salvation is by faith alone." Wesley opposed this dangerous teaching and showed that waiting on the Lord is an active sharing in all the means of grace such as reading the Bible, attending worship services, partaking of the sacraments, and doing all the good that we can.

It would certainly not be much of a relationship with other people (boring, in fact) if we placed all the responsibility on them for cultivating a friendship, while we simply sat passively by doing nothing. Likewise, a relationship with God involves our becoming responsible participants in the drama of salvation. God was patient with the human race and waited for us until we were emotionally and spiritually ready to enter a deeper and a more complete relationship with him. That time has now come with Pentecost. This is why Peter said that in past times God winked at sin but that now he commands everyone to repent and to enter into a responsible relationship with him (Acts 17:30).

This gradual and painstaking process of God making himself known in the history of Israel and finally in the history of Jesus is what theologians refer to as progressive revelation. The history of salvation recorded in the Bible took many, many years. From the time of our first parents, God gradually revealed more and more of himself until he became a human being himself in Jesus of Nazareth—of course without at the same time ceasing to be truly God. God's disclosure of himself engaged him personally in human history. Since God is a person, you would think that everybody would have expected him to appear personally. But nobody did. Not even the disciples!

The irony is that God's embodiment of himself in Jesus of Nazareth should have become the stumbling block which caused Jesus' crucifixion. In order to protect the integrity of God, the people killed the very one who was really God! This act of sacrificial love on his part shows us what it means to be a person, which we could not have known had God not given himself to us in true friendship.

Friendship means just this—the sharing and giving of ourselves in self-dedication to other persons who in turn give themselves to us. Friendship and personhood are closely linked.[2] We become authentic persons when we are mutually immersed in the lives of others whom we have carefully selected to be our friends. We may have an acquaintance with a number of people, but these are not friends in the truest sense of the term. A true friend is one who shares our deepest privacy and innermost thoughts. This level of friendship forms the meaning of our person. The meaning of ourselves develops as our capacity for friendship is increased. God's capacity for friendship is infinite, but ours must be developed.

Simply knowing about God is not enough to make us truly free as persons. For personal freedom means primarily finding our happiness in relationship with another person. Money and wealth cannot make us happy and free. To be estranged from others is to be in bondage to ourselves, inhibited, prevented from freely expressing our feelings and thoughts, feeling lost and undesirable.

The highest level of meaning is to be in relationship with God—to know him personally. This is why God "tabernacled among us" as John described it (John 1:14). Jesus is our model of this friendship. Now that God has come into human history himself, we can have a personal and intimate knowledge of him, not just about him, if we will actively wait for the Spirit of Christ. And when we develop a friendship with God, it will strengthen the bond of our human attachments as well. So it was with the disciples (Acts 1:14).

Waiting is what God now expects of us. The psalmist says, "Wait for the LORD" (Ps. 27:14). Since God has waited for us, he now wants us to wait for him. It takes time and space to get to know someone. Instant relationships are usually only superficial. That is why God wants us to count the cost to see whether we are really willing to make the effort to live in relationship with him (Luke 14:28). He wants us to choose to let him be our friend, but he wants our choice to be intentional, not just a fleeting rush of emotion. Just as God worked for countless years to build a relationship with the human race, we cannot come to him in a lackadaisical manner expecting access to his innermost life. Nor will he come to us without the appropriate preparation on our part to receive him. The essence of this preparation is an active waiting on the Lord.

Because the disciples waited in the Upper Room, they finally became more than admirers of Jesus. They had followed Jesus with a degree of loyalty during his earthly ministry, but they forsook him in the moment of his greatest trial. Betrayal is hardly characteristic of true friendship (Mark 14:50). Pentecost changed all this. For Jesus became the total meaning of their life as they experienced the pure love of God through the outpouring of the Holy Spirit (Rom. 5:5). They were empowered with courageous conviction to be faithful witnesses of Jesus Christ (Acts 1:8–9). The difference in the disciples before Pentecost and after Pentecost is the difference between fickleness and friendship.

We must see the significance of Pentecost for the formation of the disciples' spiritual life if we too are to have our own personal pentecost. The disciples of Jesus had come together in the Upper Room where they waited intentionally for the coming of the Holy Spirit (Acts 2). The Holy Spirit does not come to be with us by a chance happening like so many of our acquaintances.

Pentecost was a peak experience, a confirmation of their original commitment to be followers of the Lord. The Holy Spirit who came on Pentecost was the Spirit of Jesus Christ who now lived, not in a temple nor even alongside them as he had done during Jesus' earthly life (John 14:17), but within the depths of their emotions and thoughts. Pentecost meant for the disciples the development of a deeper and more meaningful relationship with their Lord.

Pentecost was an event that gave the disciples a new sense of continuity to their lives—but also to ours. They waited on our behalf as well (John 17:20–26). Their experience with the Holy Spirit on Pentecost was to be shared with all succeeding generations (Acts 1:8). Everyone is invited to be a part of this drama. For the point of the story is simple and is available for everyone to understand and to share: The personal infilling of the Holy Spirit is God's gift of himself to everyone who will wait and call upon his name (Acts 2:38–39). Those persons who respond make up the family of God because through the Spirit they are participants in Jesus' life story (Acts 2:44–47).

Wait for the promise. The coming of the Holy Spirit was something completely new in the history of the world. The coming of the Spirit was a sudden and transforming experience. It brought the disciples into such intimacy with God that their lives overflowed with joy that they could hardly keep to themselves. The disciples did not understand many things during the earthly ministry of Jesus, but now they understood more nearly what God had been about for years as he prepared Israel to be the means of salvation for the world. Pentecost was not an afterthought in the mind of God, and they were moved to broadcast this news to the whole world.

Peter was inspired to preach to those who had gathered in Jerusalem for the holy festival. His sermon invited them to participate in this historic occurrence. In his sermon, Peter recited those special events which God used to form the national life of Israel and prepare the way for the history of Jesus. Peter's main point was to say that Pentecost is the new event which forms our spiritual life. The Spirit permits us to share in Jesus' intimacy with God as we become a part of his saving history.

Our waiting on the Spirit will be rewarded with a fulfilling and meaningful life, a rare experience in our day, but one which is universally available. Perhaps you have read the plays which were produced a few years ago for what was called the theater of the absurd. They portrayed the sense of personal emptiness and uselessness which typify modern people who have lost their faith in God and in the values of the Christian tradition.

One of these plays was *Waiting for Godot* by Samuel Beckett. Estragon and Vladimir, the main characters, engage in chatter and pointless conversation as they wait for Godot. He never shows up. But as they wait endlessly, they engage in all sorts of meaningless antics to justify their existence:

Vladimir: *That passed the time.*

Estragon: *It would have passed in any case.*

Vladimir: *Yes, but not so rapidly.* (Pause)

Estragon: *What do we do now?*

Vladimir: *I don't know.*

Estragon: *Let's go.*

Vladimir: *We can't.*

Estragon: *Why not?*

Vladimir: *We're waiting for Godot.*

Estragon: [despairingly] *Ah!*

Peter's sermon has a word of hope to those who have lost their way. We are not waiting for Godot; we are waiting for God. We do not expect human beings alone to form the meaning of our existence; we expect the Holy Spirit to form us into the image of Christ. Our waiting is not futile because God comes to us through the Spirit of the risen Christ. And we gladly exchange the absurdity of a life without God for the joy of the Christ-filled life of the Spirit. For we are waiting for the promise.

2

THE SPIRIT OF PROMISE

> Christ redeemed us from the curse of the law, having become a curse for us . . . that in Christ Jesus the blessing of Abraham might come upon the Gentiles, that we might receive the promise of the Spirit through faith.
>
> *Galatians 3:13–14*

A promise is the most personal word which we can ever speak. It is the sincere expression of who we are in the depth of our being. It may include specific things which we say we will do in the future, but the hidden meaning of a promise is the personal offer of ourselves in friendship. A promise binds us to others as we give them our word.

The Bible is the story of God's promise to the human race. It is a story of friendship which he promised to develop throughout the course of human history. The development of this promise we call "salvation history."[1] This story of friendship begins with his promise to ancient Israel and is consummated with the gift of his Spirit on the day of Pentecost. There would have been no Israel and no Christian church had there been no promise from God.

Paul plainly says that the coming of the Spirit of Christ is indeed the subtance of God's blessing to Abraham. The entire development of biblical history had this one goal in mind—to bring us into fellowship with God through placing his Spirit within us. This is why Paul says, "Christ redeemed us from the curse of the law . . . that in Christ Jesus the blessing of Abraham might come upon the Gentiles, that we might receive the promise of the Spirit through faith" (Gal. 3:13–14).[2]

OUR PERSONAL JOURNEY THROUGH SALVATION HISTORY

To appreciate this promise of God's friendship we must highlight the main events recorded in the Old Testament which prepared the way. In an important sense, we can't simply jump into the conclusion of this story. There is no way we can really be only "New Testament Christians." To be a follower of Jesus Christ involves us in his history, and his history includes the development of God's promise to ancient Israel. This history and its events are an integral part of *our* life story as well. This means that we too must make our journey through the history of salvation.

This is a point which Jürgen Moltmann, an internationally known theologian from Tübingen, has recently made in his book *The Trinity and the Kingdom of God.* He shows that we know God as three persons because that is the way he has revealed himself in the history of salvation: through the kingdom of the Father, the kingdom of the Son, and the kingdom of the Spirit.[3]

He reminds us that this trinitarian interpretation of history has a long tradition in the church, though it is often overlooked or forgotten. In addition to those whom Moltmann names, this understanding was certainly a vital part of the thinking of John Wesley and his closest friend and coworker, John Fletcher. Wesley's sermon "On Faith" describes these different stages of faith according to the various dispensations of God's revelation. Some have the faith of the Jewish dispensation who knew God as Father; some have the faith of the followers of John the Baptist who knew Christ before Pentecost as the Son of God; and some have the faith of the apostles who knew the Spirit of Christ.[4]

The importance of this interpretation is that it helps us to see how our own growth is measured in terms of whether or not we know "the Father, and the Son, and the Spirit of Christ, in [our] inmost soul," as Wesley put it.[5] Different people experience God in different stages. For God's revelation of himself has come gradually; likewise, in our own history of salvation we too experience a developing knowledge of God.

Some know him as the one God and Father of the universe as he first revealed himself to Abraham. Many are in the church whose actual experience with God is limited to this basic awareness of him as their Creator. Even though they know about the coming of Jesus Christ, they may not have internalized this deeper revelation of God.

Yet to know God as one's personal Creator is certainly an important saving experience even if it is just the beginning of our journey with God. John Wesley reminds us that Cornelius knew the God of Abraham before Peter preached Christ to him (Acts 10). Yet Wesley says Cornelius in his heart already knew Christ before Peter's sermon to him "though [in his understanding] he knows him not!"[6] To know God as our personal Creator and Father of the universe also means we experience the entire Trinity—even if we do so in a very limited way.

Throughout the development of salvation history and as God established a deeper relationship with his people, they understood more and more about him. Some knew him more personally, such as Moses to whom God revealed his name for the first time (Ex. 6:3). Prophets like Isaiah reached a moral understanding of God unique in the history of the world. Of course the fullest revelation of God appears in Jesus Christ, and the highest level of our knowledge of him is experienced through the appropriation of his Spirit.

Many in the church have a knowledge of Jesus Christ which is limited to an objective acceptance of him as God's ultimate revelation. This is like the experience of the disciples before Pentecost. While this awareness of Christ results in saving faith, it is not enough; God's wants to fill us with the Spirit of Christ so that we become fully his.

With Moltmann, we can generally say that there are three

different stages of God's self-revelation—the kingdom of the Father, the Son, and the Spirit. These three stages of God's revelation are not three different kingdoms but a development of the one kingdom of God. In the kingdom of the Father, we surrender to his sovereignty, recognize his lordship over creation, and become his glad servants.

In the kingdom of the Son, we are adopted into God's family and become his children. Outwardly we are still God's servants, but inwardly we share in the intimacy of his family through our joint heirship with Jesus Christ, God's Son.

In the kingdom of the Spirit, our relationship to God takes on further meaning; we become his friends. This third stage of the kingdom means that we have a direct relationship to God; it means that God's promise of friendship first made to Abraham is now consummated in the fullest sense of the term. For God dwells within us through his Spirit. This means that we have true friendship with God at the highest level. This is why Jesus said to his disciples, "No longer do I call you servants . . . but I have called you friends" (John 15:15). Jesus promised his disciples this kind of friendship because they would receive the fullness of the Holy Spirit.

In his high priestly prayer, our Lord asked his Father to unite the disciples in true friendship even as they themselves were bonded in friendship. "I . . . pray . . . that they may all be one; even as thou, Father, art in me, and I in thee, that they also may be in us" (John 17:20–21). The Holy Spirit was to bind them together as one because they would be taken into the life of the Trinity. Even as the Father and Son enjoy their lives together through the unity of the Spirit, even so Jesus' followers would become a part of this friendship within God's life.

Moltmann reminds us that these stages of our relationship to God as servants, as children, and as friends do not mean that each stage can be isolated as if we could be God's servant without being his children or friends.[7] Even though Abraham lived in the kingdom of the Father, James says that he was the "friend of God" (James 2:23). In the history of salvation, Abraham is considered to be the first of God's friends.

This means we cannot simply date these stages of

salvation history in a mere chronological way, though that is certainly involved. What distinguishes these stages is the focus of each one. The focus of the kingdom of the Father is not the same as those of the kingdom of the Son and the kingdom of the Spirit. The kingdom of the Father focuses on our being his servants, but even in this stage we are his children and friends in an embryonic sense. The possibilities implicit in the kingdoms of the Son and the Spirit were already partially available in the kingdom of the Father. For the kingdom of the Father established the trend which was unfolded in the kingdoms of the Son and of the Spirit.

This is why Paul says that "when the time had fully come, God sent forth his Son" to make us his sons as well. "Because you are sons, God has sent the Spirit of his Son into our hearts, crying, 'Abba! Father!' " (Gal. 4:4, 6). Notice the two sendings. He sent his Son into the world to make us children also; and because we became his children, he sent his Spirit to dwell within us so we would feel true affection for God.

The first sending was the coming of the Son of God as a man; the second sending was the coming of the Spirit of God on the day of Pentecost to fill us with true affection. Just as there was a distinction between the sending of the Son of God and the sending of the Holy Spirit in the history of salvation, so there may be a similar historical development in our personal salvation history.[8] As our Creator and Maker, God is Father; as our Redeemer who adopts us into his family, God is Son; as our Sanctifier who binds us to himself in friendship, God is Spirit. It is possible that we can plot the development of our own relationship to God according to God's threefold revelation of himself.

The primary focus of the Old Testament is that God is our Father. In the Gospels God is revealed in his Son. At Pentecost God the Father and God the Son came to dwell within us in the intimacy of genuine friendship through the promise of the Holy Spirit. This is why the church is known as the "fellowship of the Spirit." This level of friendship with God is what Jesus promised would take place when the Holy Spirit came upon them. It is not enough for us as servants to respect God as Lord of the universe; it is not enough for us as children to respect God as the Father of Jesus Christ in whose family we are adopted children. We are faithful servants and obedient children because we are also God's friends.

This means that our relationship to God is motivated by feelings of love, not fear. As God's servants and children, we have a genuine fondness for him. We enjoy his fellowship. John wrote that we know this quality of perfect love for God because "he has given us of his own Spirit" (1 John 4:13). This affectionate quality of love is a distinctive feature of the higher level of friendship with God.

Friendship means more than just respect. It means genuine affection. Servants respect their masters because of their sovereignty. Children respect their parents and are intimate with them because of the natural blood bond between them. But friendship adds a further meaning to our relationship with God—genuine love. Friendship is respect combined with affection. The Holy Spirit indwelling our hearts inspires us with this new affection for God because his love is poured out in our hearts (Rom. 5:5).

Take the journey through salvation history once again. See how the trend of God's self-disclosure developed from the earliest beginnings with Abraham and was realized in the pentecostal outpouring of the Spirit of Christ. Discern the progressive stages along this journey and discover the specific level of spiritual growth at which you have arrived. This is of course a personal matter and not one which we can prescribe for someone else. Only we can know where we stand with God.

I will describe this journey through salvation history simply because it is a story, not a handbook of ideas and doctrines. If we are turned off by the simplicity of the biblical story, we may need to rethink the meaning of salvation. For what God offers us is friendship. This means that it is God's personal presence in history which saves us. This story, which tells us what really happened, becomes our story too as we share in God's friendship. The reliving of salvation history will help to shape us spiritually and challenge us to deeper levels of friendship with God.

GOD PROMISES TO GIVE ABRAHAM
THE LAND OF CANAAN

Formerly we knew nothing about the earliest civilizations except what was recorded in the Bible. Because in recent years archaeologists have dug up ancient cities we now know that the earliest civilization was formed in the Fertile Crescent by the Sumerians. This is the region where Abraham was born almost 1000 years later. In fact, we now know that Abraham was a common name in his day, and we also know that the description the Bible gives of the culture of that region is correct.[9]

Abraham lived in the land of Ur. God appeared to him and told him to leave his home country and go to another land. God promised that he would prosper in this new country and that his family would become a new nation. Abraham took God at his word and immediately moved to Haran on the outskirts of Palestine.

Abraham's faith in the promise pleased God. Some years after his first appearance to Abraham, God came to him again. This time he told Abraham that he wanted him to be his close friend and to walk with him with a pure and blameless heart (Gen. 12:1). God renewed his promise that Abraham's family would become a great nation and that all the people of the earth would be blessed because of them and their faith.

The rest of the world did not yet know God, but they felt a need for him. So they created images and idols which they imagined to be God. These idols were really only like reflections which people have of themselves in a pool of water; they confused God with portraits of themselves. They carved images out of wood which represented their ideas of what they thought the gods looked like. They made up stories about how they descended from the gods. They built temples where they placed their images and sacrificed animals as food for their gods to eat. These temples, called ziggurats, have been located by archaeologists.

They imagined that their gods became angry when worshipers did not give them the things they needed for happiness and fulfillment, for they believed their gods were dependent upon them. When droughts or floods or other natural catastrophes occurred, the people thought this was the gods' way of getting even with them.

God told Abraham that he must not believe in false gods since he had revealed himself personally as the only true God. This was the reason God chose Abraham to be his friend. This is why God wanted to make Abraham's family into a great nation: so that they could tell everybody else about him. God wanted everybody to know him.

Why did God not just tell everybody who he was? We do not know. But a god who is revealed in general everywhere is a god who really is not revealed anywhere.[10] The same would be true of us; if we are known in general everywhere without being known specifically in a relationship with another person in a particular place and time, then we aren't really known by anyone. We don't really think of others as friends if we know them only in general. There must be specific events in our lives which bring us together if we are to become friends with other people. Besides, it takes time to make friends. We also know that usually we get acquainted with others through the friendships which we already have.

Since God did not have friends in the world because everybody had rejected him many years before, God took the initiative to make himself known to Abraham. That is why we say that the history of salvation begins with Abraham and why God promised to give Abraham the land of Canaan as his home. God offered Abraham a contract. He would give the land to him if Abraham and his family and descendants would agree to make it their responsibility to introduce him to the rest of the world. Abraham accepted these terms.

ABRAHAM MAKES TWO NEW DISCOVERIES

Let's pause briefly for just two comments. One has to do with Abraham's sense of history, and the other has to do with his discovery of the meaning of the personal. These are two topics for which the modern world is indebted specifically to Abraham and his family.[11]

Abraham developed a sense of history which no other person had ever known. He realized that the important things in the world were not part of nature like the moon, sun, stars, the awesome hills and mountains, the storms and beautiful skies. Before the Lord appeared to him, he, like everybody else, thought these things were divine. He imagined that these natural objects were gods to be worshiped and feared.

But now after the Lord introduced himself, Abraham developed a historical sense of the meaning of the world. He realized that God wanted everybody to live in harmonious relationships and to enjoy his friendship. History is people relating themselves to each other and developing a sense of their destiny and purpose in life. Because God had appeared to him as a person and had made certain promises to him, Abraham realized that this was the real purpose of the world. He no longer believed that nature was a god, for he had come to know the God who made nature. Instead of a nature-religion made up of impersonal idols, Abraham now had a historical faith. A historical faith means having a relationship to the God who made heaven and earth and who reveals himself personally on specific occasions and in certain events in the world.

Once the knowledge of God had been lost to the human race. Now Abraham became the first person to experience this deeper understanding of the world and God. He and his family were also the first to develop a true sense of what it means to feel like a person. He no longer felt that he was just another object in the world which was used by the gods of nature to fulfill their evil and unreasonable appetites. He now knew who he was and the purpose of his life.

This was a brand new discovery.[12] The knowledge that we are persons is something which we take for granted today. So long as people thought nature was divine, human life was cheap and everything human had to be sacrificed for the terrible gods of nature.[13] Thanks to God's revelation of himself, Abraham now saw that the world was not divine; only the God who created nature is divine and people are made in his image.

This means that people are important; this means that God wants us to use the natural world as the place where we can get to know each other and develop a relationship with him that is meaningful and fulfilling because we are his children.

This is why God promised to give Abraham the land of Canaan; it would be a place in the natural world where Abraham could develop family ties and make a home for his people. It would be a place where God would be respected and loved. It would be a place where God's people could develop a sense of their personal and historical destiny. The Lord would be their God, and they would be his people.

ABRAHAM'S CHILDREN STRUGGLE FOR THEIR IDENTITY

But things did not always work out well for Abraham and his family. Some of them weren't always so agreeable as they might have been. Many times they did things which were inappropriate for a group of people who were supposed to have a relationship with God. An important part of being persons is that we have to assume responsibility for ourselves and live up to our obligations to others.

Any time people get together conflict is inevitable. But conflicts are the stuff out of which we are made.[14] Abraham's family had plenty of conflict among themselves and with other groups of people. Unfortunately much of the conflict was negative, and it was reflected in their relationship with God. But he was patient, caring, and loving in spite of this because of his contract with Abraham.

Their struggle to take possession of Canaan was often fierce and discouraging. Many years of personal growth and hard work passed before they entered the Promised Land. Their identity as a people was not something that God could just hand to them. We never become authentic as persons by simply borrowing somebody else's reality. God wanted Abraham and his family to be real people, not simply like an assembly line of plastic dolls. In order to become the people God intended them to be and to realize their potential, Abraham and his descendants had to mature in their understanding of God. That process of maturation is often painful but necessary and ultimately satisfying.

After Abraham's death, his new identity as God's friend lived on in his children. The thrilling stories of his sons are dramas about their seeking to internalize for themselves their father's faith in God. The struggles of Esau and Isaac involved a great deal of sibling rivalry, but in the end they were reconciled to each other because they shared the same history, that which the God of their father Abraham initiated (Gen. 33:4).

The story of God's friendship with Abraham and the succeeding generations is long and involved. Their captivity in Egypt, their exodus and occupation of the Promised Land, their exile from their homeland, and final return are the main features. The climax of their history is the establishment of the kingdom of David. This finally fulfilled God's promise to Abraham that his descendants would become a respected and authentic people.

A BREAK IN THE STORY

A downturn in the story appears when a drought forces Abraham's grandson Jacob to take up temporary residence in Egypt. This resulted also in a spiritual drought. They left their home to buy food in Egypt, and in the process they lost their spiritual bearings, becoming fascinated with the luxuries they found there. A break in their history occurs—except that God did not forget his promise and contract with Abraham. The low point is reached when they became slaves of the Egyptians and the pharaoh decided to kill every male child born to the Israelites, a move designed to destroy the race. Then they remembered who they were. God's promise to Abraham was that they would become a great nation, not the slaves of idol worshipers. Their identity as the people of God was to be fulfilled in Canaan not Egypt. Their destiny was to make God known to the nations of the world, not their extermination at the hands of the Egyptians. Out of this sudden awareness of who they were supposed to be came genuine conviction and repentance.

GOD TELLS HIS NAME

God gave them a strong leader in the person of Moses to lead them out of Egypt and into Canaan. Through a series of providential events Moses had been brought up in the house of the pharaoh, but he later rejected his Egyptian identity and chose to be identified as a Hebrew. When God appeared to Moses in a flaming bush, an important thing happened: God disclosed his name.[15] When he first appeared to Abraham, and later to Isaac and Jacob, he had not told them his name. Only through the process of time could such an intimate knowledge of God be understood and appreciated. That time had come.

Moses had a personal and intimate conversation with God reminiscent of Abraham's first encounter with him. God wanted Moses to lead his people out of bondage and into the land of promise, but Moses felt himself unprepared and inadequate. Besides, he thought, nobody would follow him or believe that God had commissioned him. Then Moses said to God,

> "If I come to the people of Israel and say to them, 'The God of your fathers has sent me to you,' and they ask me, 'What is his name?' what shall I say to them?" God said to Moses, "I AM WHO I AM." And he said, "Say this to the people of Israel, 'I AM has sent me to you.'" God also said to Moses, "Say this to the people of Israel, 'The LORD, the God of your fathers, the God of Abraham, the God of Isaac, and the God of Jacob, has sent me to you': this is my name for ever, and thus I am to be remembered throughout all generations. Go and gather the elders of Israel together, and say to them, 'The LORD, the God of your fathers, the God of Abraham, of Isaac, and of Jacob, has appeared to me, saying, "I have observed you and what has been done to you in Egypt; and I promise that I will bring you up out of the affliction of Egypt, to . . . a land flowing with milk and honey."' And they will hearken to your voice" (Ex. 3:13–18).

The proof to the people that God had chosen Moses to be their leader was in his personal witness to what God had said and done at the burning bush. The same God who invited Abraham to be his friend and to lead his family to the land of promise was the God who called Moses. He is the God of history and the one who directs its path.

God's call is a personal one because it is an event in our personal history; it is communicated to us through a happening in history which God initiates. We can't control the event of God's revelation because it is his event, but we can experience it and become a witness to its reality.[16] The responsibility for others believing its truth does not rest with us, but we are responsible for witnessing to it. This is an important lesson which we need to learn from Moses' experience with God as we also witness to our knowledge of him.

Their motivation to leave Egypt and enter Canaan was the expectation that this land was uniquely the place God had chosen for his earthly residence (Ex. 15:17). There he would establish a kingdom where the Israelites could enjoy the fullest extent of happiness and personal fulfillment. They knew that their reason for being was related to their belief and experience with God. This God would be their God and they would be his people. The alternative was clear: without a relationship to him who gave them their sense of identity, their hopes to be somebody with significance would be dashed.

A modern illustration of this is expressed by a recent Jewish philosopher in a small book entitled *God's Presence in History,* an account of the tragedy of the Holocaust. He reminds his Jewish readers that Hitler will yet be successful in his plan to exterminate them if they give up their faith in the God of Abraham, Isaac, and Jacob. This faith gave rise to their national identity, and this faith has preserved their existence throughout the centuries. He calls upon Jews everywhere stubbornly to refuse to do to themselves what Hitler was unable to do. To deny their belief in God would be to dissolve their history and to bring an end to their existence; this belief has been the only reason they have been able to maintain their identity throughout the centuries. Other peoples lost their national identity when they suffered the loss of their land.[17]

THE KINGDOM OF ISRAEL IS FORMED
THROUGH TWO PEAK EVENTS:
THE EXODUS AND THE CONQUEST

We now come to those peak experiences which in only a preliminary way fulfilled God's promise to Abraham: the Exodus from Egypt and the Conquest of Canaan.[18] Everything they believed about their salvation and relationship to God was explained by reference to their deliverance from Egypt and their victorious occupation of Canaan. These became the basis of Israel's national destiny and identity. Whenever the Israelites came together in worship, they affirmed their belief in the God who accomplished this miracle for them.

Imagine yourself attending their worship in the temple and hearing them recite this creed:

> A wandering Aramean was my father; and he went down into Egypt and sojourned there, few in number; and there he became a nation, great, mighty, and populous. And the Egyptians treated us harshly, and afflicted us, and laid upon us hard bondage. Then we cried to the LORD the God of our fathers, and the LORD heard our voice, and saw our affliction, our toil, and our oppression; and the LORD brought us out of Egypt with a mighty hand and an outstretched arm, with great terror, with signs and wonders; and he brought us into this place and gave us this land, a land flowing with milk and honey. And behold, now I bring the first of the fruit of the ground, which thou, O LORD, hast given me (Deut. 26:5–10).

As they recite the creed, hear them relive their history as if it had happened to them and not to their forebears. You hear them say, "We were treated harshly," not "They were treated harshly." "We cried, and the Lord heard us and saw our affliction and our oppression." And what happened? "The Lord brought us out of Egypt and he brought us into this place."

These events of the past are internalized and fulfilled in the lives of the present worshipers. The experience of their fathers now becomes their experience. The history which God initiated with their fathers is now their history.[19] The intimacy which their forefathers had with God is now their privilege to enjoy because in worship they too are called upon to participate in God's redeeming history of salvation. For in worship, the Exodus and the Conquest cease to be events of the past and become real in the present moment.

ISRAEL FAILS TO KEEP ITS PROMISE

But the story does not end here. Simply living in Canaan did not ensure that the Israelites would continue faithful to the terms of the contract. Remember that God had said to Abraham, "Walk before me and be blameless in your love for me." As a sign that Abraham agreed to these terms, he was circumcised on that very day (Gen. 17:1, 10, 24). Circumcision symbolized the cleansing of an inherited condition; the uncircumcised flesh was a symbol of rebellion against God, and its excision symbolized perfect love for God.[20] But it became apparent even after they had possessed the Promised Land that the Israelites were not able to live up to the terms of their contract with God. They may have been physically circumcised, but spiritually their hearts were unclean and their love for God mixed and impure.

Moses had recognized that their hearts remained biased toward evil and that their persistent tendency was to imagine themselves to be complete and fulfilled without a relationship with the Lord. He knew they would soon forget their part of the contract. The agreement required that they should be faithful witnesses for God in the world. God desired not only *their* fellowship; he wanted communion with the entire world. Their election was not unconditional; the promises of God are always conditioned by our obedience. Israel learned this lesson the hard way.

Faith always involves more than mere hearing with our physical ears and seeing with our physical eyes. Faith is more than information about what we ought to do and what we should know. Simply knowing the truth with our minds is never adequate to meet the needs of our spirits; nor does it guarantee that we will do it. We can never be fulfilled by attempting to discover the purpose of our lives through ourselves alone.

Moses predicted that the day would come when the hearts of the people would be turned away from their love for God and that they would go their own way and seek to fulfill their needs like pagans. God would then be required according to the terms of his contract with Abraham to drive them out of Canaan. Their destruction and exile were inevitable! (Deut. 29:16–28). Once they had a land where they could be a people with identity, but now they were devastated personally and spiritually with no apparent hope of turning things around. Their neighbors looked upon them in amazement, wondering how a people so great could now be decimated (Deut. 29:24). But Moses predicted this unfaithfulness so that when they realized what they had done they would not lose hope (Deut. 30:1).

THE PROMISE OF A NEW EXODUS
AND A NEW CONQUEST

Moses foresaw the day when they would be returned to their land and experience a new Exodus and a new Conquest.

> The LORD your God will restore your fortunes, and have compassion upon you, and he will gather you again from all the peoples where the LORD your God has scattered you. If your outcasts are in the uttermost parts of heaven, from there the LORD your God will gather you, and from there he will fetch you [a new Exodus]; and the LORD your God will bring you into the land [a new Conquest] which your fathers possessed, that you may possess it; and he will make you more prosperous and numerous than your fathers (Deut. 30:3–5).

But what good would it do to restore them to the land? Did God think that this time they would be cured of chasing after false gods? Would they not again abandon the covenant which on their behalf Abraham had agreed to? No, this time things would be different. There would be no more exile; there would be no more breaking of the contract. Everything would be different because this time God would change their hearts instead of only their circumstances.[21]

But how would it happen? How could it be that a new Exodus and a new Conquest would bring about this inner change when the first Exodus and the first Conquest failed to do so? The prophets began to explain ways this would come about. For one thing, they stopped emphasizing physical circumcision and started talking about an inner circumcision. "Circumcise yourselves to the LORD, remove the foreskin of your hearts" (Jer. 4:4). Instead of using the word circumcision, they often used the words "a clean heart."[22]

The prophets also emphasized that the Law of God would be written on their hearts, not simply on tablets of stone. It is not enough to be told what to do, for information poured into our heads does not necessarily transform our lives. It must be at work deep within us. The law given to Moses at Sinai was eventually written on scrolls, but it didn't get written into the hearts of the people. In the new contract which God would make with Israel, he had in mind something different. One prophet described it this way: "I will put my law within them, and I will write it upon their hearts; and I will be their God, and they shall be my people" (Jer. 31:33). He added,

> I will gather them [the new Exodus] from all the countries to which I drove them. . . . I will bring them back to this place [a new Conquest], and I will make them dwell in safety. And they shall be my people, and I will be their God. I will give them one heart and one way, that they may fear me for ever, for their own good and the good of their children after them. I will make with them an everlasting covenant, that I will not turn away from doing good to them; and I will put the fear of me in their hearts, that they may not turn from me (Jer. 32:37–40).

The prophetic teachings also emphasized that the Spirit of God would make fulfillment of the terms of the new contract possible. The new Conquest would involve the pouring out of the Spirit of God upon all those who would be delivered from the oppression of the nations in the new Exodus. This time when they would return to Canaan they would stay forever because God's Spirit would indwell them and enable them to love him perfectly. Not only would the land be a holy land because God had sanctified it with his presence, but his people would be holy because he had sanctified them with his Spirit (Ezek. 37:14, 23, 27–28). When this new Conquest occurs, the kingdom of David will have been truly restored even in a higher sense. For this kingdom will last forever and all who are members will have their hearts purified from evil (Ezek. 37:27–28). The sanctuary of God will not be simply in a house made by human hands, but God will take up his abode in their hearts through the outpouring of his Spirit (Ezek. 39:25–29).[23]

IN CANAAN ISRAEL ENJOYED SECURITY BECAUSE OF FRIENDSHIP WITH GOD

Often among Christian writers Canaan has symbolized the rest that awaits believers in heaven, but this is not how it is described in the prophets. The world's foremost Old Testament scholar, Gerhard von Rad, has shown that everywhere in the Old Testament Canaan symbolizes a rest and security which God's people can have here and now because of their life in God; its primary focus is not a future rest in heaven.[24] The psalmist (Ps. 95:7) calls upon his hearers to enter that rest "today," a theme which the writer of Hebrews picks up (Heb. 3:7–19). John Calvin in his commentary on Hebrews also says it is the intent of this New Testament writer to describe the complete Christian life to which God calls us here and now.[25]

If the land of rest described in Hebrews had reference to heaven, it would be a terrible thought to imagine that for the multiplied thousands of Israelites who started the journey from Egypt, only two entered the land and the remaining thousands of others were lost. Even Moses would have to be included in the number of those lost if Canaan symbolized heaven! The "rest" of faith described in Hebrews obviously has reference to the spiritual rest which is ours in this world because it is described as a present possession which one should make haste to enter *today* (Heb. 4:11).

This rest was originally described in Exodus and Deuteronomy as a physical rest following their wandering from place to place and warring with other peoples. With the psalmist a new meaning is given to it. Now it is a spiritual rest which Israel will have in God (Ps. 95:7). Or, more precisely, the prophets describe their new Conquest as resulting in a life made secure because God's Spirit indwells them and makes them holy. All of this will happen "in the latter days" when God's time has come for the establishment of his new kingdom (Ezek. 38:14–23).

The Old Testament period ends with this hope in place, but not its fulfillment. The Israelites even returned to Jerusalem and once again occupied it under the leadership of Nehemiah and Ezra. But the new kingdom of David was not yet realized; everyone was looking for a messiah who would rescue them from the rule of foreigners. By the time of Jesus' birth, the Romans were their masters.

We can now see the plan as it developed throughout the history of Israel beginning with Abraham. It was a simple concept but profound. Sometimes people have made it seem complicated. But the plan is not about ideas; it is about relationships. God wants us to have fellowship with him; he wants to be our friend; and he promised to enter human experience in the power of his Spirit.

As the prophets looked forward to that day, they knew it meant that Israel would be truly in fellowship with the God of Abraham, Isaac, and Jacob. For then God's Holy Spirit would take up his residence in their hearts in a very personal way rather than simply being present with them superficially in the outside world—as if God were present merely in a place like Canaan or in a temple. This is why Paul says that "the blessing of Abraham" is fulfilled for us today as we "receive the promise of the Spirit through faith" (Gal. 3:14). The promise of God to Abraham was really a promise of the coming of the Holy Spirit of Christ. For fellowship with God is what the history of salvation is about.

3

THE SPIRIT OF CHRIST

Christ is the man Jesus, whom God raised up. . . . He has been raised to the right hand of God; he has received from the Father and poured out upon us the promised Holy Spirit—that is what you now see and hear!

Acts 2:33, PHILLIPS

The Lord is the Spirit.

2 Corinthians 3:17

It was into a waiting world that Jesus of Nazareth was born. The prophets had said that Messiah would come and deliver Israel from its enemies. And he would be specially endowed with the Spirit.

An angel told Mary that "the Holy Spirit [would] come upon" her and that she would give birth to the Son of God (Luke 1:35–37). The earliest events surrounding the birth of Jesus were associated with the activity of the Holy Spirit. Under his inspiration (Luke 2:25–27), the prophet Simeon announced at Jesus' dedication that this boy was to be the new David, the king who would restore once again the fortunes of the kingdom. Zechariah was "filled with the Holy Spirit" and prophesied that Jesus would fulfill God's promise to Abraham (Luke 1:67, 73).[1]

A NEW EXODUS AND A NEW CONQUEST

The prominence given to the work of the Holy Spirit from the moment of Jesus' conception and birth and the events surrounding his early life illustrates the way the writers of the Gospels believed that Jesus was the fulfillment of the prophets' hope for a new Israel. The prophets believed that the coming of the Holy Spirit would be the basis for establishment of the restored kingdom. Salvation comes, they realized, not finally through the history of Israel, but through the history of Jesus Christ. The history which God had with the family of Abraham was a preparation for the history which God would have with the whole world through Jesus.

Jesus is the fulfillment of the history of Israel, and the coming of the Holy Spirit on the day of Pentecost made it possible for the contract which God made with Abraham to be personally internalized. This now meant that their hearts could be changed and their wills enabled to love God perfectly. Not only was the history of Israel fulfilled in Jesus, but he is also our fulfillment. Jesus then is the focus of the entire history of salvation and the whole world; he is the only one who can bring us into an intimate relationship with God.

The followers of our Lord were so convinced that Jesus was the intended meaning and fulfillment of God's covenant with Abraham that they interpreted the kingdom of David as only an early manifestation of the kingdom of Christ; and they interpreted the Exodus and Conquest events as a prophecy of Jesus' death-resurrection and the outpouring of his Holy Spirit upon the church. Let's trace this connection between these events in the Old and New Testaments as it developed in the minds of the disciples.

After his resurrection, Jesus appeared to two of his disciples, who did not recognize him as they walked to Emmaus. They were saddened by the turn of events which had led to Jesus' death. They "had hoped that he was the one to redeem Israel" (Luke 24:21), but his crucifixion had dashed their hopes. Jesus then said to them, " 'O foolish men, and slow of heart to believe all that the prophets have spoken! Was it not necessary that the Christ should suffer these things and enter into his glory?' And beginning with Moses and all the prophets, he interpreted to them in all the scriptures the things concerning himself" (Luke 24:25–27). Later all the disciples came together in Jerusalem where Jesus "opened their minds to understand" that he was the fulfillment of the promise of God to Israel (Luke 24:44–45).

Luke sets the stage to help us understand the event of Pentecost. He shows that Israel's history is fulfilled in Jesus' history. In his gospel, Luke shows that Jesus' death was not an accident but an important event for the coming of the kingdom of God. Jesus' resurrection was only the prelude to the outpouring of the Holy Spirit upon the church. Easter and Pentecost ushered in the coming kingdom.[2] The church was like a vestibule; it was created by the Holy Spirit at Pentecost to provide us with an entrance into the kingdom of God.

In the first chapter of the Acts of the Apostles, Luke helps us understand the meaning of Pentecost. It has often been said that we could call this record the Acts of the Holy Spirit, for it records how the Holy Spirit used historical events as the basis of what the disciples believed and taught. It is fitting that it should be a history because the life of Jesus is the fulfillment of the history of Israel, and the purpose of the Holy Spirit is to incorporate us into Jesus' saving history.

Acts contains a number of the apostles' sermons. They are simple, hardly more than a repetition of the acts of God in the Old Testament which had their fulfillment in the history of Jesus.[3] In addition to the sermons, Luke records the activity of the Holy Spirit as he directs the development of God's will through the church of Jesus Christ.

Luke's purpose in writing the Acts of the Holy Spirit is to show that the Exodus and the Conquest were fulfilled in Easter and Pentecost. Luke reports that just one week before his death Jesus was paraded through the streets of Jerusalem, the city of David, as the new king of Israel. "Blessed be the King who comes in the name of the Lord! Peace in heaven and glory in the highest!" (Luke 19:38) These same fickle people brought him to trial on the grounds that he was "perverting our nation, and forbidding us to give tribute to Caesar, and saying that he himself is . . . king" (Luke 23:2). The crowd intimidated Pilate into crucifying Jesus, but even so he was bold enough to have inscribed over the cross the words "This is the King of the Jews" (Luke 23:38).

PETER'S PENTECOST

With the stage now set for us to understand its meaning, Luke records the scene of Pentecost. It is the final event which ushers in the coming kingdom of God. The disciples are assembled in spiritual unity when they are suddenly filled with the Holy Spirit. They are enabled by the power of the Spirit to speak in the languages of all those who had assembled in Jerusalem on that day from many countries.

This fulfilled the prophets' expectation that the new Conquest and the establishment of the kingdom would be the work of the Spirit and that the kingdom would include the entire world. Their speaking in so many languages symbolized the universality of the kingdom. All the nations of the world are included and the message is to be communicated to them without delay. All national and racial barriers are now demolished. The God of Abraham, Isaac, and Jacob, and the God of Moses and the prophets is the God of Jesus who seeks to live, not in houses made with hands, but in hearts filled with the love of God. The Holy Spirit wants to take up his residence in our hearts. Through the Spirit the kingdom of God is internalized in our very being, and God's covenant with Abraham is fulfilled.

The choice of words which Peter uses in his Pentecost sermon shows that he is thinking of Easter and Pentecost as the fulfillment of the Exodus and the Conquest. Peter says Pentecost fulfills the expectation of the prophets that in the last days God's Spirit would be given to his people. As we have already seen, the prophets believed the promise that the Spirit would usher in the kingdom through a new Conquest. This new kingdom would last forever because of the giving of the Spirit; Peter quotes the prophecy of Joel to show that this is the meaning of Pentecost. The Spirit has now been poured out upon the believers of Jesus because they have experienced Jesus' resurrection in their own lives.

Peter insists that others can experience this same power of the Spirit if they too will repent and experience Jesus' resurrection life. There can be no true Pentecost for them on this day of celebrating the ancient festival until they have had their own personal Easter. They must recognize Jesus as the one who delivers from the power of evil and liberates from the captivity of sin. Without this new Exodus there can be no new Conquest. The history of Jesus must become their own personal history. Otherwise, the history of Israel is like a miscarriage, for it has no life in it.

Peter's words, "mighty works and wonders and signs," (Acts 2:22) to describe Jesus' resurrection from the dead are an exact parallel to the original Exodus event. They were used as a traditional formula to describe Israel's exodus from Egyptian captivity (Deut. 6:20–24; 26:5–10; Josh. 24:17; Deut. 4:34; 7:19; 11:3; 29:3; Jer. 32:20–21; Acts 7:36).[4] Peter also repeats the words "having loosed the pangs of death" (Acts 2:24) to link Jesus' resurrection with the Exodus. The word *loosed* is the word used to describe Israel's liberation from Egyptian bondage.[5]

The language of the Exodus becomes in the New Testament the language of Easter, for the Exodus is the central event of the Old Testament as Jesus' resurrection is of the New. The words used to describe these parallel events are "redemption" (Ex. 6:6; Eph. 1:7); "deliverance" (Ex. 3:8; Gal. 1:4; Col. 1:13); "ransom" (1 Peter 1:18–19; 1 Tim. 2:6); "release" (Ex. 6:6; Acts 2:24; Rev. 1:5); "baptize" (1 Cor. 10:1–3). As the Exodus from bondage symbolized forgiveness of sins (Ps. 130:4, 8) so Jesus' resurrection from the dead is the basis of forgiveness of sins (Titus 2:14).[6]

Peter's sermon made effective use of these commonly understood terms to refer to Jesus' resurrection. People heard his message with a clear understanding, and their hearts were convinced of its truth. Peter announced that Jesus is now the "exalted Christ" who has sent his Spirit to indwell all those who will share in his kingdom. David is not their model of the true king because he did not ascend to heaven, Peter says. Jesus did because of his resurrection from the dead (Acts 2:34), and he is the true king to whom they should give their loyalty.

"What shall we do?" the people cried. Peter exhorted them to have their own personal Easter and Pentecost: "Repent, and be baptized [the exodus event of deliverance from sin's captivity through being baptized into Jesus' death-resurrection] and you shall receive the gift of the Holy Spirit [the new Conquest of the prophet's expectation that the Spirit of God would be poured out upon all flesh and in this way usher in the final kingdom of God]" (Acts 2:38).[7] Peter showed that the promise of God to Abraham was not simply for the sake of Abraham's descendants but for the whole world, even as God had originally told Abraham. Peter said, "The promise is to you and to your children and to all that are far off" (v. 39). Similarly, Paul was later to say that the church is made up of those "who were far off" and those "who were near" and that "one new man in place of the two [Jew and Gentile]" has been created in Jesus Christ (Eph. 2:13–15).

G. E. Wright, the Old Testament scholar from Johns Hopkins University, says that the Exodus and Conquest events "are as important for the New Testament as for the Old. In Christ is the new exodus and the new inheritance."[8] Just as these events were formative for the nation of Israel, so Easter and Pentecost are for the church. Just as the Exodus and Conquest were normative experiences which every individual Israelite had to own for himself, so Easter and Pentecost are the norm for followers of Jesus Christ. As Karl Barth put it, "The New Testament witnesses . . . counted upon the Christian life only on the basis of these factors [Easter and Pentecost]."[9] Only because of Easter and Pentecost has the coming kingdom of God made its appearance in the world.

Pentecost was originally a Jewish festival which involved a ritual of dedicating to God the first fruit of the corn crop harvested in Canaan (Ex. 23:16; Num. 28:26; Deut. 16:9–11). It symbolized the life of abundance which God had promised to his people; now the coming of the Holy Spirit on the day of

Pentecost symbolized the fruit of the Spirit and abundant life in Christ.

The festival of Pentecost in later Jewish times also included a commemoration of the giving of the Law on Sinai, and Jews from all over the world assembled in Jerusalem to remember once again the giving of the Law. But Peter tells them that the prophets' expectation of the coming of the Spirit who would enable them to live obediently before the Lord had become a reality through the indwelling of the Spirit of Christ. Obedience has become now a sign of one's reception of the Spirit (1 John 3:24).

The writing of the Law in their hearts was the condition that Moses said had to be fulfilled before the kingdom could be restored in Canaan. Peter announced that the terms of God's contract with Israel were met through Jesus' death-resurrection and the sending of his Spirit into the world. This means the Law can now be written in their hearts; it is no longer contained merely in a book because the Spirit of Christ will enable them to love God with all their being and to live abundantly and obediently.

In his sermon "Christian Perfection," John Wesley showed that "when the day of Pentecost was fully come, then *first it was* [italics mine], that they who 'waited for the promise for the Father' were made more than conquerors over sin by the Holy Ghost given unto them."[10] *Wesley shows that Pentecost means it is now possible for the first time in the history of salvation for God's people to love him with all their heart,* and he says the disciples were the very first ones to experience this new possibility. This is why Wesley says that there is a "wide difference . . . between the Jewish and the Christian dispensation" because before Pentecost "the Holy Ghost was not yet given in his sanctifying graces [in full measure]."[11]

THE TRINITARIAN STAGES OF THE CHRISTIAN LIFE

Of course the Spirit of God has always been in the world. In Genesis 1:2, he is described as God's active agent in the creation of the world. In Genesis 6:3, the Spirit is God's influence seeking to bring people into conformity with his will. Throughout the Old Testament the Spirit comes upon certain individuals to enable them to do a special work of God. But the idea of the Spirit remaining with and indwelling anyone on a permanent basis is absent in the Old Testament, except for the prophet's expectation that the day would come in the future when God's Spirit would enable believers to live holy before him.[12]

Nowhere in the Old Testament is the Spirit referred to as the *Holy* Spirit in the New Testament sense. God was understood in the Old Testament as one God, but not as possessing three personal distinctions. Because of Easter and Pentecost, we now know that God is tri-personal—Father, Son, and Holy Spirit. On the basis of the Old Testament, we know that God is Father and Creator; because of Easter we know that God is Son and Redeemer; because of Pentecost we know that God is the Holy Spirit.[13]

Here the progressive nature of God's revelation of himself is clearly seen. Abraham had a deeper understanding of God and a closer relationship with him than those who came before him. Moses had a deeper knowledge of God than Abraham (Ex. 3:15; 6:3). The prophets' experience with God further deepened their knowledge and understanding. The disciples made a gigantic leap and had a greater experience of God through their walk with Jesus. But the disciples after Pentecost gained a deeper intimacy because the Christ whom they had known in his earthly existence was now dwelling in their hearts through his Spirit. Jesus had told them that the Spirit was with them but that he would later send the Spirit to dwell in them (John 14:17).

It is possible that these same stages are repeated in people today. Those who do not have the Bible have some awareness of God's existence and some possible though limited experience with him.[14] Many people know that God exists and that he is the Father of the universe. Such was the experience of Cornelius (Acts 10). Many Jews have a genuine relationship with God, but they are stalled in the process of salvation history at a point of understanding and experience which is pre-Christian, though not unChristian.

Many in Christian churches have a relationship to God which is typical of the kind of experience the disciples had before Pentecost. They are followers of the Lord, but some have only a shallow knowledge of him and they often follow "afar off" (Luke 22:54, KJV).

Some are like the Corinthians who Paul said were only "babes in Christ" and not Spirit-filled Christians (1 Cor. 3:1).[15] Harold Lindsell describes these Corinthians as typical of "carnal" Christians.

> The carnal believer is a converted believer whose life is fleshly . . . because he is under the domination of the . . . self-relying, self-pleasing nature. Therefore he is not walking in full fellowship with the Lord Jesus nor is he wholly surrendered to the Spirit of God. He is not Spirit-filled although he should be.
>
> The spiritual Christian . . . is one whose life is yielded to God and whose will is in subjection to the will of God. He is filled with the Spirit and men can see the evidences of spiritual vitality, for he produces the fruit of the Spirit in his life.[16]

Some have an experience with God which is truly "spiritual" and "pentecostal" in the New Testament sense; they enjoy a genuinely intimate relationship with God through the Spirit of Christ. As John Wesley often put it, they possess "the whole fruit of the Spirit."[17] They desire above all else to be conformed to the image of Jesus Christ. This stage of development of God's revelation of himself in the history of salvation is what the New Testament considers to be the norm of the Christian life. For "the dispensation of the Spirit" is "the dispensation of righteousness." We are now able through the Spirit to live obediently because we live in a higher stage of grace than any who came before Pentecost (2 Cor. 3:7–11). This is the meaning of Paul's advice to us "to walk by the Spirit" (Gal. 5:25).

Many specific words in the New Testament imply this higher life of the Christian. In fact, our understanding of the New Testament is impoverished because we fail to appreciate its use of Old Testament terms which refer to this higher level of grace. The concrete and physical pictures which the Old Testament words represent are the basis for understanding the spiritual and personal words of the New Testament (1 Cor. 10:11). These include *fruit, abundance, riches, blessing, promise, rejoicing, fulfillment, inheritance, kingdom, sanctification,* and many more.[18]

You can see that these terms are derived from the language used to describe Israel's experience in Canaan. This is because Jesus Christ is the new Israel. The history of Israel culminated in the history of Jesus. All that Israel expected and typified is fulfilled in Christ Jesus. We become his people, not through a physical exodus from captivity and a political conquest of a country, but through our own personal experience of Easter and Pentecost.

THE SAMARITANS' PENTECOST

This point is well illustrated in Acts 8. Philip went to Samaria and preached Christ to the people. They believed, received the word of God, repented, and were baptized into Christ (Easter). The connection between the Exodus Event and the Easter Event is suggested by the words *signs and great miracles.* As we have seen this phrase is a technical description associated with the Israelites' crossing of the Red Sea. Baptism with water refers to believers' participation in Jesus' death-resurrection (Rom. 6:3–5; 1 Cor. 10:1–4; Col. 2:12; 1 Peter 3:21–22).

Three days later Peter went to Samaria.

Now when the apostles at Jerusalem heard that Samaria had received the word of God, they sent to them Peter and John, who came down and prayed for them that they might receive the Holy Spirit; for [he] had not yet fallen on any of them, but they had only been baptized in the name of the Lord Jesus. Then they laid their hands on them and they received the Holy Spirit (Acts 8:14–17).

"Receive the Holy Spirit" is a phrase always used in the New Testament to refer to the giving of the Holy Spirit in his fullness on the day of Pentecost. In fact, this phrase is used only twelve times (John 7:39; 14:17; 20:22; Acts 1:8; 2:38; 8:14–15; 8:17, 19; 10:47; 19:2; Gal. 3:2). Another symbol of the reception of the fullness of the Holy Spirit is the laying on of hands in contrast to baptism with water which represents the new birth and repentance. Other phrases which refer to the day of Pentecost are the Spirit "falling upon," "descending upon," "being given," "poured out," etc.

Peter makes this distinction between Easter and Pentecost even more vivid in his confrontation with Simon Magus. Simon Magus thought he could purchase with money the power to bestow the Holy Spirit (Acts 8:18–19), but Peter told him that his materialistic attitude indicated a lack of spiritual preparation to receive the gift of the Spirit. Baptism accompanied with genuine repentance (Easter) precedes the reception of the Holy Spirit (Pentecost). When Simon Magus asked Peter whether he could receive the Holy Spirit, Peter said,

> "You have neither part nor lot in this matter, for your heart is not right before God. Repent therefore of this wickedness of yours, and pray to the Lord that, if possible, the intent of your heart may be forgiven you. For I see that you are in the gall of bitterness and in the bond of iniquity." And Simon answered, "Pray for me to the Lord, that nothing of what you have said may come upon me" (Acts 8:21–24).

Repentance and baptism (Easter) come before the outpouring of the Holy Spirit (Pentecost).

Peter uses several phrases here to show that he is thinking of the connection between the Exodus and Easter events on the one hand and the Conquest and Pentecost events on the other hand. "The gall of bitterness" and "the bond of iniquity" recall the Israelite bondage in Egypt (Deut. 29:18–19). Simon Magus, Peter says, still lives in the captivity of Egypt; he has never made his exodus from the bondage of sin. He does not yet know the meaning of forgiveness, death to the old life, and deliverance from sin's bondage. There can be no entry into Canaan until he has first left the bondage of Egypt.

Peter continues, "You have neither part nor lot in this matter" (Acts 8:21). The phrase *part nor lot* is also used as a technical description of Israel's possession of Canaan (Deut. 10:9; 12:12; 14:27, 29; 18:1; Isa. 57:6).[19] Acts 8:21 is reminiscent of Deuteronomy 12:12. It was by casting lots that Joshua originally divided up the land among the twelve tribes. *Lot* and *part*, along with the word *portion*, are related to the meaning of the word *inheritance*.[20] Each tribe had its "part" of the "inheritance." Peter is assuming here that the kingdom established in Canaan is a forerunner of the kingdom of Christ established as a "place" ("part," "lot," or "portion") in the hearts of believers. *We* are intended to be the place of God's dwelling, not Canaan.

Simon Magus' terrified response at the thought of his being in the gall of bitterness and the bond of iniquity is reminiscent of Deuteronomy 29:19. There Moses warns Israel that if they occupy Canaan and harbor evil in their hearts, God will punish them. Likewise, Peter warns Simon Magus against assuming that he can claim territory in the kingdom of Christ and continue to live as he did in Egypt; that would place him in real trouble with God (see Deut. 29:19 and Acts 8:23–24).

There must be an Exodus before he can receive the inheritance; there can be no Conquest until first there has been an Exodus. Simon Magus will not experience Pentecost until he has experienced Jesus' resurrected life as signified in water baptism. He has "neither part nor lot in this matter" of entering into the promised inheritance because he is still living in the captivity of wickedness and unrepentance. The power of the kingdom and the riches of the land are the privileges only of those who enter through the indwelling Spirit of Christ.

PAUL'S PENTECOST

Easter and Pentecost are everywhere assumed in the New Testament as the reason why Christians have reached the final and highest stage of the knowledge of God in this world. In

Romans 6:3, Paul writes, "Do you not know that all of us who have been baptized into Christ Jesus were baptized into his death?" He adds, "The death he died he died to sin, once for all, but the life he lives he lives to God. So you also must consider yourselves dead to sin and alive to God in Christ Jesus" (Rom. 6:10–11). Here Paul is calling us to a contemporary appropriation of the original moment of Jesus' death-resurrection.

Having pointed out to the Romans the importance of experiencing their own personal Easter in chapter six, he moves on to the importance of their having their own Pentecost in chapter eight where he describes the meaning of life in the Spirit. Romans 6 is Paul's Easter; Romans 8 is Paul's Pentecost.[21]

Romans 7 might be called Paul's wilderness experience in which he describes his experience of spiritual barrenness as he struggles with his own sense of self-sufficiency. To be freed from the power of sin cannot be achieved through perfect keeping of the Law; Paul says we will fail miserably. We must surrender ourselves completely to God and appropriate Christ's Spirit before the reality of Christ's death-resurrection becomes truly effective within us (Rom. 7:24–25).

This is also the point which Paul makes to the Galatians who seemed to be so tempted to fall back into Judaism.

> But when the time had fully come [notice the importance of history and its progressive development implied here], God sent forth his Son, born of woman, born under the law, to redeem those who were under the law, so that we might receive adoption as sons. And because you are sons, God has sent the Spirit of his Son into our hearts, crying, "Abba! Father!" So through God you are no longer a slave but a son, and if a son then an heir (Gal. 4:4–7).

Paul distinguishes between two events—"sending his Son" and "sending the Spirit." The sending of the Son made possible our "redemption" (Exodus language which prefigures Easter); the sending of the Spirit confirms in our heart of hearts that we are adopted sons of God and the heirs (Canaan language) of Abraham's blessing (Gal. 4:7).

Paul, of course, assumes a historical distinction between the sending of the Son and the sending of the Spirit. It is possible that many of us will experience a historical and time differential between our own Easter and Pentecost, though there is no reason why this has to be the case. But it certainly is true that to keep up our relationship with Christ we must continually update Easter and Pentecost in our devotional life and in worship. The main point is that we are invited to share in the highest stage of the knowledge of God through a participation in the Spirit of Christ. We all too easily assume that simply because we have believed in Christ we have automatically experienced the full blessing of the Holy Spirit given at Pentecost.

OUR PENTECOST TODAY

Have you ever noticed that the book of Acts does not have a proper conclusion? Luke simply records the history of the church up to a certain point and then lays his pen down. The last thing which he reports is Paul's freedom to receive guests while he is under house arrest. Paul uses this privilege to preach the gospel of Christ, "testifying to the kingdom of God, and persuading them concerning Jesus, both from the law of Moses and from the prophets, from morning till evening. And some believed the things which were spoken, and some disbelieved" (Acts 28:23–24, ASV).

Why did Luke stop writing without bringing the history of the early church to some sort of conclusion? The answer is obvious. Only Jesus' return to earth can bring that history to a final chapter. For the history of the church continues, and we are still invited to be a part of it.

To be sure, the final revelation of God in Jesus Christ occurred through his resurrection from the dead and the sending of his Spirit. Paul says that these two events established Jesus' authority as the Son of God (Rom. 1:4). So there is nothing more to be revealed about God since Jesus is God who came in the flesh and who sent the Holy Spirit to occupy our lives, to write his love upon our hearts, and to seal us for redemption. But the history which God began with Abraham and was brought to fulfillment in Jesus continues until —well, until God decides to end it. We must never forget this finality of revelation. Any further claim about God revealing himself is false because through the Spirit of the risen Christ God has already revealed to us all that he will until we see him face to face. Jesus is God's self-declaration. In his risen life, Jesus is the Spirit of God. Will you receive him in his fulness?

The success of his kingdom is surprising when you consider that its members have been won through the "foolishness of preaching" rather than with military force, political power, clever arguments, or claims to cultural and racial superiority. The message has been a report of good news that has happened in the world of time and space—real events which reveal God's presence in history—rather than a mere report of good views and brilliant ideas.

Yes, we are invited to receive this Good News and in this way to be a continuation of the history contained in the book of Acts. Unfortunately, many of us haven't made it into the second chapter. It's as if we are "locked on the dead center once occupied by the disciples between the Resurrection and the gift of the Holy Spirit at Pentecost," as Dr. Lloyd John Ogilvie has expressed it.[22] We may have experienced the resurrection power of Jesus' life and known him in the forgiveness of sins, but we may not have appropriated the fullness of his Spirit and the full power of the kingdom enthroned in our very being.

The choice is ours. We can receive the fullness of the promised Spirit given at Pentecost. If we want to write a new chapter to the book of Acts, the Holy Spirit is available to us today. The promise is to us as well as to the original disciples (Acts 2:39).

4

THE SPIRIT OF HOLINESS

Jesus Christ . . . was descended from David according to the
flesh and designated Son of God in power according to the Spirit
of holiness [Pentecost] by his resurrection from the dead [Easter].

Romans 1:1–4

The Old Testament history of salvation was largely a
failure for Israel. God's people were not obedient, and they
failed because they weren't holy. That is why God drove them
from the "holy land" (Zech. 2:12). For Canaan was a holy land
prepared by a holy God for a holy people.

Holiness is God's signature, the mark of his true character.
He intended that Israel should be stamped with his likeness.
You can understand why they were struck with fear at the very
thought of his presence. They were under a binding contract
made on their behalf by their forefather Abraham. The exacting
terms committed them to be "blameless" in their walk with
God (Gen. 17:1–9). Repeatedly they were reminded that their
God was holy and he expected them to be holy. "I am the LORD
who brought you up out of the land of Egypt, to be your God;
you shall therefore be holy, for I am holy" (Lev. 11:45).

Yet their Exodus from Egypt and Conquest of Canaan did
not succeed in making them a holy people. For nothing about a
piece of land produces holiness. This is why the prophets

foresaw that God would establish a new kingdom. They saw that God's Spirit would come upon the people and sanctify them.[1] This time they would be truly holy and live up to the terms of their contract with God, and this kingdom would last forever (Ezek. 36). In Romans 1:4, Paul says that this new kingdom has come. Jesus Christ is a descendant of David, but he is more than a human being. He is designated the Son of God because of Easter and Pentecost.

This new kingdom is not merely a historical extension of ancient Israel.[2] For Jesus is the new Israel which has been formed by Easter and Pentecost. We are complete at last because we dwell not in a physical place like Canaan but we dwell in Christ. Unlike living in Canaan, dwelling in Christ makes us truly holy. The terms of this new contract are not limited to one group of people, but include all the nations of the earth (Rom. 1:5–6). The expectations of this new contract are not frightening to those who are in Christ Jesus because they possess the Spirit of holiness. The Spirit guarantees that we will meet the inner conditions necessary for the privilege of living in the new kingdom.

HOLINESS AS GOD'S GIFT OF HIMSELF TO US

The Spirit of holiness came on the day of Pentecost. *He was now the Spirit of the resurrected Christ.* He no longer moved about from one person to another for temporary assignments given to specific individuals. He no longer was merely "with" people, but now he permanently took up residence "in" them.[3] His purpose was to make us saints.[4] Abraham and ancient Israel had been called of God to be holy, but they failed in their calling. Now, Paul says, we "are called to be saints" in Jesus Christ (Rom. 1:7).

John Wesley was a reformer in the church in the eighteenth century who took seriously this call for us to become saints. He preached in a chapel service at Oxford University on August 24, 1744. His text was "They were all filled with the Holy Spirit" (Acts 4:31). He titled the sermon "Scriptural Christianity." He said that the purpose of Pentecost was to give the disciples "the mind which was in Christ, these holy fruits of the Spirit." Then with embarrassing directness, he asked the theology teachers, "Are you filled with the Holy Ghost? With all those fruits of the Spirit, which your important office so indispensably requires? Is your heart whole with God? Full of Love?"

Though Wesley had regularly preached at the university, he was never permitted to do so again. His insistence that believers live truly holy lives was considered too fanatical.

In another sermon, entitled "Christian Perfection," he says that the first persons to receive the full sanctifying grace of the Holy Spirit were the disciples on the day of Pentecost. "When the day of Pentecost was fully come, *then first it was* [italics mine] that [the disciples] were made more than conquerors over sin by the Holy Ghost given unto them." He writes that "this great salvation from sin was not given" until the Holy Spirit of Christ came into the world at Pentecost.

In this sermon, Wesley calls the church to see that the purpose of Pentecost was that God might give the Holy Spirit "in His sanctifying graces." The Holy Spirit, he says, did not come at Pentecost to bestow the various gifts, for the gifts of the Spirit were already available and used before Pentecost. But the possibilities of the sanctified life now become actual because the Holy Spirit has been given to the church. He helps us to see that the kingdom of heaven is not some distant reality held for the future. For "the fullness of time is now come, the Holy Ghost is now given, the great salvation of God is brought unto men," and the possibility of "Christian perfection" (perfection of love) is now become a reality for the first time in the history of salvation. Though there is a future coming of the Lord, Wesley reminds us that "the kingdom of heaven is now set up on earth" and that those who are true members of this kingdom have experienced the sanctifying grace of perfect love. For this is the meaning of our calling to be saints.

How does this make you feel? Does the holiness of God frighten you? Indeed, if you are aware of the normal tendencies of your humanity, the very thought that we are supposed to be holy can make you feel anxious.

One day as I left New College Library at Edinburgh University in Scotland I walked passed a carrel of books where a copy of John Wesley's sermons caught my eye. So I stopped to speak to the theological student sitting there. I pointed to Wesley and said, "I see you have a good book there." He sprang to his feet and shattered the silence of the library with his booming voice. "That's a damnable book!" he exploded. He continued with his loud protest, "John Wesley's idea of the holy life has done more to ruin the emotional lives of Christian people than any single person in church history!"

I was shocked and embarrassed by his anger and apparent rudeness. People stared at us with amazement, and as I noticed the librarian beginning to look our way, I decided that that was not the time to continue our "friendly" conversation! Several days later I had a cup of coffee with this student. I learned that he was brought up in a legalistic home. His father was a minister who claimed to follow Wesley's teachings on the holy life, and he had drilled into his son all the do's and don'ts of the sanctified life. Such a serious tone of the "holy" things of Christ had so dominated his childhood that he was terrified of God. He had been so inhibited that he was afraid to breathe lest he offend the Holy Spirit and incite the displeasure of God. His way out of this emotionally and spiritually repressive environment was to break with it. He explained to me, "God accepts me for what I am and not how well I perform."

I agreed with him. This is the meaning of justification by faith through grace alone. We can do nothing to earn our acceptance with God. We are accepted as we turn to Christ. We have only to accept our acceptance. I assured him that John Wesley would have agreed with him, too, though I think he still doubted it.

A life of grace frees us from the self-defeating attitude of thinking that we can earn favor with God by our good works. But perfectionistic thinking dominates the attitude of many. All the nonbiblical religions and philosophies throughout the entire history of the world believe that we can earn our salvation or develop self-esteem through our own self-righteous efforts. Only in the Holy Scriptures is it revealed that salvation is all by grace.[5] Just as we can do nothing to earn our relationship to God, so we cannot experience self-acceptance until we feel accepted by the God of grace.

Self-righteousness is often exhibited by Christian people even though they know better. I visited in the home of a family who no longer attended church. The mother said she quit going because she had just given up on herself. "There's no way I can really live the Christian life," she said. When I asked why, she explained, "One day I got frustrated putting up new curtains in the living room, and I said some pretty bad words." Yet none of them profaned God's name. Her words may not be the kind that she would use in the presence of guests, but in the privacy of her home they seemed to me appropriate expressions of her frustration. And even if she had cursed, God forgives.

She had been brought up in the church, had heard the gospel of grace preached most of her life, and still felt that she had to earn her salvation by being good. Because she got angry in a moment of frustration and expressed her feelings with a blizzard of emotion-packed words, she thought she had offended God who must have been terribly disappointed with her. Because she was so disappointed in herself, she despaired of "trying to live the Christian life" because she could not endure such feelings of divine rejection.

This pathetic story could be repeated over and over again. We imagine that our acceptance with God depends upon our good behavior. And our good behavior is often interpreted to mean that we have no negative feelings and that we must never express them! So when they boil over into our consciousness, we quit in despair or we pretend not to feel angry. Suppression of our negative feelings makes us feel pretentious in our relationship to Christ. The price of this denial of basic human feelings is costly in terms of spiritual joy.

FEAR AS THE ABSENCE OF HOLINESS

Some think of God's holiness as a hammer that threatens us if we fail to perform perfectly. Fright is certainly understandable because the root idea of holiness in the Old Testament is "difference." God is different from the world, and there is space between what the world is and who God is. God is the Creator; we are the creatures. So in an important sense holiness does create space between God and us, and we learn to respect and worship him because of this difference.

But the problem that creates emotional space between God and ourselves is not his holiness, but our broken relationship with him. Adam and Eve felt fear when they broke faith with their Creator. Fear is a panic-feeling that tells us something is wrong about our relationship with God. But because fear is such a destructive emotion it can cause us to run away from him. This is what it did to Adam and Eve. They "hid themselves" (Gen. 3:8). It has the same effect upon us.

How do most people deal with this fear? Some become cynical about life in general. Some seek help from therapists. Some try to be philosophical about it. Some deny it. Some profess not to believe in God. Some remake God into an impersonal spirit so that they don't feel accountable to him personally. Primitive people in ancient and modern times create idols to which they offer sacrifices of food and drink and sometimes the blood of human beings. Others hide behind a pretense of good works and imagine that God is pleased with their performance. Some try to run away from God by immersing themselves in the ambitions of this world and they imagine that they are happy. And some enjoy punishing themselves with feelings of guilt and low self-esteem.

A typical textbook in philosophy of religion will tell you that fear is the least desirable motivation for faith in God. One influential thinker in the eighteenth century, David Hume, easily dismissed belief in God because, he said, it rose out of irrational feelings of fear.[6] Now, there can be no doubt that most fear is irrational, for it makes us do and think all sorts of irrational things. But Hume failed to recognize that atheism is just one of the irrational responses of fear. His easy dismissal of fear as unhuman does not make the anxiety go away, though it might help one to suppress or repress it.

Kierkegaard, the father of modern existential philosophy, was a devout Christian believer of the nineteenth century. His insight into the origin of fear is both biblical and true to human psychology. He has shown us how fear is the dreaded loss of relationship with oneself because of the feared loss of relationship with a source person (such as a mother) who gives us a sense of security.[7] God is our ultimate source person. We cannot have peace in our lives without living in the light of God's countenance, and because he is holy and we are unholy our lives are panic-driven. We feel guilty and condemned, we feel estranged and lost, we feel emptiness and meaninglessness. These feelings of fear cannot be explained away or dismissed simply because they are irrational. The only way successfully to deal with our panic-driven feelings of fear is through a restored relationship with a holy God who is also gracious.

But does God really require *us* to be holy? Surely not. Yet wait a minute. He really does! Check 1 Peter 1:15. Don't forget that ancient Israel apparently felt that God didn't really expect them to be holy. Look at what happened to them. Have you ever noticed that the Scriptures tell us that our preparation for the second coming of our Lord is through our establishment in holiness? (1 Thess. 5:23; 3:13) Heaven is a holy place prepared for a holy people who worship a holy God. Remember that Canaan was a holy land prepared for a holy people who worshiped a holy God. Because the people failed to be holy, they failed to continue in the land.

The final coming of the kingdom of God will take place in heaven. This kingdom was initiated through the Spirit of the risen Christ who was given to the church at Pentecost. We are already in the kingdom, but the kingdom will be finally established in heaven. Heaven will provide all the external surroundings necessary for a perfect existence, but earth is the locale of our preparation for this holy place. Our passport to heaven is the holiness of Christ imparted to us now through the Spirit.

You may be saying to yourself, "I am beginning to agree with your rude friend who angrily denounced Wesley!" Don't give up on me yet, for we must come to an understanding of what holiness really is. Remember that I said it was not primarily a list of do's and don'ts; our faith is not a religion of performance.

But we continue to struggle and pretend to be holy in spite of our cynical feelings. Or else we simply break out of this pretense and claim that "in Christ" we are holy even though in reality we know and admit that we aren't. We might say Christ is our righteousness and it doesn't really matter that we are unrighteous! Some interpret grace to mean a kind of license to sin. My angry friend reflected this attitude. I'm sorry to say that he admitted to me that he was living with another women out of wedlock, but he said that was all right because Christ was his righteousness!

Wrong notions of holiness can cause one to swing from a life of repressed inhibitions to the other extreme of an unrestrained libertinism. One can do whatever he feels like doing! Both are inappropriate reactions to fear. Guilt causes one person to repress normal feelings which he fears might be offensive to God, and it causes another person (or perhaps the same person at a later time) to sin openly because he says that he is free in Christ. Repressed inhibitions can cause severe anxiety disorders, resulting in a nervous breakdown. For others the inner stress becomes so great that their minds find some way to rationalize their feelings by acting them out in inappropriate ways, such as the person I met in the library.

But holiness is not performance; it is primarily a relationship. The holiness of God does indeed mean that he is different from the world; it does mean that he expects us to live as persons made in his image. And just as there is space between God and the world, so there is supposed to be space between the world and us. We are to keep ourselves "unstained from the world" (James 1:27). We are not to be "of the world." Yet we are certainly to be "in the world" (John 17:14–15). Holiness does not mean that we retreat from the world but that we infiltrate the world with the love of Christ.

In the Old Testament, the holiness of God was a fearful thing. It created feelings of distance from God because the people felt themselves so different from their heavenly Father (Isa. 6:1). God's holiness meant that he was remote (Ex. 3:5), exalted (Isa. 33:5), incomprehensible (Isa. 40:13–14), great (Ps. 104:1), terrible (Deut. 7:21), and judging (Deut. 4:23–25).

HOLINESS IS LOVE

The picture of God's holiness in the New Testament has a new face on it. It's the picture of Jesus Christ! And his facial features portray warmth and love. We now see that this affectionate quality is the distinctive feature of God's holiness. Love was always in the background along with the other expressions of God's holiness, but the embodiment of God in Jesus Christ highlighted love as the distinctive and most personal meaning of God's being.

The apostle John is known as the beloved disciple. His writings portray this warm and personal meaning of God. In his first letter, John defines holiness in terms of love. God is holy, but he is holy love. The love of God doesn't mean that God simply ignores evil in our lives. Nor does it mean that God is indifferent about our rejection of his love. The love of God is not mere sentiment; love is the caring character of God. Love means that God cares so much about us that he confronts us with our irresponsible behavior and intends to help us do something about it. John begins his first letter by defining the character of God as light and life. No sin exists in God, and those who have fellowship with God "walk in the light, as he is in the light, [and] have fellowship with one another, and the blood of Jesus his Son cleanses [them] from all sin" (1 John 1:7). Everybody has been born into this world with a sinful heart, John says. But "if we confess our sins, he is faithful and just, and will forgive our sins and cleanse us from all unrighteousness" (1 John 1:9). Even so, if we do sin, he is still our advocate and we will be forgiven (1 John 2:1).

Now all this talk about cleansing from all sin sounds absolute and too perfectionistic. What does John mean when he talks this way? Is he speaking in idealistic terms, knowing full well that we can't measure up to this standard? I don't think so. For he tells us that it is possible for us to obey God's commandments in this world (1 John 5:3).

The idea of cleansing comes from the ancient practice of circumcision which was begun with Abraham. "Flesh" represented a proud and rebellious heart, but its removal represented purity of heart.[8] This is why St. Paul often described sin as "the flesh" (Gal. 5:24). It symbolized spiritual uncleanness and represented pride and rebellion against God. The physical flesh, this skin of ours, is not sinful. "Flesh" was only a figure of speech to symbolize sin.[9] Many modern people, like ancient Greeks, think our physical bodies are evil. But that is not what the Bible teaches. God created the world, and he said it was good (Gen. 1:31). If the physical body is evil, then God could not have become a man without becoming evil at the same time. No, the fleshly body is not evil.

Moses and the prophets show that the rite of circumcision in itself meant nothing. Just because one was a descendant of Abraham and circumcised was no indication that he had a changed heart. The important thing was the reality of loving God with all the heart, mind, and soul (Deut. 30:6). True circumcision is of the heart. This is why the later prophets substituted the word cleansing for the word circumcision. They prophesied the coming of the new kingdom when love for God would be a thing of the heart and not simply a matter of ritual.[10]

This cleansing which makes it possible for one to love God perfectly is the meaning of Pentecost. This is why Peter says during the First Jerusalem Council that God is no respecter of persons; it matters not whether one is a Jew or a Gentile, for physical circumcision means nothing. The important thing, Peter says, is that the Holy Spirit cleanses (circumcises) our hearts by faith through the Holy Spirit given on the day of Pentecost (Acts 15:8–9).

BIBLICAL LANGUAGE IS ANALOGICAL

To be "cleansed from sin" is a pictorial way of saying that we have let go of our selfishness and pride and entered into a relationship of pure love for God. Both physical circumcision in the Old Testament and cleansing from sin in the New

Testament are pictorial representations. Sin is not a physical entity; it is the absence of a proper relationship to God. We are born into this world with an improper disposition toward God already formed in our minds. We develop an inner attitude of self-sufficiency as if we could get along without God.[11] The idea of sin dwelling in the heart is a pictorial way of describing this spiritual condition.

When John says, "The blood of Jesus his Son cleanses us from all sin," he means that through God's participation in human life in Jesus we are enabled through the power of the Spirit to love God with all our hearts. For the sin ("flesh") of pride and rebellion has been cleansed. We must not interpret this language in a philosophical way. John doesn't mean that we are once-and-for-all perfected in an absolutist sense. One of our tendencies in the Western world is to take everything literally. John is only describing our relationship to God in object-like words. These words, if taken literally, will confuse our Western minds.[12]

We must remember that the emphasis is on our ongoing relationship with Christ. Relationships are dynamic; objects are lifeless. Relationships grow and develop; objects are dead and deteriorate. Relationships are internal and spiritual; objects are external and physical. Yet we use objective language to help us picture the inner truth of our relationship to God. We should be aware of this use of object-language so that we don't confuse our understanding of the spiritual. This awareness is especially important to help us understand how we can love God with all our hearts and yet continue to grow in love at the same time. Our hearts are "cleansed," but they continue to be "cleansed" in our continuing life with Christ.

THE STAGES OF CHRISTIAN DEVELOPMENT

John illustrates this dynamic meaning of a developing relationship with God by citing the fact that no one is born mature. He makes an interesting comparison among little children, young men, and fathers to describe the various stages of the Christian life (1 John 2:12–14). "Little children" have their sins forgiven; "young men" have developed further in their Christian experience and become victorious in their skirmishes with the devil; "fathers" are mature and have a deeply established relationship with Christ. They have known the Father who is from the beginning. The idea of *knowing* in John's writing is more than just knowing about something. To know means to experience something inwardly. To know the Father is to internalize in the depths of one's emotions and thoughts the reality of God.

John writes so that they might know the Father, the Son, and the Holy Spirit in the very depths of their being. This is the "truth" which he wants to communicate to them and which will become a part of them. We know the Father through the Son: "He who confesses the Son has the Father also" (1 John 2:23). But John is saying that we receive more than just a relationship with the Father and Son; rather, they come to abide in us through the anointing of the Holy Spirit (1 John 2:24–26). The Holy Spirit enables us to do the will of the Father as modeled in the life of the Son (1 John 3:24). Moreover, the love of the Father and the Son is perfected within our own hearts through the Holy Spirit (1 John 4:12–13).

It is clear that John believes the love which the Father, Son, and Holy Spirit have for each other is the basis of our own personal experience of love (1 John 4:9, 12, 13). A repeated theme is that abiding in Christ through "the anointing" of the Holy Spirit involves a perfect love for God. John does not at all hesitate to show that this level of Christian experience is an expectation which God has for us. Saying, "I know him," means I keep God's Word, and "in [me] truly the love of God is perfected" (1 John 2:5). "Abiding in God" means that the holy Trinity possesses my heart. Specifically, "abiding in Christ" means loving God with all the heart, mind, and soul. "God abides in us and his love is perfected in us. By this we know that we abide in him and he in us, because he has given us of his own Spirit" (1 John 4:12–13).

John's inspired reflections on the meaning of divine love and its implications for us are at the very core of the meaning of the Christian life. Love is what God is all about; love is what our lives are supposed to be entirely about. And the whole point of the revelation of God throughout the history of salvation and culminating in Jesus of Nazareth is to make it possible for us to "abide in him" and to experience his perfect love. It is abundantly clear that our capacity to love comes from his love for us (1 John 4:19). There can be no true love without its first being divine love. Our ability to love God and each other is not natural to us nor something we can generate within ourselves. At best, our love is flawed by selfishness and the desire for personal gain. Only through an experience of the love of God can our love for each other be what God designed it to be.

John recognizes that not all Christians have a perfect love for God. Yet he believes everyone should. Read carefully the precise way that John words his plea for us to love God perfectly:

> If we love one another, God abides in us and his love is perfected in us. By this we know that we abide in him and he in us, because he has given us of his own Spirit. And we have seen and testify that the Father has sent his Son as the Savior of the world. Whoever confesses that Jesus is the Son of God, God abides in him, and he in God. So we know and believe the love God has for us. God is love, and he who abides in love abides in God, and God abides in him. In this is love perfected with us, that we may have confidence for the day of judgment, because as he is so are we in this world (1 John 4:12–17).

John's description of "fathers" (1 John 2:13) represents those who now enjoy a perfect love for God. This is why John Wesley observes that the category of fathers refers to those who know "the Father, and the Son, and the Spirit of Christ, in [their] inmost soul. Ye are 'perfect men,' being grown up to 'the measure of the stature of the fullness of Christ.' "[13]

You remember a similar distinction in Paul's letter to the Corinthians. He said they were but "babes in Christ" (cf. John's category of "little children"). Paul said that they were not fully endowed with the Holy Spirit because they were still "carnal"; a "spiritual" Christian is one who is no longer "of the flesh" and engaged in selfish pursuits (1 Cor. 3:1–3). A "spiritual"

Christian is one who is possessed by the Holy Spirit (1 Cor. 2:12–16).[14] Paul's category of "spiritual men" corresponds with John's definition of "fathers."

What are the differences among the various stages of the Christian life? Some Christians have just begun their walk with the Lord. They know him in the forgiveness of sins, but haven't matured in the love of God. Others have experienced significant growth, but haven't yet had their love for God purified. Others are truly mature Christians who have been released from all dread of God and have had their love made pure through the power of the Spirit. Yet all are the children of God. No one is a second-class citizen in God's kingdom.

When I was a young boy, a famous minister came to stay in our home while he preached a revival meeting in our church. Almost every sermon was an invitation for us to receive God's perfect love into our hearts. I could understand easily enough that God loved me perfectly, but I was troubled in my childish mind that God would expect me to love him like that. I remember being worried by the terrible thought that maybe God didn't really love me because I didn't love him well enough. I often wanted to say something to the preacher about my fears, but I bottled them up inside.

Then one day he told us a very personal story about his family who lived on a farm. One morning his younger son came in for breakfast before running off to school. As usual, he had already finished his early morning chores. While the boy was yet at the table, his father put his arms around his neck and told him how proud he was to have such a fine son. "A father couldn't want a better boy than you. I don't know how I could possibly get along without your help and the things you do to keep the farm going." He spoke in tones of deep affection.

Later in the morning the minister was in his study absorbed in his work as he busily prepared for a preaching service that evening. Suddenly he was distracted by the sound of his older son coming along the hallway with the customary dragging of his feet, for he was mentally retarded and physically handicapped.

But the minister turned once again to his studies and

didn't look up when his son opened the door and entered the room. The boy dragged himself over to his father, held out his hands to offer his father his bedroom shoes. The shoes had been taken out of the trash where he had discarded two worn-out pairs, and the son had taken one shoe from each pair.

Looking up with a bit of annoyance because of the interruption, the father saw a look of love on the face of his retarded son. "I stood up," he told us, "took off the shoes I had on, and put on those mismatched and worn-out bedroom slippers. I then reached over and pulled my son as close to my body as I could and gave him a hug like I never had before. I told him I loved him with all my heart and that no father could be more proud of his son than I was of him."

He then shared with us some of his feelings about having a retarded son. He had felt so saddened and hurt that his first-born was handicapped. Now it would be impossible for the boy to live up to the expectations which most fathers have for their sons. But in time he learned that a retarded child can teach us much about the meaning of life. He learned that life is not made up of success in achieving goals and high expectations. He learned that having children was more than their becoming what a father wants them to be. His retarded son taught him how to love and that a loving relationship is the only thing in life that ultimately matters.

I never forgot this story. And when I begin to fear that my love for God is not good enough, I remember that in spite of my inadequacies God accepts me. We might not be able to do the family chores so well as some members of God's family can. We might not be able to relate to other members of God's family so normally as others. We might not receive a lot of affirmation and attention as others do. But our heavenly Father places his strong arms of holy love about us and speaks to us in tones of infinite affection.

God doesn't measure our worth in terms of our perform-ance. For perfect love is the quality of our relationship to God, and not a measurable quantity. He asks only that we receive the Spirit of holiness. We don't need to be afraid, for holiness is the pure love of God.

5

THE SPIRIT OF LOVE

I appeal to you . . . by our Lord Jesus Christ and by the love of the Spirit.

Romans 15:30

No human emotion is more powerful than that of love. No human need is so great as the need to be loved. No bond with another human being is so strong as the bond of love. No human pain is so intense as the pain of love. No trait is more characteristic of people than their capacity to love. "Love makes the world go 'round." Without it we are nothing! (1 Cor. 13:2)

LOVE MAKES US REAL PERSONS

Most people would agree with this, but many don't often stop to ask, "What is love?" They assume that they know what it is. But in spite of a ravenous appetite for love, we act as if everything else is much more important. We seem to be so much more obsessed with success, sex, prestige, entertainment, money, drugs, and power. These obsessions only reveal to us our confusion over the meaning of love. We want love, but we seek almost everything else.

Freud advised people to be picky about whom they love. He assumed that most people don't have a sufficient amount of energy to be loving toward everyone.[1] Some of his followers, like Erich Fromm, disagreed, but they admit that only a few ever achieve a genuine capacity for loving.

What is love? It is more than a good effort, more than a pleasant emotion, more than knowledge. Love is the likeness of God in our hearts. It is the essence and character of real persons. Nothing matters so much as love; if we lack it, we are as nothing.

Many assume that love is just being lovable. So we concern ourselves with such matters as dressing attractively, behaving in an agreeable manner, and making sure that we always put our best foot forward. We seem easily to confuse love with sex appeal, social and professional success, and money. One of the great illusions of Americans is our belief that love can be bought. Money makes us "lovable" because of all the nice things we can buy for our family.

The most popular opinion is that love means being sentimental, romantic, and sexually responsive. The typical lyrics on the popular music charts contain endless references to the need for love and its fulfillment as the reason for existence. Physical love is portrayed as an instant fix for all of life's problems. Whitney Houston's popular song "How Will I Know That He Really Loves Me?" has no answer except a feeling that "we fall in love everytime we see each other." Feelings of romance, sentiment, and physical closeness are the only apparent meaning and proof of love.

But Paul tells us that love is a choice, a feeling, and a knowing: "If there is any encouragement in Christ, any incentive of love, any participation in the Spirit, any affection and sympathy, complete my joy by being of the same mind, having the same love, being in full accord and of one mind" (Phil. 2:1–2). Love is a choice; we are invited to share in "the same love." Love is an affection and a feeling of sympathy. It is a motivation. Loving is knowing others in the intimacy of their mind and a oneness with them in spirit. More importantly, love is a participation in the Holy Spirit who enables us to be truly loving persons.

The sentimental love of sex and romance, the special love

of our children, the love of family members for each other, the love of our friends are all expressions of divine love. Whatever human relationship we enjoy is enriched by the love of the Holy Spirit who genuinely makes us feel one with God and others. For the Spirit forms our capacity for truly loving.

One of the most inhibiting emotions which reduces the feeling of love is guilt. A person who has felt the loving acceptance of our heavenly Father and been empowered by the Holy Spirit to be "real" in his inner being is a person who can enjoy the privileges of love. God's unconditional acceptance of us and the assurance of his love branded onto our feelings through the Spirit free us from the crippling effects of guilt. This freedom comes to us as a gift, and it cannot be earned by our good behavior. We have only to accept it. "There is therefore now no condemnation for those who are in Christ Jesus" (Rom. 8:1). When we are paralyzed because of guilt and cannot love freely, we can repeat this verse over and over again until its truth releases us from the grip of condemnation.

LOVE IS OUR CAPACITY FOR TRANSCENDENCE

We don't develop as normal persons if we put distance between ourselves and others. Love is our capacity to reach beyond ourselves to penetrate the lives of others and embrace them as part of our own reality. Love gives us depth because we become more than just individuals. Through love we transcend the immediate moment of our own feelings and thoughts and enter sympathetically into the hearts and minds of our friends and family. We share the pictures of our mind and the feelings of our heart with others, and they in turn open up the galleries of their lives to us.

We give up our right to privacy (deny ourselves) in order to reach out and include our friends, and then we in turn find ourselves through the experience of a loving relationship. This is why Jesus once said that unless we deny ourselves we cannot be his friends. With this kind of transcendence and transparency, we will experience the bonding power of love.

We have already said that God's self-declaration to Abraham revealed for the first time in human history the real meaning of the personal. An important implication of this "discovery" of the personal was the feeling that Abraham stood over against the reality of God; he stood alone. He was an *I* over against the *Thou* of God. A by-product of Abraham's acquaintance with the distinctive personality of God was his awareness of himself as a personal *I*. With this awareness came a feeling of his own spiritual transcendence and moral responsibility.[2]

The importance of Abraham's self-discovery cannot be overly emphasized for us today. For this personal dimension of our human life could not have been felt and understood until we were first fully known and understood from beyond ourselves by an all-knowing God. Even secular humanists acknowledge that belief in one God as Father was the first decisive step forward for the human race in its search for the true meaning of the personal.[3]

Primitive religions represent the infant stage of the human race when it could not distinguish itself from mother nature. Just as an infant does not make any distinction between itself and its mother, so primitive religions represented the way which human beings experienced themselves as part of nature. Primitive peoples identified themselves with animals by wearing animal masks and by worshiping totem animals. These nature religions show that they did not yet have a feeling of being separate from nature. They were not able to distinguish between spirit and nature.[4] Consequently, they did not recognize themselves to be "persons" with a sense of individuality and spiritual uniqueness.

They were driven primarily by fear. Love was by no means a typical quality of their gods; rather the gods in turn were driven by jealousy, lust, and contempt. The religion of the Bible is the only religion which developed a belief in a personal God who is not dependent upon the world for his existence; it is the only religion which believed that God merely spoke the world into existence through the power of his word; it is the only religion believing that an invisible God whose existence is totally independent of nature became visible in a human being,

Jesus of Nazareth; it is the only religion believing that a personal Creator expressed his love through self-sacrifice.[5]

The reason for this is that biblical religion is the only one which taught that the universe had a face on it. Other systems believed that even their gods were subject to the brutal force of blind nature. But the God of Jesus is a personal being who created the world and redeemed it; he is not a blind force.

Love in its truest dimensions could not be known without the revelation that the God of creation is the God of redemption. He is a person. That's why we can know ourselves as persons. Modern psychology is living off the borrowed experience of the Christian faith. Its search for the meaning of persons is motivated by a Christian understanding and cannot be achieved without a corresponding understanding of God.

LOVE IS DEVELOPED THROUGH INTERPERSONAL RELATIONSHIPS

We do not become loving through a mere act of the will, pleasant sensations, or by merely getting to know pieces of information about another. We do not develop a loving disposition through reading books on how to love. Love is a quality which develops from healthful and meaningful interpersonal relationships. Our model for becoming loving persons is not an abstract principle; it is not an aesthetic and pantheistic union with a faceless universe. Some thinkers have talked about love in this impersonal manner. Love is not merely a psychological idea, a goal, which we can achieve through self-help techniques.

Our Model of love is a personal being—the Holy Trinity. "Beloved, let us love one another; for love is of God, and he who loves is born of God and knows God. He who does not love does not know God; for God is love" (1 John 4:7–8). Throughout his writings, John shows that we come to know God the Father through the revelation of his Son by means of the Holy Spirit (1 John 4:13–14). "God is love" does not mean simply that God is loving; God is love because he is a unity of three persons in one relationship. Love assumes the existence of someone else. If God were merely one, he would be static, boring, and uninteresting to himself. Indeed, he would be lonely.

To be a person carries with it the meaning of interpersonal relationships, the meaning of empathy and affection for others. No one can truly be a person if he lives isolated from other persons. We are "personal" because we are also "social." God would not be the truly supreme *personal* being if he were merely one person because he would be all law with no love. He would be insensitive, autocratic, and harsh will with no affection. This is what the god of Islam is—all law and will without love. "God is love" means that God is truly personal because he is three persons in one relationship.

We must be careful not to imply by this that God is a neurotic with three personalities. He is not three independent centers of self-consciousness; he doesn't appear under the guise of three different people. He is not three gods; he is one God. He is like a triangle which has three sides but is one object.

The Father is Father because of the relationship he has with the Son; the Son is the Son because of the relationship he has with the Father; the Holy Spirit is the personal unity of the Father and Son. God is one in interpersonal relationship, and the bonding quality of this relationship is the love of the Spirit.

John's first letter is a beautiful description of God's love which he has within himself as an interdependent relationship of Father, Son, and Holy Spirit (1 John 2:22–24; 4:7–18). Notice that God's love is not an immature sense of dependency. The Father doesn't drain the life out of the Son nor does the Son do the same to the Father. There is a mutual sense of respect for each other as distinct persons, but there is also a recognition that each is a part of the substance of the other. Jesus said, "The Son can do nothing without the Father." Each has his own identity; at the same time they are interdependent. A dependent love is immature, for it uses and sucks the life out of another person for its selfish purposes. In God we see the model of mature love of three persons who are interdependent and reciprocally related.

We learned all this from God's self-disclosure. God is the Father as Creator; he is the Son as Redeemer; he is the Holy

Spirit as Sanctifier. The Father is the Source of everything; the Son is the Model of everything; the Holy Spirit is the Agent of God in the world who makes real in us what is true in the Father and what is seen in the Son.[6]

In John's gospel, Jesus told his disciples that he and his Father would come to them and take up permanent residence in their hearts through the Holy Spirit. No longer would God be confined to living in a temple or in a physical place like Canaan. Instead of this superficial kind of relationship, the Father and the Son would send the Holy Spirit to dwell in the disciples and they would be one with each other even as the Father and the Son are united in love by the Spirit (John 16, 17).

The Holy Spirit is like a real estate agent or broker whose task is to take a piece of property which belongs to somebody else and turn it over to us. This is what the Holy Spirit does. He takes the human "properties" of Jesus and passes them on to us—his love, his joy, his peace, his patience, his goodness, his self-control. These "properties" of Jesus are all transferred to us without charge; we have no down payment to make and no monthly payments. His pieces of "real estate" are free for the asking and taking. They are gifts of God the Father; they are "subdivided" in Jesus of Nazareth who is the perfect model of these properties of love, joy, peace, patience, self-control, and goodness; and they are "brokered" to us through the agency of the Holy Spirit.

This of course doesn't mean that only Christian people know how to love. In fact, Christians often fail to love. This isn't the fault of divine love but of our slow appropriation of it. God's love is the only reason why any expression of love exists in the world. Without God's love there would literally be no world at all. Creation is the expression of his love. Love is the inevitable "cause" of God's creating the world in the beginning. He didn't need the world as if he were dependent on it psychologically for his well-being.[7] But his act of creation was as spontaneous and inevitable as our breathing, as inevitable as parents desiring to have children.

A distraught father once said to me after I had preached on the love of God, "I wouldn't have had a son if I had known what a heartbreak he would become." Perhaps not, I thought, after I listened to his story. But I reminded him that it's part of our nature as persons to take risks, and having children to love is a risk most of us are willing to take. Then I tried to add a word of encouragement: "That's the risk God was willing to take with us because he is love. Even though God knew that the human race would disgrace him, he still created us as persons with free choice to love. God knew of this possibility in advance, and this is further evidence of the power of love to express itself even though we may be brought to disgrace." But as I looked that father in the face, I saw his hurt, his pain. He was not able to hear a word I said, and I sensed that what hurt him most was not the disgrace but the feeling for his son. That father would gladly have exchanged places with him because he loved him.

In moments of such grief, words fail to alleviate the pain of love. Before I left, I prayed with him and was thankful that he had given me a chance to share in his sorrow. For the pain of love I saw in his eyes was the same love which God has for us.

If it were ever true that God created us because he is love, it is even more true that because he is love he sent his Son to die to save us. The death of the Son of God was the pain of love which God the Father felt for us. He did not spare himself; he did not show vindictive feelings against us because we had disgraced him. But he embraced our fallen humanity and fully shared in the consequences of our sin. He felt the sorrow and grief of our situation even though we were blinded and unaware of his love.

> O Love divine, what hast thou done?
>   Th'immortal God hath died for me!
> The Father's co-eternal Son
>   Bore all my sins upon the tree!
> The Son of God for me hath died:
>   My Lord, my Love is crucified.
>   Charles Wesley

This self-sacrificing quality of Calvary love was just as inevitable as the love which caused God to create the world in the first place. He exchanged places with us so that he could feel our aloneness and we could feel his love. Nothing is more transforming for our sense of worth than love, and nothing is more compelling for one who loves than sacrificing oneself for the sake of the loved one.

We are truly renewed as persons because we now share in God's interpersonal relationship of love which he has within himself. We know God because he knows us in our fallen human condition and because he has given us his Spirit who will make possible our love for and knowledge of God. Paul says, "What person knows a man's thoughts except the spirit of the man which is in him? So also no one comprehends the thoughts of God except the Spirit of God. Now we have received not the spirit of the world, but the Spirit which is from God, that we might understand the gifts bestowed on us by God" (1 Cor. 2:11–12). This is a fantastic insight! We are taken into the life of God and know him truly and most intimately because we have been given his Holy Spirit. We know God because he knows himself in us through his Spirit. This is not a knowledge about God, but of God himself.

This is the same insight which Jesus shared with his disciples before Pentecost. He promised them that his love and the Father's would be given to them through the Holy Spirit because "we will come to [them] and make our home with [them]" (John 14:23). This means that we are changed into loving persons because we share in the same love which God the Father, the Son, and the Holy Spirit have for themselves.

This means that love is interpersonal. But just having interpersonal relationships does not make us truly loving persons unless they have the quality of God's pure love which binds us together. Human love in itself does not have this pure quality of divine love; it is flawed by selfishness. This is why religious humanism does not succeed.

THE CHURCH IS GOD'S WAY OF DEVELOPING OUR CAPACITY FOR BECOMING LOVING PERSONS

I do not mean that some measure of love is not possible unless one has received the Spirit of Christ. We often hear of inspiring incidents of sacrifices which even non-Christians make on behalf of others. History is filled with thrilling stories of human love. But even these instances are expressions of the love of God, traces of God's love left over in the hearts of marred humanity. We could not exist for a day without love. Love, as Plato put it, is the longing for immortality.[8] It is the natural evidence that God exists. But the purity of love and its redeeming quality is most clearly seen in the self-declaration of God as Father, Son, and Holy Spirit. And the most visible expression of God's interpersonal love is the power of God's Spirit working in us through the community of faith.

This community of faith was created by the coming of the Holy Spirit on the day of Pentecost; we call this community the church, which means the ones who have been called to share in the Spirit-filled life of Christ. The Holy Spirit dwells within our very being, generating the loving of God within us, and inspiring us to be witnesses of his love to the whole world. Through the loving fellowship of the body of Christ, believers are a witness to the possibility of everyone becoming a loving person. For love is the first fruit of the Spirit. The Spirit who dwells in us inspires us to pass God's love on to others. This is the evidence, John says, that we truly belong to God (1 John 3:16–18).

Though the church is the most visible expression of God's love in the world, this doesn't mean that we are perfect role models. Only Jesus is. And it often happens that we don't always say or do the most appropriate things either. Just because we have received the Spirit of Christ's love doesn't necessarily mean that his power is instantly released into our lives in such a way that all our personal problems are resolved. What we have experienced in our hearts may take a while to be released in our feelings and thoughts.

THE PATIENCE OF THE INDWELLING HOLY SPIRIT TEACHES US HOW TO LOVE

For the rest of this chapter, I want to address those who seem to have great difficulty in developing their capacity for becoming loving persons. You may become uneasy or over-whelmed with a sense of guilt every time you read or hear someone talking about the love of God. You may feel like a spiritual failure because you are troubled with difficulties in relationships. I cannot give you a remedy, but I offer the following reflections.

The process of emotional healing often requires the loving care and personal attention of other Spirit-filled believers. This in fact is what being part of the body of Christ is all about. This is why the Spirit distributes within the body different gifts of ministry so that we can be bonded together in mutual love and develop as mature persons (Col. 2:19; 3:14; Rom. 12:1-11).

Unfortunately many of us seem at times not to be mature loving Christians. Sometimes genuine love gets mixed up with a pretentious way of relating to others in order to manipulate them through guilt. We turn on the charm to give the impression that we are selfless and inordinately generous. This is so insidious because we are usually unaware of what we are doing to ourselves and to others. Through the appearance of being loving and yet making others feel guilty, we are often unconsciously learning how to control the actions of our friends and loved ones. "Love" can do awful things to people. In the name of love, some have been driven to despair, hate, and an inability to love truly.

One well-known philosopher of ethics believes that the Christian virtues of faith, hope, and love are an example of "vengeance gone underground." He says that we embrace the so-called virtues of love and faith because we are emotionally weak and feel threatened by the strength of other people's egos. So we try to inhibit others by making them feel guilty. This in turn makes us "strong" because we are able to control them since we have made them "weak." So he says that love is really self-hate which has been driven beneath the surface of our consciousness but masks itself through the pretense of love.[9]

His criticism is surely overdone, but he does have a good point. We often compensate for our negative feelings by projecting a good appearance. This is normal and acceptable, but it becomes an illness spiritually and emotionally when we refuse to deal openly and honestly with our feelings. When this happens, we become pretentious rather than authentic persons, and love may degenerate into exploitation of others for our own gratification, or we may compensate for a lack of genuine love through acting as though we are super-spiritual, super-kind, and super-loving.

Often this inappropriate expression of love is rooted in hidden feelings of hurt going back to early childhood. I once developed a pleasant association for a brief time with a construction worker who was helping to build my home. He enjoyed taking his morning breaks talking to me about John Wesley's teaching on Christian perfection. For the first few days and each time we met he would speak about the joy of knowing the Lord in the fullness of his love. Then he would weep profusely. I am not an emotional person, but I respect those who are. This man, however, was so overcome with emotion that I was unnerved by his involuntary crying.

He told me that he had been reared in a home with inflexible and strict rules of conduct. His father had only passively been involved in his life, while his "saintly" mother dominated everybody. He shared with me a secret which he had never told anyone else. His now deceased mother had practiced a type of punishment which she said she used in order to ensure that her children would grow up to respect God. Whenever the least bit of back talk occurred or the slightest suggestion of disobedience showed itself, she promptly smacked him in the face and locked him in the cellar for two hours.

I felt that this hurting man didn't want to recognize the wrong his mother had inflicted on him. He obviously believed that she was a saintly woman whose love for him had made a devout Christian out of him. But I suspected that lurking beneath his involuntary tears of joy which he shed whenever he spoke about the love of God was a deep hostility toward her. This caused an overwhelming sense of guilt since he had been taught that such feelings for his mother were inappropriate for a Christian. His claim of loving God in part was a mask to hide his rage toward her.

I am sure that this man experienced a measure of God's

love and grace in his life, though his life was torn by relational strife. His fellowworkers were dismayed by his capacity for great generosity and thoughtfulness on the one hand and an equally great capacity for indignation over the slightest provocation on the other. His overreactions would always be immediately followed by apologies and a seeking for forgiveness. He had carried hidden feelings of anger for many years, and he coped by appearing to be very loving, thoughtful, and kindhearted. But at times his stress level became so great that he exploded with indignation.

We easily hide from our true feelings by pretending to be different from what is really going on inside us. We drive resentment down deep within our hearts and pretend it isn't there, but our troubled relationships are a reminder that we have fooled only ourselves.

It is important to note that hate is not necessarily contrary to love. The opposite of love is indifference, not hate. Some things we ought to hate, and an eight-year-old child being placed on several occasions in a locked cellar appropriately hates his mother's actions. I think the same is true with children who are slapped in the face by their parents. God may have made a boy's seat an appropriate place to be spanked, but surely not his face. One's face is the most personal part of the body, and it is insulting and damaging to a child's sense of personal worth and self-esteem to be struck in the face.

I have no doubt that this man knew the love of God in his heart, even though unknown to himself he had buried feelings of resentment toward his mother, his father, and possibly even God. But God understands even when we don't. It is possible for a consecrated Christian to have buried feelings of hurt and injury stemming from bad relationships.

A Christian ought not self-consciously to harbor and nurture bad feelings toward others and act out feelings of anger in an intentional and premeditated way. The Holy Spirit cleanses our hearts from such attitudes. But at the unconscious level, where we are not in control and where feelings lie buried beneath the surface of our conscious and rational life, are hidden memories that in subtle and unconscious ways still influence our behavior. We are able by the Holy Spirit to deal with these unconscious motivations as they surface, but there is an important sense in which we are not responsible for what goes on inside that subterranean level of our being. Through the helping love of mature and responsible laypeople in the church, along with those trained in pastoral counseling and Christian psychology, God can heal us of these buried memories of the past through his Spirit.

My friend never had that opportunity, and I'm sorry to say that his life came to a sudden end from a massive heart attack. I wasn't surprised, given the intense stress he lived with. I was told that unflattering comments were privately made at his funeral about his "hypocrisy," his "pretense" about being a Christian, his "sharp tongue" being silenced by his death, etc. I was saddened because I knew perhaps what nobody else knew. But I rejoiced to know that this man was received by a gracious and loving heavenly Father who is pure love and perfectly understands.

It's easy enough to be loving when all the necessary support and influences are there for us, but to attempt the experience of love when you have been emotionally abused and spiritually whipped with guilty feelings all your life is a far greater accomplishment. Some of the greatest models of sainthood are not the obvious ones, for too often they have found it easy because of the many good influences in their lives. But those whose lives have been crushed by the harsh hand of ugliness and the misfortunes of birth and environment yet who still dare to love God in spite of their emotional pain and unresolved feelings of anger, these are the unsung heroes of faith. These maladjusted persons often feel a far greater degree of love and grace in their hearts than those who may not have had to contend with inner struggles of hurt and injured emotions. God has much more patience with them than we do. This is why we need to be kind even to ourselves by not beating our own heads with a blackjack of guilt feelings if we discover that our relationships are often troubled with moments of inappropriate temper and such "sins of surprise," as Wesley called them.

Even though the science of psychology was not so developed and its insights not so well known in his day, John Wesley was careful, considerate, and understanding enough in his preaching and writing to show that many dear souls had been made perfect in God's love in their hearts even though they continued to struggle with emotional and personal conflicts. God judges us, not on the basis of an impossible perfect performance, but on the sincerity of our love for him. This is why Wesley once said that a person made perfect in love may at the same time be afflicted with maladjustment problems associated with "nervous disorders." He also cautioned against setting the standard of Christian love so high that most would despair of achieving it. He further cautioned against assuming that Christians are not subject to mistaken perceptions and faulty judgments.

I do not intend to say that we shouldn't attempt to work through our relational problems; maturing in grace means that in fact we seek to be more and more like Christ in our behavior and performance. It also means that daily we need to seek forgiveness and the restoring love of Christ. This is why Wesley reminds us that, no matter how mature we might be as Christians, we always stand in daily need of the atonement of Christ.

At some point many Christians do experience the cleansing flow of the Holy Spirit washing over their emotions, and are freed from hidden anger and secret hurt. Often these hurt feelings are more hidden from us than from our friends and loved ones, and this is where the helping and caring members of the body of Christ can be important resources for our emotional healing. They can help us see what we would not dare see by ourselves.

Christ has chosen his body, the church, to be the channel of grace for us. This is a personal world which God created. This means that we are responsible for each other. To develop into the kind of persons God wants us to become requires our own personal involvement and responsibility. Ordinarily, God does not provide us with an instant and automatic solution to our personal problems. An important aspect of our development is to accept responsibility for what we are both in our thinking and feeling. This is possible through the caring relationships we develop within the community of the Spirit, the church.

I remember a psychiatrist friend once saying, "Thank God for our human ability to compensate!" Genuine love is the love of God revealed in Christ. This love can be genuine within us through the power of the Holy Spirit, but sometimes we compensate for a lack of genuine love by pretending to love when we really don't. The problem is not that we don't want to love, but that we are inhibited by buried hurt feelings which often paralyze or restrict our capacity to love. The power of the Holy Spirit working through the interpersonal relationships within the body of believers gradually changes our pretense into genuine release of God's love throughout our being. With appropriate nurturing relationships, love heals all hurts, and it begins at Calvary. That is where the Creator of the world became the Redeemer of earth people who had lost their capacity to love.

In his prayer for the Christians at Ephesus, Paul shows that this spiritual capacity to love is developed through the power of the Holy Spirit.

> I bow my knees before the Father, from whom every family in heaven and on earth is named, that according to the riches of his glory he may grant you to be strengthened with might through his Spirit in the inner man, and that Christ may dwell in your hearts through faith; that you, being rooted and grounded in love, may have power to comprehend with all the saints what is the breadth and length and height and depth, and to know the love of Christ which surpasses knowledge, that you may be filled with all the fulness of God (Eph. 3:14–19).

6

THE SPIRIT OF HOPE

May the God of hope fill you with all joy and peace in believing,
so that by the power of the Holy Spirit you may abound in hope.

Romans 15:13

Hope is one of three Christian virtues along with faith and love (1 Cor. 13:13). Love is the personal character of God, and it is the foundation of hope and trust. Faith is love trusting; hope is love expecting (1 Cor. 13:7). All three virtues are eternal whereas some gifts of the Spirit will cease to exist (1 Cor. 13:8–9).

The origin of hope is the promise of God to Abraham (Rom. 4:18). The capacity to hope is a gift of God's grace (Rom. 4:16). The power to hope comes from the Holy Spirit (Rom. 15:13). Hope is defined as "beholding the glory of the Lord" and "being changed into his likeness" (2 Cor. 3:12–18). Hope is the present expectation and guarantee of our future relationship with God in heaven (1 Peter 1:13, 21). Without the present and future dimensions of hope in God, human life is a pity (1 Cor. 15:19). Paul reminds the Christians at Ephesus of their former life as Gentiles when they had "no hope" and were "without God in the world" because they were "separated from Christ" (Eph. 2:12).

HOPE IS AN EXCLUSIVE CHRISTIAN VIRTUE

Hope is a Christian virtue, not just a subjective feeling and a pleasant emotion. Hope is the character of love to expect what God has promised. Hope provides us with our sense of human worth and leads us to believe in the promises of God. This hope is more than just a psychological attitude; it is an objective experience of the transcendent reality of God in Christ. Hope is no mere personal feeling; it is an assurance of our eternal relationship with God.

Those outside biblical faith know through a general revelation of God that we should possess at least four virtues: wisdom, courage, temperance, and justice. What they don't know about are the Christian virtues of faith, hope, and love. For these are available to us only through Jesus Christ.

Not even Old Testament believers fully understood these virtues because Christ had not come. This is why a pessimistic attitude is expressed by the Psalmist: "In death there is no remembrance of thee; in Sheol who can give thee praise?" (Ps. 6:5) God's presence among his people was the "hope of Israel" (Jer. 14:8), but the certainty about life beyond the grave was often imperfectly understood. This is why the psalmist grieves over the meaning of death because hope seemed to be gone. Job once asked, "If a man die, shall he live again?" (14:14) He observed that when a tree dies it has the chance of sprouting again, but "man dies, and is laid low: man breathes his last, and where is he?" (14:10) He then asks, "If a man die, shall he live again?"

This feeling of despair is later transformed for Job into an attitude of hope because he sensed that a relationship with the eternal God means that he too will live forever. "I know that my Redeemer lives, and at last he will stand upon the earth; and after my skin has been thus destroyed, then without my flesh I shall see God, whom I shall see on my side, and my eyes shall behold, and not another" (Job 19:25–27).

Death is an awful and ugly experience even though there is a trend today to dress it up as something natural and normal.

Paul labels it the number one killer of human hope, and declares that Christ himself will destroy it (1 Cor. 15:19, 26).

The disciples felt the disappointing experience of the death of a loved one when their dreams and hopes had been swept away by the crucifixion of their Lord. They had expected him to be "the one to redeem Israel" (Luke 24:21). They later discovered—rather, Jesus showed them—that he was indeed the hope of Israel and the hope of all humanity because he conquered death.

Death is our enemy because it brings to an end our relationships with loved ones. This is why the resurrection of Jesus brought such joy to the hearts of the disciples: their Lord whom they loved was alive (Matt. 28:8). And because he is the Lord of life and conqueror of death, they too would share in his immortal life in a fellowship of love forever.

Our life with God beyond this world is always described in the New Testament as a fellowship of saints in union with Christ. Notice this relational emphasis in Paul's description of the second coming of our Lord:

> The Lord himself will descend from heaven with a cry of command, with the archangel's call, and with the sound of the trumpet of God. And the dead in Christ will rise first; then we who are alive, who are left, shall be caught up together with them in the clouds to meet the Lord in the air; and so we shall always be with the Lord (1 Thess. 4:16–17).

The relationship of the "togetherness" of believers with Christ is the hope of the Christians, depicted as a banquet scene in the book of Revelation when God's people will sit down together at "the marriage supper of the Lamb" (19:9). The featured host is Jesus himself: "They shall see his face, and his name shall be on their foreheads" (22:4). This is the meaning of the hope of eternal life—enjoying the fellowship of Jesus and the love of God's family forever and ever. Amen!

GOOD REASONS FOR THE HOPE EVERLASTING

Relationship with God is what makes eternal life so desirable. Those who think of it primarily in terms of the extension of life miss the whole point of the Christian hope. The attention is on our relationship to God, not on ourselves. Our activity then will not be self-serving, but God-serving. Our time then will be spent in worship of God, not in praise of ourselves.

I am puzzled when I hear someone say that he has no desire for a life beyond this world, yet this is the attitude of many secular people today. I have talked with many of them and I have listened to their reasons; I have read their philosophies and observed their arguments; and I have come away with a feeling of sadness that they don't seem to appreciate the eternal meaning of their own personal relationships.

Many "proofs" have been offered to support the idea of life after death. But I suspect that so much attention has been devoted to this belief, not because we have proved it, but because we have such strong intuitions of immortality rising from our relationships with loved ones. So thinkers try to prove it with their heads because they first believe it so strongly in their hearts.

I can't help but wonder also whether some try to disprove the belief in immortality for the same reason. Could it be that their relationships with loved ones are less than desirable? Could it be that their present existence is so miserable that the idea of its extension into another life would be terrifying?

If that is so, then belief in immortality would not be a hope for them but a fear. That in itself would be "hell" for some if we simply defined immortal life in terms of the mere extension of our existence. Hell in a real sense is separation from meaningful relationships. Sartre in *No Exit* described hell as other people we have to live with, an experience which is common in our modern world, as divorce statistics plainly show.

Several hundred years before the birth of our Lord, Plato was the first thinker to try to prove immortality through reason. He offered complicated and clever arguments which have inspired many people ever since he wrote *The Phaedo*. He said that his motivation was to find "the best and most dependable theory which human intelligence can supply, and use it as a raft to ride across the seas of life" (85:c). He believed that we were left to figure this out for ourselves since the "father of the universe" (*Timaeus,* 28:c) is unknown and since we have no divine revelation (*Phaedo,* 85:c). Plato often refers to our relationships as the basis for our intuition of immortality. He defines love as a longing for immortality (*Symposium,* 206:e).

I can understand why some would find his way of thinking objectionable, for his reasoning is not always convincing. Perhaps the most threatening thing about his belief is that the gods will judge us in that life according to our behavior in this one. So he stresses the importance of education to teach us how to live here and now. He also thinks our present education will assist "the newly dead at the beginning of his journey there" to adjust to his new surroundings (*Phaedo,* 107:d).

Since most people have found their attempts to relate to others troublesome at different points in their lives, it would be unnerving to think of going into the next world carrying with us our present personality and individuality and trying to make new adjustments there. If you feel you have adjustment problems here and now, imagine what they will be like when you cross into the next life as a total stranger and have to fend for yourself!

It is no wonder that Paul says non-Christians are without hope in this world because they have no sure hope in God. The hope of the Christian is that the meaningful and loving relationships that we have developed here will be enriched and fulfilled in the life we have with God there. *The hope we have is a reassuring one because we have received the power of the Holy Spirit to love God and each other here and now, and we have the inner assurance that our inheritance awaits us there* (see Eph. 1:13–14). We have hope because we have the promise of God that he will be our God and we will be his people.

This is a sure hope, not a hunch cleverly devised by complicated reasoning. For the resurrection of Jesus Christ from the dead (Easter) is an event in history witnessed by those who knew him most intimately during his earthly life and who later came to know him in their inner hearts by the power of his

Holy Spirit (Pentecost). We have a reason to hope which is more than mere logic; we have an intuition of eternal life which is more than a human feeling for immortality. That reason is found in the person of the risen Jesus who is God's promise made to us in the history of salvation; that intuition is the indwelling Spirit.

A sure hope is not commonly found in many modern people, but some degree of hope is certainly an important part of being human. The testimony of the history of the human race is clear in its feeling that life after death is an expectation. Even when this intuition of immortality is rejected, one can't live without some kind of hope. Modern medicine recognizes that death is the consequence of radical hopelessness. Even those who say that they don't believe in God admit that hope is the virtue which gives meaning to human life. One well-known Marxist philosopher says that modern unbelievers like himself who attempt to live a meaningful life without God are living off the "borrowed credit card" of Christian faith. For there is no motivation "to keep the head high and to work" with a confession of unbelief.[1]

Another influential thinker frankly says that when you look at all the intellectual problems which philosophers seek to resolve, there is only one that matters—suicide. Is life really worth living? His answer is that there is no good reason except the mere choice to do so![2] Another widely known philosopher simply dismisses the idea of personal existence beyond the grave because he can find no good "reason" to believe in such a hope. But he is still sure that life is worth living![3]

"Why?" we might ask, "is there such a problem among some intelligent people with belief in the hope everlasting?" Are they simply deceived, or is it really foolish and immature to hope in this way?

OUR CAPACITY TO HOPE IS ROOTED IN EARLY FAMILY LIFE

The problem goes back to a more fundamental issue. The reason why the hope of eternal life has lost some of its logic for many is because relationships in family life have suffered from a disintegration of love. For the quality of early family life is the foundation for the hope of eternal life.

Erich Fromm, the world-famous Swiss psychiatrist who died in 1980, once said that "no objective observer of our Western life can doubt that love—brotherly love, motherly love, and erotic love—is a relatively rare phenomenon."[4] This is exactly why the hope of life everlasting doesn't seem to fit into the expectations of many people. For they have no experiential basis in their early family life for appreciating the meaning of loving relationships.

Almost everything we believe as adults is rooted in our earliest relationships in life. Our perceptions of the world and the interpretations which we place upon them are all filtered through life experiences. Of course, our beliefs are not merely subjective, but our emotions and feelings which rise out of human relationships condition the way we see things. And when our early experiences are largely negative and lack the support of loving relationships, the ideas which we hold about the world and ourselves are going to be formed accordingly. Actually, I should say "de-formed" instead of "formed."

This connection among the relational, the spiritual, and the personal is often ignored. We like to imagine that our ideas and beliefs are the product of our reason alone. But that rarely is the case. The Bible assumes that our basic beliefs are formed during our childhood; it assumes that children are molded by their parents' set of spiritual values and beliefs. This is why Moses specifically placed responsibility on parents to teach God's will and purpose "diligently to [their] children" (Deut. 6:7).

Clinical studies have shown the lasting influence which mothers and fathers have upon their children. Every child when he matures is a synthesis of his parents. Fromm describes a mature person as an adult who has become his own mother and father, and an immature person as one who experiences considerable difficulty in reconciling these two competing influences. The result, he says, is often a neurosis.[5]

A MOTHER'S LOVE IS THE
FOUNDATION FOR HOPE

Other clinical studies show that the first few years of a child's development will form his character and pattern of relating for the rest of his life. The face of the mother and her gaze into the infant's eyes will make the difference between an adult in later life who is able to love and one who isn't. Evidence points to the particular importance of a mother's face in a child's developing sense of self-acceptance and personal identity.[6]

The prolonged absence of the mother's face makes the infant feel that he must die, for his security and very being are entirely dependent upon the mother's attention. The cry of the infant when the mother disappears from the room expresses the child's fear that his very being will disappear. The loss of love is the loss of being.

The mother represents unconditional love; she is the source person for being alive. She makes the infant feel good about himself. She is the source of life's inspiration. She instills a joy of living within the infant. She makes the infant child feel loved simply because he is, because he exists—without any conditions attached.

The infant feels no difference between himself and his mother. The picture of a nursing infant at his mother's breast is the symbol of the bond between mother and child; it is the child's sense of union with himself. Unless the mother reinforces the infant's well-being by attending to his needs, he will experience troubled relationships throughout his life. Emotionally the infant will feel depersonalized through neglect, and his growth will be stifled and "fixed" at an early level of immaturity.

A hidden feeling of rage against being thrown into an objectless world disturbs us in adult life if as infants we felt abandoned, greatly neglected, and failed to see mother's loving face. Our coping technique will be one of anxiously clinging to others in our adult years, or an impersonal detaching of ourselves from others in lonely isolation. In both instances, the bruised self will feel insecure, unloved, and skittish about relationships. The intensity of our need for unconditional love in our adult years will be so great that we will overreact in our relationships, with the result that our need for love will be frustrated almost every time.

The inseparable attachment of the infant to the mother begins even before birth, but it continues for several years thereafter. The most important need during these early years is the need to be loved, to feel the mother's thrill of his very existence and to hear the whispers of warmth and caring. Otherwise the child will in all likelihood never learn to love. Here in this mothering relationship he learns to think of himself as a person of inherent worth; he is loved not because he deserves it but simply because he is a person. This feeling of unconditional love is the normal infant's experience of being, and mother's face represents the source of being.

A FATHER'S EXPECTATIONS ARE THE MEANING OF THE CHILD'S HOPE

But the second most important need is the father's guiding voice.[7] The father is not so significant a part of a child's earliest experience with himself as is the mother. But the father represents a further need within the child—the need to think, to discriminate, to become aware of law and order, and to begin to develop one's own moral responsibility to be a distinct person. The father's voice represents authority, guidance, and adventure.[8] Mother's face represents security and love; father's voice represents the need to begin to cope with life's problems and its challenge to become somebody. Mother's face represents being; father's voice represents becoming. Mother's face reflects love; father's voice projects hope.

Mother's love does not restrict the infant's need to become independent; father's hope for the child does not overpower his development with an authoritarian and fearful tone of possible rejection. Mother's unconditional love does not exclude the need for the child's growth and moral development; father's hope includes the quality of unconditional love of the child along with the expectations of what the child is supposed to become through the development of his own potential.

As the child develops into adulthood, he learns to synthesize within himself the love of the mother and the hope of the father. An emotionally healthy adult has integrated mother's self-acceptance and father's encouragement to be all that he can be and not to be satisfied with anything less. Love and hope are the essential qualities of personal maturity.

INABILITY TO HOPE IS ROOTED IN FAULTY PARENTAL MODELS

In this description of the roles of a mother and a father in the development of a mature adult, I have appropriated some conclusions from studies in psychoanalysis which illustrate important biblical insights about the meaning of parent-child relationships for the development of our relationship with God.

Fromm in *The Art of Loving* has a brief and insightful discussion of this theory of human development. He does not discuss parental roles strictly in terms of the virtues of hope and love as I have sketched here, but those elements are evident. What is conspicuously missing in his analysis is the biblical virtue of faith. For him a mature adult is one who has faith in his own capacity to act in accordance with his love for himself and the expectations which he has adopted as appropriate for himself. The spiritual dimension of faith is completely missing in his analysis of the meaning of personhood.

Fromm believes that faith in God robs us of personal maturity. Why? Because he interprets our belief in God as a repetition of our childish need for protection from feelings of helplessness. The idea of God as a Father is a "childish illusion," he says.[9] He claims that in the maturing of the human race, belief in one God as Father was a necessary psychological stage which brought us out of our identity with and immersion in mother nature. So belief in one God was psychologically a step above the belief in many gods because it represented the emergence of one's own identity distinct from nature. Fromm believes that the final stage of maturity is total self-reliance without clinging to the need of a father figure. He believes that we are emotionally stalled at an early infantile stage of development if we lack this personal faith in our own independent resources for living. So Fromm advocates the personal virtues of faith, hope, love, but he dismisses their connection with faith in God.[10]

I understand in part why he does this. Too often our relationship to God is developed from an inadequate modeling of love and hope in our parents. For one reason or another we didn't feel unconditional love, even though our mothers may have loved us unconditionally. Perhaps we interpreted our fathers to say that they would love us if we earned their respect and lived out their expectations and hopes for us. In this process, we somehow felt left out. Our needs didn't seem important; we got little attention at all—except the negative attention we attracted through crossing our parents.

As we grew older, our relationships were often fraught with difficulties because they were developed out of our own panic-stricken needs to be loved and to be respected for what we wanted to be instead of what father hoped for us. The intensity of these needs made us anxious; consequently, our ability to relate to others in normal ways was rendered almost impossible. Throughout adulthood, feelings of harshness, coldness, insensitivity, bitterness, indifference, and self-hate have dogged our steps. This is not the exceptional experience; these feelings are the baggage most people carry around every day. For this reason psychoanalysts say that the capacity to be loving persons is rare.

As a result, this shaky foundation of our being gets projected on to our concept of God. Many people turn to him and develop an immature relationship there. This immaturity is a result of imprinted attitudes we improperly learned from mother who was an inadequate source of our being and from father whose stern or wimpish voice threatened or diminished our sense of self-esteem. In our panic-driven need for security, attention, and respect, we now look to God as a Father who rescues us from our helplessness.

In spite of our unconscious and hidden rage against God

because of our feelings of personal injury inflicted upon us, we turn to him in prayer in a childish manner of dependency expecting him to solve our problems for us. We hope that he will hear us, but if he doesn't we conclude that we have not pleased him. Such feelings of God as vindictive are not uncommon among us. And so the game of pretense and unreality goes on.

Fromm is right to call this view of God a childish wish. I am surprised, however, that because of this common and inadequate response to God, Fromm could so easily explain him away as harmful to our maturation. Why shouldn't our view of God be an inadequate one, given the harmful and injuring relationships of early moral and spiritual development? How can one's perception of God be otherwise if one has not been able to internalize a mother's spirit of love and a father's strength of hope?

A British pastoral counselor and psychoanalyst, Frank Lake, gives us a much more discerning evaluation of this situation. Among scholars who have written in the area of pastoral care (including Wayne Oates, Howard Clinebell, and Seward Hiltner), Professor Thomas Oden in his recent book *Pastoral Theology*[11] singles out Frank Lake as "most exemplary." Oden, a theologian from Drew University, says that Lake is "regrettably little known" in this country. Lake's insights as a psychiatrist and his knowledge of the Bible and theology combine to make him the most significant writer in pastoral care and counseling whom I have ever read.

Lake shows that the bitter memories of unloving faces and stern voices "are the beginnings of man's distortion of the truth about the ultimate personal reality, God Himself." With rare insight, Lake shows that "this is where the lie is first told about God, the lie which bedevils humanity, which determines our solidarity with the race in ignorance, pride, fear, anxiety, despair, idolatry and lust, unbelief and murderous hatred of God Himself."[12]

ATHEISM IS A PROTECTIVE DEVICE AGAINST EMOTIONAL PAIN

One of the distortions of our view of God is atheism. In atheism you don't have to live with inner rage against God since he doesn't exist. But then you have to create another childish illusion of achieving independence from father and throwing him out of the house. Atheism is our childish wish to get rid of our heavenly Father so we don't have to deal with our inner feelings and thoughts. Instead of clinging to a father who, we hope, will rescue us from our helplessness, we detach ourselves from our heavenly Father. We deny his existence so that we are no longer threatened with feelings of anger toward him because of personal injuries which he permits life to inflict upon us.

A panic-driven retreat and detachment from God as Father is just as immature as a panic-driven clinging of dependency. Often thoughtful people and professional scholars take this detached view of the meaning of the world and seek to carve out their own meaning in life by creating a world of "ideas." That way they won't be burdened with the responsibility of developing an intimate and personal relationship with God.

Intimacy may be intolerable for a hurting person who has felt rejection in the formative years of childhood. And a relationship with the Almighty may not be an emotionally appealing experience for this very reason. To feel the closeness and love of God as a Father is difficult if one bears resentment and hurt toward one's parents, even if it is driven underground in the unconscious life. God created us in such a way that we cannot really love him if we don't love at the human level, especially our own flesh and blood (1 John 4:20).

THE HOLY SPIRIT—GOD'S VOICE OF HOPE

But the unconscious rage remains and the game of pretense goes on—until we hear the good news that our lives can be free of pretense, ugliness, and the drivenness of panic-stricken feelings of dependency or detachment. For we are offered through membership in the family of God an adult knowledge of God in the face of Jesus Christ whose voice is the Holy Spirit. The face of Christ is "unveiled," as Paul puts it, so that we really see God in the "splendor" of his glory (2 Cor. 3:12–18). And the Holy Spirit is God's voice who calls us to be changed into his likeness and enables us to experience the inner freedom which comes from relationship to the Lord (2 Cor. 3:17–18).

Paul defines hope as the spiritual freedom of becoming in reality what we are potentially in Christ (2 Cor. 3:12). Our earthly mother represents a gracious and loving God who is "our Mother." Christ, like an earthly father who teaches us to set up our goals and expectations from life, represents our potential and hope. His voice is the Holy Spirit who is our Counselor and Guide (John 14:15, 26) enabling us to become mature Christians. Maturity is the synthesis of mother and father, of love and expectations. Likewise, the Holy Spirit is the synthesis of God the Father (Mother) as the source of our being (love) and God the Son as the Example of what we are expected to be (hope). Christian maturity begins with our personal experience with God the Holy Spirit who is this synthesis of love and hope.

It is no wonder then that Paul says that faith, hope, and love are the lasting essence of the Christian life. For faith is our personal synthesis of hope and love. Love is the foundation; hope is the structure built on love; and faith is the home. Faith is what we are; it is the assurance of things hoped for (Heb. 10:22; 11:1); it is the indwelling love of Christ (Eph. 3:17–18). Faith is love trusting and hope realized.

THE "I-MY-SELF" IS A SYNTHESIS OF FAITH, HOPE, AND LOVE

When we refer to ourselves as "I-my-self," we are describing this personal synthesis of faith, hope, and love. "Self" represents the spirit of mother (love) who has given us a sense of our well-being; "I" represents the strength of father (hope) who has given us an awareness of our own ego; "my" is the relational component of the human spirit and represents faith which is our capacity to trust and enter into meaningful relationships.[13]

Whenever our feeling of love ("self") or hope ("I") is reduced, faith ("my") in our capacity to have a meaningful relationship is threatened. Those who experience difficulty in human relationships can often trace their problem back to a difficulty in feeling loved by mother or being deprived of hope by father. And those who have difficulty in their relationship with God have the roots of their spiritual immaturity in these early childhood experiences. Our parents are intended to be our role models in the development of our maturity. For our awareness of the world, ourselves, and God is filtered through their examples. This is the way God intended it.

The reason for God's plan is obvious, for this is a personal world which God made. He is our ultimate model of personhood. We are all on the way to becoming persons, a painful process illustrated by the trauma of birth both for the infant and the mother. We are a community of persons in relationship with each other and in this way we become the persons we hope to be.

When this personal dimension of our growth is minimized during our earliest experiences, the path to maturity is often blocked. Thus we will likely develop distorted views of ourselves, others, and God. These distortions are in effect depersonalizations. The "I-my-self" becomes an undifferentiated "Imyself" without the inner qualifications suggested by the hyphens. One is all "I" without a source person to give a sense of "self," and there is no "my" because there is no interpersonal relationship. Depersonalization is the loss of the self due to feelings of isolation. Depersonalization means an individual "I" without a self or a meaningful relationship with others.[14]

A repersonalization can occur when individuals are placed in a relationship with others who can become for them father, mother, brothers, and sisters. These family relationships can provide the home atmosphere for the fulfillment of our original needs of love and hope. This new home setting is exactly what the church as the family of Christ is all about. We enter through the Holy Spirit into human relationships of faith and trust because our fathers, mothers, brothers, and sisters in the Lord communicate to us the love of God and the hope of Christ. This new spiritual relationship involves not a reprogramming, but a repersonalizing, of the "Imyself" into an "I-my-self." The original de-forming circumstances of our earliest life experiences can be transformed into a re-forming of our identity into the image of Christ.

INTELLECTUAL DOUBTS OFTEN TELL US MORE ABOUT INADEQUATE RELATIONSHIPS THAN ABOUT ACADEMIC KNOWLEDGE

It is customary for some to think that a decline in traditional beliefs, such as a personal God and the hope of the resurrection from the dead, is a product of more enlightened thinking in the modern world. But I suspect that a major reason is a corresponding decline in traditional family life in contemporary society. Without the model of a family where mother's unconditional love and father's hopeful expectations exist in a union of mutual trust, the basis for developing a mature "I-my-self" and the hope for an enduring and eternal relationship with family, friends, and God is absent.

I'm not saying that everyone who has doubts is emotionally troubled. A point usually comes in everyone's life where he must begin to think, ask questions, and find answers for himself. This is part of the maturation process; it is part of the process of becoming one's own person. I suspect that many of our problems with Christian beliefs are relational rather than intellectual.

As a seminary professor, one of my major responsibilities is to help students develop an adult interpretation of Christian faith. Most of my time has been committed to providing students with the academic tools necessary for learning to think responsibly about their faith. Over the years I have become more and more convinced that responsible thinking is more than learning the rules of logic and developing the art of reasoning. While these are indispensable for becoming able ministers of the gospel, I have found that many of the faith problems my students have rise out of the relational conflicts of early family life. I have been particularly struck by the number of times students having difficulty in their studies speak of considerable conflict with their fathers. The problem is usually one of communication. Such students often have difficulty with motivation and the development of a clear sense of direction for their future vocation.

Some students lack a mature sense of divine call into full-time Christian service partly due to the absence of a close bond with their fathers. This is evidenced by those who have difficulty obtaining ordination because they cannot communicate to their boards of ordained ministry a clear-cut statement of their reasons for entering the ministry. Their lack of a clearly defined vocational goal as minister is indicative of their lack of a well developed "I-my-self." Their hope for the future is unclear.

Early in my teaching career in the seminary a post-graduate student came to my office. He had been a missionary for several years and was now home on furlough and had enrolled in a few refresher courses in theology. He explained that he was bedeviled with serious intellectual problems regarding belief in God. He felt guilty for preaching to others what he himself no longer was certain of. "I'm ready to quit," he said to me with some degree of defiance. "I've tried to believe in Christ; I've preached now for ten years. I'm even supposed to be a missionary, but I haven't managed to convince myself of the truth of what I have preached to others."

He continued, "I have come to you as my last resort. I need some intelligent and convincing reasons why I should believe in God and why I should devote the rest of my life preparing others for the future life." It was obvious that a major concern of his was whether or not life had a sense of direction and final purpose to it. We talked about several books which might help him. He agreed to read them and to meet with me weekly for discussion. At our next meeting, we exchanged greetings and engaged in a bit of chitchat when he suddenly exclaimed, "I've been really seriously thinking about killing myself!"

I had not suspected the seriousness of his problem. He had from all outward appearances an ideal marriage and a lovely family. He had been successful as a missionary and was well appreciated by his church family. Then he said, "Let me tell you about my father."

We never did talk about theology. But I heard an awful story of the time when he was a fourteen-year-old son of a dearly loved father who failed him. His father had been an active layman in the local church and highly respected as a Christian and as a successful businessman. One day he returned from work to tell his wife and son he was leaving. He packed his belongings and left. The very day the divorce was finalized he married another woman in the church family with whom he had been having an affair.

This boy's idol was destroyed and along with it his own "I-my-self." I listened to the agony in his voice as he cried, "I still can't believe he left us!" The grief in his voice sounded as though he had evaporated into nothingness. Love for his mother and the need to protect her from the hurt became his only reason for living. She was a devout Christian for whom he wanted to do whatever he could to ensure her happiness. So one day he told her that he had decided to become a minister. But now after a number of years he realized that all this was a mistake. "I never really had a call to preach. I was only trying to please my mother. The only way out of this mess, as I see it, is to end my life. I have no reason to live."

It became obvious that his doubts about God's existence stemmed not from intellectual problems but from deep emotional pain associated with a father who had abandoned him and his mother during his adolescent years. The path to healing for this missionary came through many weeks and months of Christian counseling and the loving support of his wife and church family.

The very word father made it impossible for him to feel any desire to have fellowship with his heavenly Father. All the anger and hurt experienced from his earthly father was unconsciously projected onto God. Who would want to believe in the existence of a God as father when the very thought brought memories of hurt, rejection, and pain? Would you want to believe in a heavenly Father if your only model was one who callously rebuffed you and destroyed his relationship with you; who destroyed your ideal of what you wanted to be like when you grew up; who crushed your spirit by rejection, banished you from his very presence, and demolished your model of perfection?

The Scriptures make it plain that fathers have a priestly responsibility for their children in bringing them to God and setting a proper example for them to follow. The first and most fundamental thing that we learn about God is that he is our Father. He represents the very meaning and purpose of life. Our goals and the potential we see for the future depend upon our relationship to him as our heavenly Father and to our earthly fathers who instill within us our hope in God.

THE HOLY SPIRIT IS GOD'S GIFT OF HOPE

Pentecost marked an important date in salvation history for our relationship to God, for that is when we received "the promise of the Father." The Holy Spirit is our heavenly Father's gift of hope to us. The Father did not abandon us (John 14:18), but sent the promised Holy Spirit into the hearts of believers that we might have reason to hope. He is our Counselor, Guide, and Teacher (John 14:15, 26). The Holy Spirit is the voice of hope in our hearts who reassures us of the eternal relationship we have with God (Rom. 5:2, 5). The Christian hope is not simply perpetuation of our existence, but our transformation into the likeness of Christ and enjoyment of fellowship with the family of God in a renewed world that has no end (Rev. 22:1–5). Paul says that our hope cannot be disappointed because "God's love has been poured into our hearts through the Holy Spirit [who] has been given to us" (Rom. 5:5). The Holy Spirit is God's guarantee in our hearts of unending fellowship with his family (Eph. 1:18; 2 Cor. 4:5).

The final conviction for our hope beyond the grave lies in this relationship with God. This is the point which Jesus made to the Sadducees who disbelieved in the future life. Ironically, they believed in God but didn't believe in the life hereafter. Jesus reminded them that God is the God of the living and not of the dead. And if God is the God of Abraham, Isaac, and Jacob, then they too must be living (Matt. 22:32). This relational proof is our most convincing proof for the hope of the life everlasting which the indwelling of the Holy Spirit impresses upon our hearts. This proof is reasonable because it is a necessary implication of our life with God here and now. It is also an implication of the eternal quality which we feel so strongly implied in our relationships with loved ones. But it is more than a logical implication; it is an inward certainty we have through the "power of the Holy Spirit" (Rom. 15:13).

7

THE SPIRIT OF POWER

You shall receive power when the Holy Spirit has come upon you.

Acts 1:8

Jesus promised his disciples power to be his witnesses when the Holy Spirit came upon them. Power is the energy to act in harmony with the kind of person we really should be and want to be. The power of the Spirit is the kind of power which enables us to affirm our feelings and thoughts with courage and to assert ourselves with authority in an appropriate way. This kind of spiritual power releases us from the inhibiting fear of self-doubt and from the bondage of others' opinions. A timid person often is afraid of others because of an insecurity about himself. A powerful person in the best sense is someone with strength of character who has persuasive power with others.

This of course doesn't mean that Spirit-filled Christians are flamboyant or necessarily extroverted. In fact, they may be quiet and even shy. But the baptism with the Holy Spirit does mean that Christians have the power to be—to be spiritually authentic in Christ. And nothing speaks to others more forcefully about who we are and whose we are than our sense of self-authenticity. Our body language and the tone of our voice will convey to others our sense of spiritual being in Christ.

But we often fail to be in control of our emotions and thoughts. We allow negative emotions to dominate us: jealousy, resentment, impatience, arrogance, and fear. The power of the Holy Spirit is given to us so that we can take control of our lives instead of being driven by negative feelings. Before Pentecost, Peter was too timid when under stress to own up to his relationship to Christ (John 18:25–27). When asked about his friendship with Jesus at the Lord's trial, Peter was panic-stricken with fear and felt powerless to be true to his own identity.

Before Pentecost, Mary felt resentful toward her sister, Martha, and complained bitterly to Jesus about her apparent insensitivity. Martha was devoting herself to Jesus in worship instead of helping with preparations for dinner. Mary was powerless to put her priorities in order because she was driven by the more practical need to do good deeds rather than to stop long enough to receive God's grace as revealed in Jesus (Luke 10:38–42). Perhaps Mary hoped to impress Jesus by what she was doing for him, and she resented the attention he was giving Martha.

Before Pentecost, John could be harsh, impatient and vindictive; he wanted God on one occasion to destroy those who dared to disagree with him (Luke 9:54). Another time he inappropriately spoke sternly (Luke 9:49–50). Once he and his brother, James, arrogantly asked Jesus to give them a place of preference over the other disciples when Jesus came into his kingdom (Matt. 20:20–24). After Pentecost, the disciples were no longer driven by these negative feelings. The disciples possessed inward power to be in control of their new life in Christ through the Spirit. They were released from those inhibiting emotions and were now able to be all that God wanted them to be.

To be sure, there were conflicts and misunderstandings among the disciples after Pentecost, but a shift in the tone of their lives became noticeable. Only one thing ultimately mattered to them—laying down their lives for the sake of the gospel. Their power to be this kind of committed believer was the direct result of their infilling with the Holy Spirit. This is the essence of the Spirit-filled life—conformity to the image of Christ.

This is the only way we ever achieve our truest sense of personal being—through the power of the Holy Spirit. But our generation places emphasis on the need for personal and emotional fulfillment as an end in itself—apart from Christ. The result of such self-preoccupation in our culture is a tendency to psychologize human life and to deny our spiritual transcendence. Unlike Paul, the secular goal can be expressed like this: "for me to live is myself!" We are consequently better schooled today in psychology than in the Christian faith. We are more familiar with the language of the social sciences than Christian theology.

THE TRIUMPH OF THE THERAPEUTIC

A newspaper recently reported on just how common psychological terms have become and how they are used in ordinary conversations of the average person. Despite the high cost of therapy, the article stated that a large number of people regularly seek treatment for the anxieties which sap their emotional energy and keep them from being fully functioning individuals. A major trend in society is now to accept psychotherapy as a normal experience which most of us will receive at some point in our lifetime.

It used to be that we learned Bible verses and could quote them freely in moments of spiritual need; now we learn psychological terms and use them to try to understand our motivations in moments of stress and anxiety. It used to be that the local preacher was the person we turned to for help with our personal problems; now we turn to the analyst and therapist. It used to be that we talked about Abraham, Isaac, Jacob, Moses, and Jesus; now we talk about Freud, Jung, Adler, Rogers, and Maslow. It used to be that we affirmed our faith as expressed in the Apostles' Creed, "I believe"; now we prefer to express our emotions contained in our private experiences, "I feel." It used to be that we used words like sin, conviction, conversion, regeneration, sanctification, and faith; now we use words like maladjustment, stress, insight, coping, development, orientation, reinforcement, and integrity.

One recent sociologist refers to this shift in our attitude as "the triumph of the therapeutic" over the religious.[1] People today want to feel good; they want emotional fulfillment; they are concerned about practical and everyday issues of living meaningfully in relationship with themselves and others. Their central concern is to preserve themselves from feelings of panic and emptiness. The religious attitude of our more traditional culture assumed that one is born to be saved; the psychotherapeutic attitude of our secular culture assumes that one is born to be pleased. It used to be that we felt we were inadequate and powerless without the grace of God; now we are told that we must discover our sense of adequacy and power for living from within ourselves.

Nineteenth-century philosopher Friedrich Nietzsche was a patron saint of that way of thinking. He heralded the beginning of such secular thinking with his poetic description of the superman whose motto was "will to power." The figure of the superman is one who owns responsibility for himself and derives the power for his successful living through a personal affirmation of his own inner resources.[2] Almost any secular university course in ethics requires students to read Nietzsche because of the dramatic effect of his poetic language. He challenged his readers to liberate themselves from inhibitions of the Christian religion and to become strong in their resolve to be themselves and independent of God. This attitude of self-affirmation is what he meant by "will to power."

Jesus said that we will have power to be what God wants us to be when the Holy Spirit comes to dwell in our hearts. Nietzsche said we will have power to be all that we can be when God is driven out of our minds and out of the world. He believed that we can never be fulfilled as persons until we get rid of our belief in God. His central argument is that belief in God renders us powerless to achieve the greatest expressions of our personality. Why? Because to believe in God is to incur an inhibiting sense of guilt. So he taught that atheism and a sense of innocence go together; belief in God and feelings of guilt necessarily exist together.[3] He concluded, therefore, that to believe in a personal God meant to become necessarily weak and powerless as feelings of guilt damage our self-esteem and inhibit our powers of self-affirmation.

Nietzsche's attitude was extreme, and even secular writers shy away from his reactionary atheism. I would not have mentioned him except that his influence on many continues. The spirit of Nietzsche lives on in the thinking of secular therapists, secular ethicists, and even some theologians. The supposedly good insight which Nietzsche offers to the modern world is the belief that we are adequate within ourselves to be truly human and authentic without belief in a personal God whose very existence would threaten and unsettle us psychologically.

Who can deny that living in today's world takes a lot of personal courage? Certainly many people are deprived of a good sense of well-being because of wrong notions about God. Because of this, they feel defeated, guilty, and inadequate to maintain any sense of equilibrium. Religion for them has become a burden. Their guilt-ridden and joyless religious experience is a neurotic failure to respond to God's offer of power for living through the Spirit. They haven't experienced the liberating power of the Holy Spirit who genuinely frees us to be ourselves. Some suffer especially from the false notion of a vindictive God—an all too common inhibiting experience for religious people. These defeated Christians have neither the arrogant spirit of Nietzsche nor the humble spirit of Christ. They choose to feel inferior and persecuted through anxious feelings of guilt and shame, and they complain about the way life treats them.

This neurotic obsession with feelings of inferiority is certainly not the meaning of Christian humility. We become truly humble through the Spirit when we recognize realistically our inadequacy and then find that we are transformed by the power of God into authentic persons. Most of us know that an arrogant spirit is really a feeling of inferiority disguised as superiority. Those who project themselves onto others as confident and superior are usually only masking a hidden feeling of inferiority. Despair and pride are like two sides of the same coin, but a humble spirit is an authentic feeling of knowing and being what we really are through the power of the Holy Spirit. A self-effacing feeling of worthlessness is not the self-perception of the Spirit-filled Christian.

Therapists can often only encourage their patients to compensate for their feelings of inferiority by getting them to focus on their good points and helping them to achieve a sense of confidence and self-sufficiency through their own efforts. This works-righteousness approach to self-salvation is arrogance even if we do dress it up with words like authenticity and self-reliance.

We can be thankful for the writings of philosophers and psychologists who have formulated categories to help us understand ourselves. I am appreciative of this, and we should be glad for any help we can get to resolve our hurting and damaged emotions. Being Spirit-filled does not necessarily resolve our personal problems, but the solution to our anxious feelings must begin with God. This is the point which I am trying to make, and this is why I offer a word of caution here.

One well-known theologian, Paul Tillich, wrote three volumes in systematic theology, one on each person of the Trinity. The interesting thing is that his volume on the Holy Spirit was a serious attempt to substitute the categories of modern psychology for the traditional language of the Bible.[4] Life in the Spirit is reinterpreted along the lines of psychoanalysis with its emphasis on personal reorientation and fulfillment. He confused the Holy Spirit with the human spirit, spiritual fulfillment with psychological fulfillment.

This confusion is widespread in the church. Part of the reason for this tendency is that we have been so programmed by secular society to think in terms of "my needs," "my feelings," "my goals." We have been pressured, especially since the eighteenth century, to trust in our intellectual powers and to insist on our right to a life of personal fulfillment. Somehow the relevance of a personal God has become lost in favor of psychological self-analysis.

SPIRITUAL POWER IS MORE
THAN PERSONAL FULFILLMENT

One of the many psychological terms commonly heard in our daily conversations is fulfillment. "My job is not very fulfilling" is a complaint made by many who rise early in the morning day after day going through the same old tiring routines. They come home at the end of the day emotionally drained and unable to relate to other members of the family because of exhaustion caused by emotional stress.

Why is there such discontent in our affluent society? Why are so many people emotionally and spiritually unfulfilled, especially in a day when so much attention is devoted to the satisfying of personal and emotional needs?[5] Has any civilization been plagued with more severe cases of anxiety than ours? The more we try to satisfy ourselves the more intense our anxiety becomes.

But could this just be the problem? Are we looking for fulfillment of our needs without turning to the spiritual resources necessary for that? Jesus once asked a question relevant to this problem: "What shall a man give in return for his life?" (Matt. 16:26) In our culture the question is now phrased this way: "How can my priorities be rearranged so that I can be personally fulfilled? How can I actualize my true potential?" The idea of the immortal soul has been dropped from the thinking of many, but they cannot ignore the need to discover the meaning of their existence. How can I exist with some sense of significance in the midst of a world that is largely impersonal and uncaring? The very way of phrasing implies that God is not a part of the answer, for the question betrays an interest, not in knowing God, but in knowing oneself. "How can I have a meaningful life?" is the question psychotherapists encourage us to explore for ourselves, often without assuming any need for spiritual direction. It used to be that we went to church to find out about God; now we go to the therapist to find out about ourselves.

One psychologist who has received a great deal of attention from the public because of his professional writings on the meaning of human existence is Abraham Maslow (d. 1970), a long-time professor of psychology at Brandeis University. Maslow studied the lives of prominent historical people like Baruch Spinoza, Thomas Jefferson, Abraham Lincoln, William James, Albert Einstein, and Eleanor Roosevelt. He also studied the lives of a select group of college students. His purpose was to discover the characteristics and behavior of those students who seemed to have the highest degree of self-fulfillment. They supposedly were the healthiest one percent of the population, they showed little evidence of neurosis or psychosis, and they were making good use of their talents and capabilities.

Maslow discovered that these people, whom he called "self-actualizers," usually experienced "peak experiences" of self-fulfillment. A peak experience is one of happiness, a temporary, non-striving, non-self-centered state of perfection and goal attainment. Those who were asked about their peak experiences described them in terms of wholeness, perfection, aliveness, uniqueness, self-reliance, and the values of beauty, goodness, and truth.[6]

Maslow's description of self-fulfillment is a psychological substitute and secular restatement of the Christian meaning of spiritual formation and sanctification. The fruit of the Holy Spirit in the life of the Christian is love, joy, peace, patience, kindness, goodness, faithfulness, gentleness, and self-control (Gal. 5:22–23). The Holy Spirit is God's guarantee to us that we belong to him and that our lives take on eternal significance. Through the indwelling Spirit we now become all that we are intended to be; we are self-actualizers because we are God-actualizers. Through Christ we experience feelings of wholeness, perfection, and true being.

This specific Christian content is just the element that is missing in Maslow's description of the self-actualizer. The spiritual has been spiritualized away. His description of peak experiences is faulty in that he explains away the true meaning of religious experience. How? Maslow has intentionally psychologized the meaning of the religious. All that remains in his description of the peak experience is the purely private feelings of the individual in his solitariness.

This Jewish psychologist rejects the relevance of a personal God who supernaturally reveals himself in history. He says that "the core-religious experience" is a feeling of ecstasy which does not depend on any particular revelation of a personal God. He says people used to believe that their peak experience originated with a supernatural revelation, but we now know that it is an experience which is normal, human, and natural. For him all religions are the same in their essence. We need only to eliminate their cultural and historical setting, and then we can see that religious belief and language are universally concerned about one thing—personal fulfillment. Once we have peeled away their "localisms in time and space," we can see that there is no difference between the religious and the psychological goal of happiness and fulfillment.[7] He makes no distinction between religiously-induced and psychologically-induced experiences. For those who have trouble permitting themselves to enjoy peak experiences, Maslow suggests hypnosis or psychedelic drugs as a possible alternative.[8]

I have been helped in my own understanding of the psychological dimension through study of secular writers like Maslow. I have no quarrel with the psychotherapeutic goal of personal fulfillment and emotional maturity. I applaud their efforts to enrich our understanding of the meaning of our existence. And it is certainly not unchristian for us to use secular terms to explain our faith.

Christians have always been willing to use the language of any culture to explain faith in God. The earliest Christian writers, such as Justin Martyr, freely borrowed the language of pagans to explain their faith in Christ. Augustine used the words and ideas of pagan writers like Plato and the Stoics to express his faith. Christians believe that God has placed a measure of truth in the minds of everybody since we were all made in his image.

But the danger always exists that we may unwittingly permit wrong notions to creep into our beliefs when we use words and insights of nonbelievers to explain our faith. When we use these words, we have to stretch their meaning to say things which the nonbeliever was unable to say and did not know about. We must be careful not to allow the secular to supplant the Christian components. This can happen all too easily. We find ourselves talking about salvation in terms of personal fulfillment, and before we realize it we have unconsciously dropped God out of the picture. Even though we may continue to use the words of the Bible like *justification* and *sanctification,* it is easy to forget that their meaning has something to do primarily with our relationship to the reality of God. We have been programmed by our psychologically-minded culture to think of God as one who can be used to make ourselves feel good and emotionally satisfied, and the focus of our experience easily becomes ourselves rather than Christ. We may actively seek a religious type of emotional satisfaction which we call spiritual fulfillment without really counting the cost of true discipleship.

If we were to follow Maslow, we would settle for that kind of experience. He makes a sharp distinction between the prophet who has a peak experience and the theologian who wants to report that original revelation in words. Maslow rejects the attempt to verbalize our peak experiences in formal statements.[9] Religious experience is entirely a private affair of the spirit for him. He rejects all religious beliefs about supernatural realities. The need to witness to someone else about one's faith in Jesus Christ who died and rose again would be considered intellectually naive and psychologically inappropriate. Such witnessing is considered disrespectful because it is trying to push one's ideas onto somebody else.

He says that those who attempt to express their faith in a logical and rational way are "anti-emotional" and cannot have genuine peak experiences. They do not become self-actualizers, for their ideas about God preclude the possibility of such an experience.

Maslow's insight into the problem of doctrine sometimes preventing one from having a genuine experience of faith is valid. We can certainly have a good understanding of what we believe intellectually about God, but faith is much more profound than that. We should not allow our ideas to be substitutes for actual experience. Paul warned us to be careful not to have a form of religion without the power (2 Tim. 3:5). After all, evil spirits know the truth even though they do not embody it (James 2:19). Knowing correct doctrine and having right notions and perceptions are not the same thing as experiencing genuine faith. There is no spiritual power in merely knowing ideas and doctrines.

The problem is that secular pyschologists offer us only the idea of self-fulfillment, only an imitation of the real thing. Keep in mind the strong similarity between a psychotherapeutic description of personal fulfillment and the Christian doctrine of salvation by grace through faith alone. In fact, we could say that they both express the same thing but independently of each other. Yet this is not quite the case. For modern psychology borrowed its basic insights from the Judeo-Christian tradition. The significance of the personal and the relational meaning of our existence are distinctly Judeo-Christian contributions. No other religion and no other philosophy offered such a clear understanding of the significance of the individual as does biblical faith.

SPIRITUAL POWER IS MORE
THAN SELF-ACCEPTANCE

Rudolf Bultmann (d. 1976) was a prominent theologian and highly respected New Testament scholar who opposed orthodox Christianity and rejected the idea of supernatural revelation. Yet almost all theological seminary professors and certainly most former seminary students who are now pastors have studied his writings. The extent of his influence may be surprising since he seemed to be opposed to almost everything the church traditionally believed about the Bible and its teachings. One reason why he has been so influential is because of his work in the New Testament. But perhaps the main reason is his sophisticated attempt to reformulate Christian belief by using modern existential-psychological categories. He reinterpreted faith to mean self-acceptance.[10]

Bultmann believed that biblical language which described the spiritual world, such as living eternally with God in heaven, was simply a mythical way of talking about becoming self-actualizers. New Testament talk about faith in the risen Lord was the disciples' attempt to express their hope of achieving a better understanding of themselves and actualizing their human potential. In other words, the disciples were limited in their thinking in their day because they did not have available a more scientific worldview. Bultmann believes we know better today because we supposedly have a more adult understanding.[11]

In a later chapter, I will discuss this unscientific way of using science to tear down traditional Christian belief. For now, I want to illustrate how his use of secular psychology has at times undermined Christian belief because he has defined faith in terms of human potential and self-fulfillment rather than in terms of Christ-fulfillment. Bultmann does not even mean the Jesus of history when he speaks of Jesus Christ.[12] To be sure, Bultmann believes a real man named Jesus lived in the historical past. But Jesus for us today is only a symbolic expression for describing our "event" of self-understanding and self-fulfillment.

The "event of Jesus Christ" is a figure of speech which means for Bultmann only a peak experience; it has nothing at all to do with what really happened in the past. He rejects all historical events as having any relevance for our salvation today. His reinterpretation of Christian belief is a psychologizing of the biblical faith. Nothing supernatural remains. Though Bultmann was not influenced by Maslow, his writings on the meaning of Christian faith for today reflect a general trend among theologians and pastors who follow in an uncritical manner the lead of secular psychological thinking so widely accepted in our Western culture.

You might wonder why people like Bultmann still call themselves Christians. The answer is simple. They have been brought up in the Christian faith and have been members of the church all their lives. They have experienced something of the reality of faith, even though they later developed a misunderstanding of it through wrong perceptions of so-called enlightened thinking. They feel that their Christian training and background have something to offer to the modern world.

Bultmann recognizes this when he says frankly that the modern understanding of human existence was not "discovered apart from the New Testament." He adds that modern thinking is clearly indebted not only to the Bible but to Christian thinkers like Luther and Kierkegaard for its understanding of the personal.[13]

Many liberal churches share Bultmann's perspective. They frankly reinterpret the Bible according to his understanding of faith. For them, faith means self-understanding rather than a personal relationship with a supernatural, personal God. The Bible for these "Christians" is not a record of saving historical events of the past which can be shared by us today. The Cross of Jesus was a tragic event which happened to an innocent and good man, and it became the occasion for his friends to be shocked into a new awareness of the meaning of their own existence. But as an event of the past it has no supernatural meaning for us. At best, it can be a symbol for us to accept our finite existence and to go ahead and live out our true potential in spite of the final reality of death. Easter was not really a historical event but a psychological event, something that happened only in the emotions of the disciples and not a real perception of their minds.

This is a tragic misunderstanding of the dynamic of faith. But I can't help but wonder how close we traditional Christians get to that point of view when we allow our psychological categories to replace biblical words to describe our faith in Christ. *The ideal of personal fulfillment and self-understanding is a myth if the Spirit of the risen Christ has not come into the world and indwells our hearts.* Paul said it quite plainly: "If Christ has not been raised, your faith is futile and you are still in your sins" (1 Cor. 15:17). It is a case of wishful thinking to believe that we can hope to achieve a meaningful existence in the here and now when all our efforts, all our relationships, all our hopes and dreams, all our tears and laughs are ultimately brought to nothing. Paul succinctly says, "If in this life only we who are in Christ Jesus have hope, we are of all men most to be pitied" (1 Cor. 15:19).

To propose the idea of affirming ourselves and realizing our potential without the benefit of divine grace may appear to be an adult perspective, but in reality it is nothing more than a childish fancy. To talk about self-fulfillment apart from a personal God is to make ourselves gods. The attempt to achieve our potential through self-affirmation is counterproductive. We cannot feel complete in ourselves nor do we feel complete through our human associations and relationships. Human beings make lousy gods! Only God can be a god! He alone is self-sufficient and capable of enabling us to feel complete and perfect. So God alone is God. That is why he became truly human. Our completeness and our fulfillment are in Christ alone. The New Testament is clearly devoted to the importance of our personal fulfillment in life. In writing to Timothy, Paul instructs the young man as an evangelist and pastor to see to it that individual needs of his people are met. Our task, Paul says, is to make sure that everyone is offered an opportunity to be made perfect and to be completely fulfilled in Christ (2 Tim. 3:17; see James 1:4).

Paul is preeminently the apostle of the Spirit.[14] His major emphasis is to live in the Spirit, to walk in the Spirit (Gal. 5:25), to bear the fruit of the Spirit (Eph. 5:9; Gal. 5:22–23), to be filled with the Spirit (Eph. 5:18), to be sanctified through the Spirit (2 Thess. 2:13), and to be inwardly formed and sealed with the Spirit (Eph. 1:13).

The spiritual dimensions of our personal fulfillment are Paul's first concern for Christians. It is not enough to know that our sins are forgiven and that we have been accepted by God, as important as that is. Paul can think only of our personal appropriation of the meaning of our acceptance in Christ. The truth that we are saved by faith through grace alone must be internalized in the depth of our being through the indwelling of the Spirit of Christ. But this spiritual dimension cannot be reduced to a mere psychological experience. It is more than just personal fulfillment; it is sharing in the power-giving life of the Spirit.

PERSONAL FULFILLMENT IS IMPOSSIBLE APART FROM SALVATION HISTORY

One prominent sociologist, Philip Rieff, believes that Christians will continue to use psychological terms to describe the meaning of faith, but he is convinced that this trend will only further undermine belief in Christian experience. If the important thing is the actual psychological experience of knowing oneself and appropriating one's true potential, why do we need to believe in an invisible and supernatural world? Why do we need to insist on holding to archaic beliefs which hardly any thinking person today can believe with any sense of intellectual integrity? For him, it is only a matter of time before the psychological completely eliminates the traditional Christian view of salvation.[15]

This is similar also to the point of view of Bultmann and a majority of those who embrace a liberal interpretation of Christian faith.[16] They ask, "Why do we need to believe in the historical events of the Bible? Faith is something that is entirely private and personal and has nothing to do with real events that might have happened in the past. Why be so narrow-minded as to insist that our faith depends on a particular event of the past? After all, faith is an inward certainty and should not be linked to belief in a probable event of the past. We must eliminate the localisms and particularisms of the Bible and preserve only its emphasis on human development and moral values."

I will discuss this point later. For now I want to point out that the historical basis of faith is something that cannot be given up without the complete loss of Christian faith. The attempt to eliminate all "localisms" and all historical events of the Bible, as Maslow and Bultmann try to do, and to preserve only the ideal of self-fulfillment is a total misunderstanding of the meaning of our humanity.

The goal of personal fulfillment is not something which can be achieved in a private and autonomous way. We were not made to be a Robinson Crusoe, destined to live alone on an isolated island. Who we are is communicated to us through relationships we share with others in our community. Our

participation in the history of our family and community form
the meaning of our personal existence. Can you imagine any
meaning in your life apart from your family and personal
history? Any significance we feel about ourselves is directly
linked to relationships we have had with significant persons in
our lives, while feelings of low self-esteem stem from inadequate relationships.

This point is humorously but sadly illustrated by an
experience I once had on a plane. I was hardly aware of the
woman who sat beside me because I was preoccupied with my
reading. But within a few minutes she introduced herself, told
me where she was from, where she was going, and how many
former husbands she had. Her trip on this occasion was to meet
one of them in Florida and accompany him to the Bahamas for a
short vacation. I briefly acknowledged her introduction and
turned again to my reading. But this did not please her! She
made a point of the fact that she intended to intrude into my
"space," as she put it, and that I was for the duration of this
flight a part of her vacation whether I liked it or not. Her
extraordinary forwardness surprised me, and not knowing
exactly what to say, I simply smiled and replied, "Oh, I see."
She answered with humor in her voice, "No, you don't really
see." At that point she reached out her hand and lifted my
glasses off my face! "Now you really can't see, can you?" she
said. You can imagine just how uncomfortable I felt in that
situation. I had never before been approached in such a manner
by a stranger, and I hope that I never will again.

I politely replied, "Oh, I can still see a little bit, but if you
will give me my glasses back I think I can see a whole lot
better." She immediately took off her glasses and before I knew
what was happening she had placed them on me! "Now you
can really see!" she said with a great deal of emotion. Her
glasses were tinted. "Now everything looks rosy and bright,"
she explained.

For the remainder of the two-hour trip I listened to her
history of broken relationships and broken promises made by
those who were closest to her—beginning with her father and
including her friends and three husbands. She had no one in her

life, including her mother, who she felt really cared about her. Her history had been one of drifting from one relationship to another. She had no continuity in her life; no peak experiences which gave a sense of meaning to her existence. She was a drifter with nowhere to go and no one to receive her. Life had become so cruel to her that the only way she could stand to look at it was through rose-tinted glasses!

I tried to talk to her about God and his offer of a relationship to us in Jesus. Her response was, "The idea of God never made much sense to me." I think I understand what she meant. She had experienced very little of the meaning of intimacy which comes with meaningful relationships. How could I possibly expect her to understand the meaning of a relationship with God? She did not have the experience in her background to comprehend what I was talking about. Her life history was a series of frustrated expectations which gave her little purpose for living.

Coping with life is not easy for one who does not know the meaning of intimate friendships. And without intimate friendships there can be no peak experiences of self-fulfillment. Part of the tragic situation of this woman was that she did not consciously perceive that she had any relational or spiritual problem. She did not really know herself even though she had told me all about herself. She imagined that she was a happy and fulfilled person, but was totally oblivious to her true condition as a "poor, blind and naked" human being (Rev. 3:17). Just as she imagined her world to be a happy and bright place as viewed through her rose-colored glasses, so she pretended to herself that she knew the meaning of personal fulfillment. For her therapist had assured her that she was really quite normal.

The Bible is a case history of God's relationship with the human race. And it has been a stormy one with ups and downs, ecstasy and tragedy, of promises made and broken. It is a history of people unable to live together in harmony with their families and neighbors, a story of violence, maladjustment, rejection, and death. The Bible makes no attempt to cover up the muddle which the human race, including God's chosen people, has made of life. Critics are surprised to find that in the New Testament no attempt is made to hide the blemishes, warts, and maladjustments of even the disciples of Jesus. The Bible deals in realities, not illusions.

If it were not for the mercy of God, all of us would be totally blind to the unhappy situation of our self-centered lives. We would simply have to cope the best we can in the midst of a world that is cruel and uncaring. Coping sometimes means that we have to blind ourselves to reality; otherwise we could not endure it. This is why the Bible describes the condition of sin as like a state of blindness. We choose to be blinded to reality rather than to have to endure the emotional pain of knowing that we are not living up to the potential of human excellence; this damages our sense of self-esteem. So we imagine that we are better off than we really are, that we are sufficient in ourselves and have no unmet needs. Like Nietzsche, we believe that we can manage well enough on our own.

But God has not left us alone nor condemned us to a life of pretentious self-fulfillment. The most exciting thing about the Bible is that it is a case history of grace, salvation, trust, and personal fulfillment in Jesus Christ. It is a history of God's taking the initiative to open a relationship with us so that we could come to see ourselves for what we really are—lonely, inadequate, and anxious—and what we can become in Christ— whole, adequate, authentic.

We could never endure the sight of what we are without the loving care of our heavenly Father. The law revealed at Sinai would be too terrifying for us to recognize if it were not for the graciousness of a loving God who assures us of his acceptance of us in spite of what we are in our fallenness. "I am a sinner" is not an insight which comes to us naturally through introspective analysis. We may instinctively sense something is wrong inwardly, but we are unable to diagnose our spiritual situation apart from the Holy Spirit.[17]

My point is that we do not find God through our own efforts. The religions of the world are the creative product of those who are driven by the need to find meaning in life. But the Bible is a history of God revealing to us our need of him, and he initiates the means through which we can come to know him. It may be difficult to understand how our salvation can depend upon something that happened in a specific place and time many years ago. This "scandal of particularity" (as it is sometimes called) is the very thing which Christians cannot give up.[18] Paul said that to the Greek philosophers, preaching that says our faith is dependent upon Jesus was "foolishness," and to the Jews it was an "offense," but that to those of us who believe it is the power and wisdom of God (1 Cor. 1:21–25).

It is ironic that Abraham Maslow, who possessed such rare insights into human psychology, failed to perceive the genuinely spiritual needs which go beyond the mere ideal of self-actualization. It is also ironic that he was born a descendant of the Old Testament patriarch Abraham but did not share the faith of his biological forefather, and that he stressed the importance of our developing our own sense of personal identity through self-implementation but failed to see that we can appropriate our identity only through knowing the identity of God. The notion of *self*-fulfillment is as much a myth as the imaginative creations of ancient mythological religions.

Paul put things in proper focus: "For to me to live is Christ!" (Phil. 1:21) Christ alone is our adequacy. Through the power of the Holy Spirit we are enabled to be his witnesses because we have been refashioned in his likeness. To be a witness is to tell whose you are and whom you serve. After Pentecost, the disciples found it possible to affirm themselves by living up to their full potential in Christ, and they could now assert their true feelings and thoughts without fear because they were filled with the love of God. The power of the Spirit is an uninhibiting life of freedom in Christ.

8

THE SPIRIT OF MIRACLES AND GIFTS

God . . . bore witness by signs and wonders and various miracles and by gifts of the Holy Spirit distributed according to his own will.

Hebrews 2:4

I remember being electrified by the testimony of a well-known lawyer who told of his excursion into a South Carolina town over a weekend to hold a layman's revival. A friend of his arrived on Sunday night in a private plane to fly him home following the service. He was exhausted from demands of the meetings and welcomed this quick transportation. He could get a good night of rest before having to face another work week. About an hour into their flight his friend announced that they would have to land for refueling. But the Christian lawyer insisted that it was unnecessary because they were servants of the Lord, and God would certainly take care of them. This was especially so since the lawyer had worn himself out in the Lord's work of the weekend. So they flew on low fuel for another hour before landing in Charlotte. "Check the fuel tank," the lawyer ordered the mechanic who had come to service the airplane. He stuck a dry cloth into the tank. "It's bone dry!" he exclaimed.

"When you're filled with the Holy Ghost," the lawyer

shouted to us in that Methodist congregation, "You can demand that God prove himself by working miracles every day in your life!" Clearly this is not the meaning of the Spirit-filled life. Nor are these kinds of sensational "miracles" the reason why we believe in the gospel. A Baptist minister's wife was sitting close by. She whispered, "That sounds more like the sin of presumption to me!" I agreed.

In Hebrews, the writer says that we believe the gospel of Jesus Christ is "a great salvation" because, first, it was "declared" by Jesus Christ; second, because his disciples were witnesses of what they heard him speak; and third, because of "signs and wonders and various miracles and by gifts of the Holy Spirit" (2:1–4). These "proofs" of our faith are given in the order of their importance—Jesus' words, the words of his disciples, and then miracles and gifts of the Holy Spirit.

THE GIFTS OF THE SPIRIT WERE SIGNS OF THE NEW KINGDOM

Even before Jesus' birth, Israelites believed that the manifestation of spiritual gifts would coincide with the coming of their Messiah.[1] This is why Matthew, Mark, Luke, and John reported the miracles and signs as they told the story of Jesus. Simeon, a devout man, "prophesied" when Jesus' parents presented him to the Lord in the temple (Luke 2:22–29). Elizabeth and Mary "prophesied" about Jesus' birth (Luke 1:39–56). After the Holy Spirit came at Pentecost, Peter said "prophecy" would once more be restored (Acts 2:17). Our Lord exercised the gift of healing and performed numerous miracles. On one occasion, doubting Pharisees asked Jesus what "signs" he would give to indicate that he was God's anointed (Matt. 12:39). This expectation that the gifts of the Spirit would be restored when the Messiah came is the reason that the Lord told his disciples to "preach the kingdom of God and to heal" (Luke 9:2).

Have the gifts of the Holy Spirit ceased to function in the church today? This is a bothersome question for a lot of people.

But nowhere in Scripture are we led to believe that these gifts were restricted to first-century Christianity.

DIFFERENT GIFTS FOR DIFFERENT NEEDS

In 1 Corinthians 12:4–10, Paul lists gifts of the Spirit. These are, first, the ability to speak words of wisdom and to have good perception concerning special situations; second, the ability to have advanced knowledge or an intuition concerning events which are about to happen or may have already happened; third, extraordinary faith for special situations; fourth, power to heal; fifth, power to perform miracles (Acts 13:11); sixth, prophecy or the ability to foretell events (Acts 11:27f.; 21:10) or forthtell God's Word (Luke 1:67ff.; Acts 19:6; 21:9); seventh, the ability to recognize the difference between evil and good spirits; eighth, the ability to speak in different tongues; tenth, the ability to interpret these different tongues.

Later in the same chapter (1 Cor. 12:28–31), Paul makes another list of gifts or offices in the church: apostles, prophets, teachers, workers of miracles, healers, helpers, administrators, and speakers in tongues. In Romans 12:4–8, Paul has yet another list of gifts: prophecy, service, teaching, exhortation, the ability to make financial contributions (see also 2 Cor. 9:7; James 1:5), aiding, and acts of mercy. In Ephesians 4:7–11, Paul lists these offices: apostles, prophets, evangelists, pastors, and teachers. In 1 Corinthians 7:7, Paul identifies singleness as a gift which God may bestow on believers. Peter identifies such gifts as hospitality, speaking the oracles of God, and rendering service (1 Peter 4:10–11; see Acts 6:11).

There is no reason to believe that these passages give us a complete list of spiritual gifts. Why? Because Scripture does not indicate that it is doing so, and because the needs of the church may vary from one generation to another. There are as many gifts of the Spirit as there are special needs which develop in the church.

THE GIFTS OF THE SPIRIT ARE
REINFORCEMENTS
OF OUR FAITH IN CHRIST

Little else is taught in the New Testament about the specific gifts of the Spirit except that which is mentioned in these few passages. Explicit instances where the gifts were practiced are recorded in the Gospels and in the book of Acts; Jesus and his disciples regularly healed and performed various kinds of miracles. Acts records numerous instances where the gifts were expressed. These supernatural happenings played a supporting role in the preaching of the gospel, but they were not the substance of the gospel. The apostles didn't focus attention on the gifts, but on the Giver of the gifts. Jesus chided the Pharisees for looking for miracles and signs (Matt. 16:4). Faith comes by hearing the word of Christ, not by the sensational performance of miracles. "Faith comes from what is heard, and what is heard comes by the preaching of Christ" (Rom. 10:17).

Jesus once told a parable of a rich man and a poor man. The rich man died and went into the next world without God. The poor man died and was taken into paradise. The rich man cried out for relief from his pain, but it was too late. He had chosen to live a selfish and godless life in this world, and now an eternal chasm separated him from the fellowship of others. Thinking of his five brothers, the rich man begged that the poor man might be raised from the dead and be sent to warn of this place of torment. But Abraham replied, "They have Moses and the prophets, let them hear them." If they refuse the Word of God, they will not be persuaded even if someone were raised from the dead (Luke 16:27–31).

The rich man thought otherwise. His earthly life had been dominated by the things which he could touch and see and possess. Truth was physical for him. It could be measured in quantitative terms. But Abraham says that truth is inward and spiritual. Faith is a matter of belief in the heart, not a matter of physical proofs. We are saved by faith through the Word of God. Miracles may serve as a supporting base for faith, but no one is ever saved simply because of a miracle. "If they do not hear Moses and the prophets, neither will they be convinced if some one should rise from the dead." Look at what happened after the raising of Lazarus. That miracle failed to convince critics that Jesus was God's anointed servant.

Then there was Jesus' resurrection. The chief priest and other leaders in the community refused to believe. Indeed, the only ones who accepted the fact of the risen Lord were those who were already believers, and they believed only as Jesus came to them and opened their eyes so that they could perceive him. Until that moment, Mary had mistaken him for the gardener. She reported to the other apostles that she had seen the Lord, but Luke says, "These words seemed to them an idle tale, and they did not believe them" (24:11). When the risen Lord appeared to the disciples on the road to Emmaus, they mistook him for a stranger even after talking with him at length—until he opened their eyes.

An agnostic philosopher once said that he would be inclined to believe in a supreme intelligence if he should hear a voice speak to him out of the sky, predicting unlikely events which would later happen. This is of course a superficial notion of faith. We can't dictate to God the terms upon which we will believe. But this attitude is reflected in some who flock to sensational religious meetings where demonstrations of the gifts of the Spirit will supposedly serve as props for their faith.

The plain statement of the Bible is that faith in God is communicated through his Word. If any refuse to hear the preaching of Moses and the prophets, if one will not listen to the preaching of Christ, neither will he truly believe should miracles be performed.

Paul put it this way: "It pleased God through the folly of what we preach to save those who believe. For Jews demand signs and Greeks seek wisdom, but we preach Christ crucified, a stumbling block to Jews and folly to Gentiles, but to those who are called, both Jews and Greeks, Christ the power of God and the wisdom of God" (1 Cor. 1:21–24). Paul frankly says that the gifts of miracles which the Jews demand and the gift of wisdom which the Greeks seek are not the basis of a personal faith. But the preaching of Christ is.

This means that the trained scholar has no advantage over the layman.[2] The most spiritually gifted is no surer of his relationship to God than the less gifted. Faith is as readily accessible to the simple as to the genius, to the uneducated as to the educated, to the foolish as to the wise, to the poor as to the rich.

A DISTINCTION BETWEEN GIFTS AND FRUIT

We are spiritually formed primarily through the *gift* of the Holy Spirit and secondarily through the *gifts* of the Holy Spirit. For there is a difference between the gift and the gifts.[3] The *gift* of the Spirit is God himself fully indwelling our minds and hearts. The *gifts* of the Spirit are special abilities and talents with which the Lord endows us for the good of the body of Christ (1 Cor. 12:7; Eph. 4:12).

We must also recognize a difference between the gifts of the Spirit and the fruit of the Spirit.[4] There are many gifts of the Spirit and not each person possesses the same gifts. But there is only one fruit of the Spirit. Notice that in Galatians 5:22–23 Paul specifically says, "The fruit [not fruits] of the Spirit is love, joy, peace, patience, kindness, goodness, faithfulness, gentleness, self-control." Everyone is supposed to possess the whole fruit of the Spirit, but not everyone possesses all the gifts of the Spirit (1 Cor. 12:4–11). This is why Peter says, "As each has received a gift, employ it for one another, as good stewards of God's varied grace" (1 Peter 4:10). If we neglect our gifts, then the body of Christ suffers.

THE GIVING OF THE GIFTS ARE BY GOD'S CHOICE ALONE

The gifts of the Spirit are "distributed according to [God's] own will" (Heb. 2:4). Paul also makes this point clear in his instruction to the competitive Corinthians. He chides them for boasting about their gifts when in fact these gifts are "gifts" and not personal achievements: "Why do you boast as if it were not a gift?" (1 Cor. 4:7)

Their attitude about the gifts of the Spirit were in direct contradiction to the fruit of the Spirit. He could not write to them as believers endowed with the fullness of the Spirit (1 Cor. 3:1) even though they possessed the gifts of the Spirit. Our Lord in his Sermon on the Mount also said that it was possible to possess the gifts of the Spirit without the Spirit: "On [judgment] day many will say to me, 'Lord, Lord, did we not prophesy in your name, and cast out demons in your name, and do many mighty works in your name?' And then will I declare to them, 'I never knew you; depart from me, you evildoers' " (Matt. 7:22–23). Balaam was a person in the Old Testament who possessed the gift of prophecy, but he was morally unregenerate (Num. 22).

Paul wrote his letter to the Corinthians because of a number of problems which existed in their fellowship. It has often been said that the modern church is regrettably not like the New Testament church. But an examination of the problems which confronted the Corinthian fellowship indicates that their problems and ours are not all that different. Their difficulties included jealousy (1:10; 3:3), immorality (5:1), lawsuits against each other (6:1), lack of self-control (7:5), divorce (7:10–16), legalism (7:17–24), idolatry (10:14), abuse of the Lord's Supper (11:17–33), and a denial of the resurrection (15:12). And the list is really much longer. One of their greatest problems was their unspiritual attitude about the gifts of the Spirit. Each seemed to think that his particular gift was a sign of his special importance.

Paul says no to this. God chooses how he will divide up the gifts for the improvement of his church. They are not necessarily the result of our own asking. While it is all right to ask for certain gifts, he reminds them that it is by God's choice alone that the gifts are distributed to the body of Christ (1 Cor. 12:11).

SOME GIFTS ARE MORE
IMPORTANT THAN OTHERS

The apostle tells the Corinthians to be more focused on "the higher gifts" of the Spirit (1 Cor. 12:31). Paul specifically says that their priority list was different from the Holy Spirit's. They prized particularly the gift of tongues, but Paul twice listed it as the least important gift (1 Cor. 12:27–31). And he omits it from his list of gifts in other instances (Rom. 12:3–8; Eph. 4:9–14).

Perhaps their obsession with this one gift stemmed from their culture. Delphi was a neighboring Greek city with a pagan temple whose priestesses spoke ecstatic utterances. Their babblings were supposed to carry the message of the god of the underworld, Hermes. The great Socrates got his "call" to be a seeker after wisdom from one of the oracles of Delphi in the fourth century B.C.[5]

The Greeks were lovers of wisdom and sought after "mysteries." They prized their religious heritage and held the oracles of Delphi in high esteem. Now that the Corinthian Christians had been saved out of this pagan background, it is possible that their liking for the mysterious was carried over into their new Christian surroundings. The ability to speak in tongues and the apparent gift of knowledge and wisdom made them feel superior.

Paul doesn't reject the gift of tongues, but he wants it to be kept in proper perspective. He admits that on occasion he speaks in tongues. But it is not that which ought to be so highly prized. The apostle says that instead of giving excessive attention to the gifts of the Holy Spirit they ought to seek "the more excellent way" of love. Love is the primary expression of the fruit of the Spirit. "If you are going to be excessive in anything, be excessive in your love, not in your emphasis upon the gifts," is the tone of Paul's instruction (1 Cor. 12:27–31).

But this doesn't mean that the gifts of the Spirit are therefore unimportant. Indeed, Paul says that they are of utmost importance "for the equipment of the saints, for the work of ministry, for building up the body of Christ" (Eph. 4:12). He adds that we should use the particular gifts which God has given to us (Rom. 12:6). But if these gifts of the Spirit are to serve a meaningful function in the spiritual community, they should be exercised with a Spirit-filled temperament.

ALL CHRISTIANS ARE SPIRIT-GIFTED

Does every Christian have a particular gift of the Spirit? Yes. Nobody has all the gifts, but everybody has some gift which is practiced from time to time. Without the distribution of the gifts, the body of Christ would be incomplete. If some member in the body of Christ fails to exercise his gift, the whole body suffers.

One question often asked is, "How can I discover what my gifts are?" Sometimes this is asked in a tone of desperation as if one is not a good practicing Christian if he isn't consciously aware of the particular gift which God has given to him. But I suspect that most people aren't aware of their gifts even though they practice them regularly.

When I was in the ninth grade and living in a small town in South Georgia, a friend invited my older brother and me to go fishing in a pond on his parents' farm. Instead of walking to the pond from their house, we took an ancient tractor which was on its last legs. My brother, who knew nothing about tractors, drove us down and onto the dam. Since it was impossible to drive all the way across, my brother decided to back out. And he did! Right off the dam! We jumped to safety within a split second of our lives, terrified.

When our parents arrived at the scene of this near-fatal accident, my mother told us that the Holy Spirit had warned her the previous day that something awful was going to happen to her children. She was so overcome with concern that she left the house, went to the church, knelt at the altar, and prayed for our safety. And she didn't leave the church until she felt a reassurance in her heart that God would protect us. Though I have never heard her claim to possess it, my mother at that specific time possessed the gift of knowledge.

Some believers may be generally endowed with a gift on a

more permanent basis, but many Christians are temporarily gifted for whatever specific situation might rise. Paul possessed the gift of healing on some occasions but not on others. When a serpent fastened itself on Paul's hand on the island of Melita, he was not hurt. When he visited the home of Publius on the island, Paul healed his father of a fever. "When this had taken place, the rest of the people on the island who had diseases also came and were cured" (Acts 28:5–9).

Yet there were times when Paul did not heal. He said to Timothy, "Trophimus I left ill at Miletus" (2 Tim. 4:20). Why didn't Paul heal him? He certainly needed his help. And if Paul's thorn was an illness, neither his physician nor the Lord healed him of it (2 Cor. 12:7).

The performance of miracles and the exercise of the various gifts of the Spirit were obviously a part of Paul's ministry, but there is a remarkable silence in his letters about the gifts of healing except in this one passage in 1 Corinthians 12. Only rarely does he mention the gifts of the Spirit at all; his obsession was Christ and our being remade in his likeness. This is why Paul devoted most of his writings to encouraging Christians to walk in the Spirit of Christ instead of focusing on spectacular demonstrations of miracles and signs.

Luke emphasized the Holy Spirit's direction of the missionary work of the church. It is a misreading of his record to think that he focused primarily on miracles and the gifts of the Spirit. His interest was to show that the church, which was begun at Pentecost, was the fulfillment of the Old Testament history of salvation. The theme of Acts is the proclamation of Christ as Savior and Lord. The miracles and signs played an important but secondary and supportive role.

Of course God performs miracles today. But if we become obsessed with miracles and signs, we may be guilty of what Jesus once said to the Pharisees: "An evil and adulterous generation seeks for a sign" (Matt. 12:39). Why did our Lord say this? Because the Pharisees pressed Jesus for more signs as ground for faith, and they used his refusal as an excuse for their unbelief. An obsession with miracles can become a substitute for faith in Christ.

PRACTICE YOUR GIFTS WITHOUT FANFARE

Spirit-filled Christians practice their faith without drawing attention to themselves. With humility they receive the gifts of God and fulfill their divine calling without fanfare and show. They do not focus on their gifts as if they have something which others don't.

Jim is a local merchant and an active Methodist layman. He has never had any formal training in seminary, but he has preached in many churches across this country, and he is highly respected in his hometown. One of his gifts is healing. He has prayed for the healing of many people, and the Lord has honored his spiritual service. I have never heard this dedicated Christian say that he has the gift of healing or the gift of faith. But he doesn't need to. The purpose of his lay ministry is to help people come to know the Lord and to experience his fullness.

Once as we drove home together after a Sunday morning service, I told him about a young man who had recently felt called to be a missionary and who was visiting in several churches in the area to seek support for his ministry. He had just been taken to a hospital with a possible eye disease. Jim felt that we ought to visit him. We walked into his hospital room and immediately sensed the man's deep distress. His wife stood by his bed with tears in her eyes. They were far away from their friends and families. He had several years earlier given up an important teaching position in a state university in preparation for the mission field. He had asked his family to share much personal sacrifice for his calling. Now it appeared that he might lose his sight.

Jim reached out his hands in compassion and love to this missionary couple and prayed for God's healing grace. I sensed the love of God flowing out of his heart into theirs. I saw discouragement turn into faith. I saw despair transformed into hope. The look in their eyes and the joy on their faces indicated that they had been touched by the Holy Spirit

The miracle in this act of ministry was in the timing of the Holy Spirit We came at the exact moment of their greatest need. My friend had exercised the gift of knowledge in recognizing the urgency of our visit at that moment. I saw him exercise the gift of faith which inspired this couple to a new sense of God's presence in their lives. I saw him exercise the gift of healing as he prayed for the complete restoration of this man's eyes, a request which God fully honored. Today they are doing the work of God in Africa.

I'm sure that Jim never stopped to think about which gifts he was practicing—or that he was *using* any gifts at all. I've heard him preach many times and known him for many years. If I were to ask him about his spiritual gifts, he would be surprised at such a question.

There is no indication in the book of Acts that the apostles kept tabs on their gifts. They were simply open to the inspiration of the Spirit to serve as the need arose and the situation required. Paul put it briefly: "I decided to know nothing among you except Jesus Christ and him crucified" (1 Cor. 2:2). He rejected any interest in appearing to possess the gift of wisdom when he came to Corinth "proclaiming . . . the testimony of God" (1 Cor. 2:1). He said that the true "demonstration of the Spirit" is not in the endowment of particular gifts but in the authenticity of our faith-relationship to God (1 Cor. 2:4–5).

We develop a growing relationship with Christ when we do so intentionally. But often we employ spiritual gifts unintentionally. As we are filled with the Holy Spirit, God decides which gifts he wants us to have for the good of the Christian community. "As each has received a gift, employ it for one another, as good stewards of God's varied grace" (1 Peter 4:10).

9

THE SPIRIT OF TRUTH

I will pray the Father, and he will give you another Counselor, to be with you for ever, even the Spirit of truth.

John 14:16–17

One summer our kids complained that vacation had gone too fast and school was starting too early. Here it was already August 15 and the time for fun and freedom was over. Now the serious stuff starts. To reinforce the bad news that their summer party had ended, their teachers dared to give them homework and tests during the very first week of classes! Our oldest boy complained, "I don't see why our teachers think this stuff is so important!" I reassured him and the others that truth is always important and that if they expected to be successes they needed to pay attention to what the teachers were trying to impart to them.

I had misgivings about my pep talk, for the first test which our seventh grader had was over the scientific method. Truth, she was told, is always the result of our own thinking. We never believe anything is true simply because somebody tells us that it is. She was given the seven simple steps to discover truth: state the problem, collect information, make a hypothesis, make observation through experimentation, record the facts, analyze the data, and draw conclusions. Then you have the truth! Or do you?

The Bible of our secular culture is the scientific method. Truth is impersonal and the means of getting to it are impersonal. If we can see it, smell it, hear it, touch it, and taste it, then we can believe it!

But don't you believe it! Some recent scientists themselves have been telling us that the truth about our world depends largely upon the personal interests and attitudes of the scientists. Michael Polanyi is a world-famous scientist who has reintroduced the personal element into the scientific method. His great book *Personal Knowledge* shows us that a strong faith element inheres the method of knowing used by scientists.[1] A trusting attitude is as important as a probing and critical mind in the scientific pursuit of knowledge.

TRUTH IS ROOTED IN OUR CAPACITY FOR TRUST

The Old Testament word for truth is often translated "faithfulness" (Ex. 34:6). This implies that the primary meaning of truth has to do with trust. *The Bible teaches us that truth in the highest sense of the word is our personal trust in the faithfulness of God and in the goodness of his creation* (Deut. 32:4). This is the point which Alfred North Whitehead once made in his book *Science and the Modern World*. He says that modern science is indebted to biblical faith because it teaches that the world was made for man to understand and to have dominion over because God created it for our benefit.[2] The scientific method was not so likely to develop among other religions because they believed the world was like a god whom they must worship along with their idols; but the Bible teaches that the world is different from God and we are to use it responsibly for our purposes.

God not only acted in creation; he acted in history. The creation of the world provided the space for him to place man and woman where they could in time develop a relationship together as well as with him. With Abraham the history of salvation begins. This history, which formed the bridge between God and us, was fulfilled in Jesus Christ. Now we must ask ourselves whether this record is reliable.

One of the most prominent theologians today, a man widely known and respected for his scholarship, is Wolfhart Pannenberg, who teaches at the University of Munich. He has shown that the scientific method as practiced in the field of historical studies indicates that this salvation history is true. He concludes that the main events in the record are so highly probable that to doubt them is unreasonable. Like the scientist Polanyi, Pannenberg has shown that our capacity to know depends upon our personal assumptions and on our sense of values.[3] These personal values provide our minds with the proper attitude to discover the truth about what really happened in the past.

He shows that the claims of Jesus to be God, the tradition about the empty tomb, and the appearances of the risen Jesus are reliable historical happenings. If scholars doubt that these events really happened, it is not because they use the scientific, historical method in interpreting the Bible. It is because they choose not to believe because of reasons of ideology.[4] Much of Pannenberg's reasoning about the veracity of the recorded events is based upon Paul's reports, especially the evidence Paul produces in 1 Corinthians 15. No respected biblical scholar literature doubts that Paul wrote this letter around A.D. 55, even if he doesn't believe what Paul said.[5]

No document has ever been so exposed to a more careful and thorough scrutiny as the Bible. In fact, Ernst Cassirer in *The Age of Enlightenment* has shown that it was a scholarly interest in the historical nature of the Bible which led to "the rise of the modern historical consciousness."[6] By this phrase, scholars mean that in the modern world historians engage in a more careful scrutiny of what really happened in the past and they examine historical documents with a more thorough analysis and critical examination than was done in the pre-modern world.

We have already seen how secular psychologists recognize that the meaning of the personal in the modern world is derived from the Bible with its emphasis on a personal God. We have seen that scientists acknowledge their debt to the Bible for the emergence of the scientific method. Now we are pointing out that the historical-critical method is the outgrowth of biblical faith.

The Bible has been put through severe tests by scholars because it claims to be primarily a history of salvation. All that we believe about God is communicated to us through these events of history. And there are certain facts in this history which no critical scholar, whether liberal or conservative, has any doubts about today. These facts include the disciples' witness that Jesus believed himself to be God and that the disciples believed Jesus was raised from the dead and the tomb was empty.

But this is where history becomes a problem for some critical scholars. They remind us that just because the disciples believed these things doesn't mean that they really happened. This of course is right. But Pannenberg has shown that only a confirmed skeptic would doubt that they really happened, and if they are doubted, it is not because of insufficient historical evidence. The problem is with the scholar who has an attitude problem about belief in the existence of a God who is capable of acting so personally in the world.

There is obviously a difference in the way that the Bible was written and the way modern scholars write history. But the difference is not because the latter write better history; it is only that they write from a different perspective. To them history is a collection of impersonal facts which they offer the reader along with interpretations of how the facts may fit together. But biblical history is a drama of God's revelation of himself to specific individuals on specific occasions. The story isn't intended to be an impersonal and impartial report of historical occurrences.

The Bible does not take an indifferent attitude toward truth. Truth is what the Bible is all about. It understands the importance of testing the veracity of what is reported to be true (Deut. 13:14), and that truth is more than simply the way something may seem to be or appear (Acts 12:9). It understands that truth is based upon fact (John 5:31–32; 8:13–14; 21:24; Titus 1:13; 3 John 12).

Holy Scripture distinguishes between myths and historical events.[7] Peter plainly says that he is writing about the events of salvation history which really happened because he was an eyewitness to them. He writes, "We did not follow cleverly devised myths when we made known to you" the thing which we heard and saw in the life of Jesus. This is why he says, "I intend always to remind you of these things" so that you will be "established in the truth" (2 Peter 1:12–19). The Bible understands the importance of certainty regarding actual events in the history of salvation. This is why Peter says he is "more sure" of the word of God than even the prophets of the Old Testament were because "we were with him on the holy mountain" when God spoke words of approval of Jesus as his Son (2 Peter 1:18).

Likewise, John is certain of what he says concerning Jesus because he had been an earthly witness of the things that Jesus did. He appeals to the evidence of his five senses as proof of his testimony: "We have heard . . . we have seen with our eyes . . . we have looked upon and touched [him] with our hands" (1 John 1:1). Luke wrote his gospel because he wanted to "compile a narrative of the things" that happened to Jesus. He did this by writing down those facts which "were delivered to us by those who from the beginning were eyewitnesses" (Luke 1:1–2).

Luke's method was in one sense scientific because he intended to examine the evidence and to follow it "closely" and then "write an orderly account" of the truth (1:3). This analysis of the facts would then assist Theophilus to be able to "know the truth concerning the things of which [he had] been informed" (1:4). Facts, information, reliability, careful analysis, honesty, observation, responsible conclusions, testing hypotheses—all these were basic underlying principles in what the Bible reports as having happened in the history of salvation. These reports could not have been sustained by the church for a moment if they had been proved false.

Then why doesn't everyone believe in the resurrection of Jesus? Why doesn't everyone believe that he is the Son of God?

Why is the truth of God's revelation so widely doubted in the modern world? Surely the problem must be the lack of sufficient evidence; otherwise, more people would have less difficulty believing.

But wait a minute! Belief is no more difficult today than it was in Jesus' day. Even the disiciples found it impossible at first to believe that he had come back from among the dead. Remember that they considered the women's report of having seen Jesus to be no more than an "idle tale"—until Jesus showed himself to them as well (Luke 24:11). Thomas also doubted the resurrection—until the evidence was presented to him and he believed (John 20:25). One of the myths popularized by modern scholars is that the Bible has an unscientific and uncritical attitude about miracles. The biblical writers were not mythmakers. They made a point of dissociating themselves from mythical religions (1 Cor. 8:4).

What, then, is our modern problem with belief in the truth of Jesus Christ? The answer goes back to an even more fundamental problem. Truth is primarily a matter of trust. It is an affair of the heart before it becomes a concern of the mind. Our more scholarly attitude does not make faith so difficult for us today; it's our inability to trust.

In fact, as we have said, the Old Testament word for truth is often translated in our English Bible as "faithfulness." This personal component is the basic meaning of truth, not the impersonal attitude which is often assumed in the scientific method. For our perception of truth is never something that results simply from observing facts and then drawing impartial conclusions. The guiding factor in our perceptions is our attitude. *Our attitudes are always formed out of the human relationships which we have developed.* When we interpret our experiences, whether as scientists, historians, psychologists, or theologians, we always do so from the standpoint of our life experiences.

The idea of absolute proof is a myth. Not even missile-launch accuracy is absolute accuracy. Besides, for daily living we don't require that kind of evidence. Our human relationships would be torn by distrust and suspicion if we related to others on the basis of this kind of absolute evidence. In the same way, a believing and trusting attitude in the responsible witness of the disciples is involved in the meaning of our trust in Christ. A distrust of their witness is a more fundamental distrust in Christ. We can't have faith in Christ and at the same time distrust the witnesses of his saving life.

But even the capacity to trust in Christ is by the power of the Holy Spirit. Faith is the gift of God. It comes by hearing his Word. This is why Paul has said that our perception of the truth of Christ is a discernment of the Spirit (1 Cor. 2:14). This is why Jesus told the Eleven that the coming of the Holy Spirit would give them power to understand his teachings (John 14:26).[8]

Faith is not a mere subjectivism; it is not saying that we believe in spite of a lack of historical evidence nor that all truth is merely a matter of one's preference. Nor is it enough to believe that this truth is reasonably based in the events of salvation history. But for us really to believe we must enter into relationship with the God of history who promised our forefather Abraham that we could enjoy eternal fellowship with him through faith in his promises.

The indwelling Holy Spirit is the guarantee (2 Cor. 1:22) of the truth of God and provides us with the attitude of faith; he enables our minds to understand that the witness of the disciples is true. This personal and relational dimension is what turns the probable events of history into *the inner certainties of faith*. This trusting relationship makes the difference between those who perceive the history of salvation as a reliable and true revelation of God in Christ and those who don't.

I find it ironic that some of the makers of modern thought acknowledge their indebtedness to the biblical faith for their ideas, but then fail to commit themselves to a personal trust in God. I earlier showed how psychologists such as Erich Fromm recognized that we are indebted to the biblical view of God for the emergence of the modern meaning of the personal. We have seen that Whitehead agreed that biblical faith in the God of creation was the necessary background for the development of modern science. Yet neither Fromm nor Whitehead believed in the personal God of history who made these truths available to us today.

Some modern scholars apparently are willing to reap the benefits of God's revelation without accepting him as the truth. They want to know the meaning of the personal; they want to know the meaning of the universe. But they don't seem to want to know the God of the personal and the God of the universe. They believe that truth somehow evolved out of the impersonal make-up of the world, yet they admit that without a belief in a personal God modern truths would not have been developed.

TRUTH IS OUR PARTICIPATION IN GOD'S HISTORY

The main point which we have emphasized in this chapter so far is that truth is an attitude of trust in the faithfulness of God. The second main point is that *salvation is history*.[9] When Paul speaks of our being saved through the "sanctification by the Spirit and belief in the truth" (2 Thess. 2:13), he means that we share in the saving events of Jesus' life through the power of the Spirit. For truth is not an assortment of ideas which we swallow like candy. *Truth is the event of Jesus Christ whose life-history includes us.* This history includes ideas and doctrines, but the reality is the history itself.

Ancient Greeks believed that nothing new ever really happens; they thought of history as just an endless repetition of events. Many secular people today think that history records development from a cluster of matter into higher forms of life, with personal life at the top of this impersonal evolutionary development. But in the Bible, the truth about human life developed in real history as the Israelites were formed as a community of people under the guidance of a personal God. This is why personal relationships were so important to them, and this is why the future was more real for them than the past or the present. For the promises of God always had them looking toward the future.

The meaning of history with its forward-looking attitude is a basic meaning of truth in the New Testament as well.[10]

Jesus' teaching on the coming kingdom of God implies that the truth about our world will be revealed in the future. Though the kingdom has come, it is yet to come. All of Jesus' teachings reflect this attitude about the future.

The hope of the future coming of the Lord indicates that this forward-looking attitude is the key to understanding the New Testament. Yet the coming of the Holy Spirit on the day of Pentecost means that the future is already here, even though it is still to come. The existence of the church as the community of the Spirit is the arrival of the future in the here and now. The history of salvation is the story of our life which we now have with God in Christ. God's existence spans the distance of the finite distinctions between the past, present, and future. For example, Abraham was justified by faith in Christ even before Christ was born (Rom. 4:22–25), and we are told that we have the future inheritance now even though it is still future (Eph. 1:13–14).

History is the development of the past, present, and future. But it is our future which gives direction to the present. It is customary to believe that our present life is a result of the continuing influences of the past. But the Bible assumes otherwise, for God, as the power of the future, directs the present events of our lives. Past events, such as Easter and Pentecost, are important because they were also anticipations of the future which we will have with God. So our attitude toward the future is more basic than our attitude about the present and past. Yet the way to get to the future is through the past. "Back to the future" is an important biblical idea; we reach our future with God by way of Easter and Pentecost. So past events in time, like Easter and Pentecost, are not merely past. For these events as they really happened in their original setting are available to us in our personal history today.

I hesitate to use this word *history* because history was a class we had to take and were glad when it was over with. I remember a homespun poem scribbled on the flyleaf of my textbook in the tenth grade. It expressed the sentiments of a lot of students: "When I die, bury me deep. / Bury this history book at my feet. / Tell Mr. Warren I'm at rest, / And won't be back for the history test!"

History in its highest sense does not mean a list of events and dates. These are only secondary meanings. History is the story behind the events which shape the lives and thinking of persons. History is not merely a record of events; it is reality. History is the life of the soul; it is the meaning of persons in relation. *Truth is history; it is the story of our life with God in Jesus Christ by the power of his Spirit.*

In an important way we span the past, present, and future all at the same time because we are spiritual beings made in the image of God. In another sense, our feet are planted on the ground of the present world because we are finite. Time is not only like a line which can be divided into past, present, and future. Nor is time like a spinning wheel that goes only in a circle. Time is really like both without being either one. We are aware of a sequence of events which we label as past, present, and future. Yet we sense that the past and the future are with us in the present moment.

Though our present experience is influenced by past events in our lives, we demonstrate that we are persons rather than mere animals because we live our lives from the perspective of the future. We refuse to be chained by the past and are free to be open to the future possibilities of our existence. Time is primarily a forward-looking experience for us. We are not content with what lies behind us, but we are always reaching out toward the future. Without this sense of movement toward a future goal, we would be without a sense of history.

History is the spiritual dimension of our being; it is that characteristic of our lives which makes it possible for us to relate to others. History is the arena of life's engagements. Events in the world are historic because history is a quality and an attitude which forms the meaning of our personal existence.

Because we are able to project beyond ourselves through time into the past and future we are able to stand outside the present. We can even look back at ourselves from an outside perspective. Our capacity for history means that we can be open to others, experience their inner life, and see ourselves as others see us. We have a dimension of freedom to be available for others in a thoughtful manner, unlike animals and things. Most of all, this means that we are available to God and that he is available to us.

Because history is the spiritual meaning of our existence, it is not easy to illustrate or define. The spiritual world is something we can point to and affirm without understanding it completely. The Bible is a record of its historical manifestation, but it does not try to define it or prove it logically. The Bible assumes that God is the cause of all things and therefore has a personal existence independent of the world (Acts 17:24–25). He does not need the world for his existence, though the world could not exist without him.

God is *who he is* (Ex. 3:14); he does not need someone else to help him realize his potential. He already is his own potential.[12] Because God is a person who is the larger reason why everything exists, the world is personal. God intends for us to become real persons through the history which he has developed with us.

Now all this might seem far removed from us. What does it matter what history is? Well, not very much if we are talking only about a theory. On the other hand, it means a lot if we wish to understand how the events in the Bible can be saving for us today. Are the events in the life of Jesus only memories for us to recall? Or do they still exist in the present moment as an extension of the past? For example, is the resurrection of Jesus merely an event of the past or does this once-for-all event in the past still exist as a reality for us to share in today? If so, how is it possible? How can the past live on for us today?

One thing about the history of Jesus seems clear in the New Testament. We must experience for ourselves the events of his resurrection and the outpouring of his Spirit. These once-for-all happenings must be personally appropriated today. They are not buried in the past as if they once happened and then ceased to be. They live on in the present, and our relationship to God is dependent upon our participation in these saving acts of God. I repeat, we are saved only if we as well as the apostles experience Jesus' actual death-resurrection and the giving of his

Spirit (Rom. 6:8; Acts 2:38). Easter and Pentecost in their original happening are available to us through the power of the Spirit. We really die with Christ, are raised to newness of life, and are empowered by his Spirit given on Pentecost. His history must become our history if we are to develop a relationship with God.

BACK TO THE FUTURE

I don't know how our real participation in the past can be clearly defined. After all, spiritual realities exceed our ability fully to comprehend, but perhaps an illustration will help us. Dr. Wilder Penfield is a world-famous brain surgeon. His pioneering efforts with epileptic patients have made a lasting contribution to neuroscience. He was the first scientist to deal in direct observation of the human brain in fully conscious persons. Many of the results of his studies are included in his book *The Mystery of the Mind*.[13]

Surgery on epileptic patients required that they be fully conscious. Their scalps were injected with a local analgesic to prevent pain and no sedative or anesthetic was given. The surface of one hemisphere of the brain was exposed enough for study and possible excision to cure the source of abnormality which caused uncontrollable discharges of energy leading to epileptic attacks. The patients, awake and alert, were able to guide the surgeon's hand throughout the operation. He explained to patients each step of the process, and they told the surgeon what they were experiencing.

An important part of the process involved the use of a stimulating electrode. Its function was to seek out the site of brain irritation. With the electrical stimulation of the interpretative areas of the cerebral cortex, the patients reported actually reliving with exact detail the visible, audible, and feeling dimensions of previous experiences. At the same time the patients were fully conscious of being on the operating table.

This doubling of their consciousness within a single awareness of what was happening to them provided for Penfield a conviction that the mind was distinct from the brain. The brain is a physical organ, but the mind is nonmaterial. The brain is like a computer which stores information, but the mind is the inner essence of the person which thinks, knows, and enjoys self-awareness. Penfield's distinction between the mind and the brain (body) is a traditional belief which of course is assumed in the Scriptures as well.

The mind refers to that part of the human spirit which allows us to know ourselves as we really are. The mind is our spiritual capacity to stand outside of ourselves and look back at ourselves; we can project ourselves into the past and relive events in their original form; we can move beyond the present into the future possibilities of our existence.

This is the meaning of spiritual freedom; we are not immersed in the processes of nature. We are not only conscious of our surroundings as animals are, but we are self-conscious. To be self-conscious is to be conscious both of our surroundings and of the awareness of this consciousness. Animals seem to be conscious only of their surroundings but not conscious of themselves. This is why they are motivated only by instinct, but humans have the capacity to choose. This is why we are moral, spiritual, and physical beings all at the same time. As an illustration of this paradox, think of Paul's comments about someone who in a vision may have been carried beyond his body into the heavenly realm (2 Cor. 12:2). Though we are finite and our bodies exert a restraining influence upon our spirits, we are also capable of transcending the present moment.

Though Dr. Penfield does not write as a Christian, he believes in the nonmaterial make-up of our true selves. He argues this point on the basis of scientific observation. In all of his brain operations on epileptic patients, he has probed extensively with an electrode but has found no evidence that self-consciousness can be identified with any part of the brain. To be sure, one may lose consciousness if the brain receives a physical blow, but the capacity of a person to organize his thoughts and feelings within his mind as a single experience seems to be a spiritual and not a physical activity. Dr. Penfield believes that the doubling of consciousness in his patients which results when the electrode probes the memory-storing cells in the brain implies this belief.

The first memory flashback was reported to Dr. Penfield in 1933 by a mother. As the electrode touched her interpretative cortex, she said that she was suddenly aware of working in the kitchen and hearing her little boy's voice as he played in the backyard. She also heard familiar neighborhood noises. Another patient reported being at a baseball game in a small town watching a little boy crawl under the fence to get inside the ballpark. Another patient told of hearing musical instruments. She hummed the melody which she heard, and the tempo was correct. Penfield restimulated her over thirty times, trying to mislead her. Each time she heard and relived the very same experience, and her humming started each time with the chorus and on to the verse. On another occasion, a young South African patient in surgery expressed amazement "that he was laughing with his cousins on a farm in South Africa, while he was also fully conscious of being in the operating room talking to the doctor." Penfield's studies with over a thousand patients have led him to the conclusion that though the contents of consciousness are dependent upon the activity of nerve cells in the brain, the awareness of ourselves is not.

This brain research illustrates two things. First, it suggests that we are more than our bodies. An increasing number of brain scientists insist on this fact. We have a spiritual center which cannot be located merely in the brain. Second, it illustrates how the past lives on in the present. We have buried many things beneath the level of self-consciousness that are still a part of who we are because they influence our feelings and thoughts. The striking thing in these experiments is that the events of our past are not recorded in a superficial manner. *The pictures, feelings, sounds, smells, and tastes are still there in their original form.* Memories are not just records. Memories are the real events themselves. Nothing in our past is mere "history" which we can simply and conveniently forget. For all events which catch the attention of the mind are remembered, and they continue to influence our personal history whether or not we are fully conscious of them. Like it or not, all the events of our lives continue to inform and form us. For our past is forever with us—except as it is transformed by our spiritual participation in the history of Jesus.

Even as our minds span the distance in time and preserve our past for the present, so God's mind is the basis of the unity of the whole sweep of the past, present, and future happenings in the world. What occurred once for all in the past is preserved in the mind of God in its original form. God does not sit on the sidelines as a neutral spectator. This is his world and his creation. He is deeply involved in all the events of the entire world. He cares deeply what happens to us and what happens to his creation. The Bible is clear that God is emotionally involved with us. He is grieved when we sin against him, and he rejoices when we live in obedience to his will.

Sins of our past along with any damage which they have inflicted upon our spiritual and emotional life cannot be eradicated simply by divine fiat. Not even God can wipe the slate of our lives clean willy-nilly, though he has thoughts and feelings and is affectionately bonded to us. He worked for thousands of years to transform the history of the human race before our redemption and sanctification could be achieved. He expended an infinite amount of energy to save us from our sins and heal us of our damaged feelings and wrong thoughts.

This is the meaning of the gospel. The Spirit of Jesus Christ has come to indwell us and to make us an integral part of the life of God. He does this by inviting us to participate in God's history of salvation. As we respond to this offer of grace, once again the events of Easter and Pentecost, which are eternally preserved in the mind of God, are relived and bring salvation and healing to our life history. As we are incorporated into God's history, we begin to find ourselves released from the pain of the damaging memories which haunt us.

Our lives up to this point may have been dull beyond telling or as painful as that of an abandoned child with no history of security and love. But if we will trust, God will change our history by his redeeming and sanctifying presence. *And that's the truth!*

10

THE SPIRIT OF PEACE

To set the mind on the Spirit is life and peace.

Romans 8:6

Recently my youngest daughter turned the car radio to her favorite popular music channel. A new song had just hit the top of the charts and its cheery melody sung by Bobby McFerrin repeated over and over again these simple words: "Don't Worry! Be happy!" The popularity of this song speaks of the crying need for peace among our youth, for they feel stressed out in a world where adult unreality has left them feeling insecure and anxious.

Contentment is not a common experience today. Our anxiety has reached a level of intensity previously unknown in the history of the world. No society has ever been so drugged, no time in history has ever been so emotionally stressful, and no people in any culture have ever been so obsessed with the need for peace.

If material prosperity could buy peace, it would have been easily purchased in the counseling rooms of therapists and around the bargaining tables of political diplomats in our affluent world. Instead, our wealth has often succeeded in only hiding from us our anxiety. Yet we hear as Jeremiah did in his day of futile programs which will bring "peace, peace, when there is no peace" (Jer. 6:14).

What does it mean to have peace with God? Simply, it means to live in the light of his countenance. *Peace is a relational quality; it comes through looking into the face of God.* God gave to Moses a benediction which the priests were to use when the community gathered for worship, a blessing which promised peace if they lived in the light of God's presence: "The LORD bless you and keep you: The LORD make his face to shine upon you, and be gracious to you: The LORD lift up his countenance upon you, and give you peace" (Num. 6:24–26).

PEACE IS THE GIFT OF A PERSONAL GOD

Of course many seem to know the meaning of peace today without faith in a personal God. Contentment, we are told, is an inner attitude which the self-reliant must achieve for themselves. In a television interview with Barbara Walters, Don Johnson was asked for his philosophy of life. He replied, "Expect nothing, and do everything simply for the love it. This way you'll never be disappointed." This secular idea of peace as the result of learning to hold down one's anxiety levels by fixing realistic goals is the best that many can hope for in a world that has lost the meaning of a personal faith in God.

Some are not satisfied with a strictly nonreligious view of life, but they don't go so far as to believe in a personal God. So they affirm the existence of a larger dimension to our world than merely the physical universe. But this larger dimension seems to be more like an aesthetic experience. God is Beauty, Order, and Truth, but not a person with self-awareness. When we die, God offers us peace from our life struggles by assimilating us into his (its!) being. This "beautiful thought" about the meaning of religion really brings to an end everything immortal about our human relationships.

Such an "intellectual" attitude about resting in peace at death was recently expressed in the popular television series "Family Ties." An acquaintance of the family had died, and after the funeral service the father reported to his children his more enlightened view of resting in peace. Deity for him was not a "heaven-and-hell kind of personal God." Rather, he said, "I believe God is like a great spirit which pervades the whole world." He explained that to be at peace means to rest from the troubles of the world and to be immersed in the spirit of the world. Then we will no longer have to exist as individuals.

This religious point of view, advocated on a popular family program, was portrayed as a more thoughtful expression of faith in God. I find it ironic that this depersonalizing of God and of ourselves was dramatized on a popular family program stressing the importance of lasting and meaningful relationships.

Many nonchurched people hold such an impersonal view of God, but it is not a new belief. In fact, one of the most influential religious beliefs in the Western world held this point of view: Stoicism. Stoicism, which developed in the third century B.C., was a combination of the best from a variety of philosophies and religions and a powerful movement among the more educated during the era of the Roman Empire. Among the most significant Stoics was Emperor Marcus Aurelius.

Stoicism was the greatest rival of Christianity during the latter's earliest days because its philosophy appeared to be intellectually compelling and emotionally satisfying.[1] That was a politically explosive time with a great deal of upheaval in society. People looked for peace in the midst of a world in turmoil, and a major attraction of Stoicism was its answer to the problem of fear. This philosophy of consolation offered comfort to the "wise" who lived thoughtful lives. God, the spirit of the world, was beyond suffering, and the wise who meditated on God could also rise above suffering. This mental participation in the divine offered release from anxiety and in its place peace of mind.

Stoicism had many good points, but its major difference from Christianity was its view of God as an impersonal something and its attitude of retreat from life. The Stoics believed that we simply have to resign ourselves to the way the world is and then heroically rise above it by thinking of God.

It attempted to speak to the relational problems and conflicts of its world by advocating universal brotherhood. It addressed the personal and emotional problems of life. It elevated the importance of education and the need to live with integrity. But it lacked one dynamic. It had no personal God and no history of salvation. Consequently it lacked the one intellectually compelling and emotionally satisfying component in life—the personal dimension.

We exist authentically as persons as we are known by the divine Person. We have already said that this feeling of personal integrity first emerged from the relationship God developed with us in the history of salvation. Knowing God makes us feel that we are building relationships which will last for eternity. Peace comes to us, not through engagement with an impersonal divine spirit, but through relationship with the living God of Jesus Christ.

Peace results not from suppression of our fears, but from deliverance from the fear of death, sin, and condemnation through a restored relationship with the God and Father of our Lord. Fear is the enemy of peace. Fear is the most damaging and depersonalizing of all human emotions. Fear was the very first negative human emotion; it surfaced immediately after Adam and Eve disobeyed God. They were afraid and hid themselves (Gen. 3:10). Fear is first and foremost a feeling of a dis-relationship with others and with oneself.

Freud didn't know what to make of this ultimate fear of all fears. His psychoanalytical practice consisted primarily of treating people's specific fears and phobias.[2] Irrational fears, like fears of high places, closed spaces, and insects as well as more serious ones such as fear of commitment are all rooted in this one ultimate fear—the loss of relationship with God.

Adam and Eve were afraid because their relationship with God had been violated. This resulted in a sense of loss of their personhood. So they hid themselves from God. Fear always makes us feel less than a person. That is why it is the most intimidating of all emotions. We are by God's design persons only to the extent that we engage in relationships with other persons. Parents, because of their disrelationship with God and their disrelationship with their children, have ever since Adam and Eve passed this fear to their children It was this disrelationship which Stoicism failed to understand, and it offered no hope for reconciliation with a personal God.

I am amazed at how widespread Stoicism is today even if we don't call it by that name.[3] It is portrayed as the thoughtful person's religion on television family programs, in university classrooms, and even in many theological seminaries. Its fundamental appeal is that we become authentic persons through the thoughtful cultivation of our intellectual life. Supposedly, our intelligence bestows upon us our sense of personhood. But the Bible makes it clear that we become true persons through our relationship with God. We were made in his image so that we can become persons through a participation in his life. Developing our ability to think, while invaluable, can create distance from others and from ourselves when it becomes a retreat from having to live in the real world of relationships.

The mind is certainly an important part of being a person, but a stoical philosophy of life is a retreat from having to engage other minds in personal relationships. The irony is that Stoicism insisted that the real world is like one simple drop of water and that we are to be merged into it. You might expect, with its emphasis on world brotherhood, that it would have said that the real world is a community of persons. Alas! It doesn't. Stoicism means the ending of all relationships. Its ultimate goal is not the affirmation of our human relationships, but their demise. Even suicide was considered to be a proper act of self-affirmation, for its goal was the loss of individuality by merger with the oneness of the world soul.

If the real world is only like a drop of water with no distinctions in it, then it is merciful that their god was not imagined to be a self-aware person because he would have been extremely lonely! But if the world beyond is really lifeless, then there is no fellowship, no hope, no love, and no faith. The Stoics wanted to be free from fear. They wanted to have peace of mind. But they retreated into an inner world of loneliness. Instead of their meditation on God making them feel like persons, it really resulted in depersonalizing them. Any time we cut ourselves off from others, we are depriving ourselves of the essence of our humanity. The Stoics had peace at any price as their goal even to the exclusion of developing relationships for the world to come.

The failure of the Stoics to appreciate the meaning of the personal is reflected in their descendants today. I am thinking particularly about an increasing belief among many in the church who embrace process theology. This belief is derived largely from the philosophy of Professors Charles Hartshorne and Alfred North Whitehead. Some Christian theologians have been particularly impressed with their philosophy as a means of interpreting faith.[4]

Their brand of Stoicism says that God offers us consolation precisely because he suffers with us. Professor Whitehead calls God "the great companion—the fellow-sufferer who understands."[5] Unfortunately, there isn't a lot of comfort in this abstract notion of suffering. To Whitehead, God is not a person who is conscious of his own feelings and thoughts. Like the Stoics, Whitehead's god is the great soul and spirit of the universe. This god is not the personal creator of the world who exists from eternity. Instead, he, or it, is also in process of development just as we are, except in a greater sense. He is not the Father of our Lord Jesus Christ whose Spirit of peace has been sent into our hearts.

One of the earliest theologians in our day to adopt this "new" way of interpreting the Christian faith was Paul Tillich. He undoubtedly is also the most creative and informed of all the process theologians. The religious world was shocked when Tillich's extramarital affairs were widely publicized shortly after his death.[6] But this was no real surprise to his seminary colleagues who knew him well. His ethical system permitted infidelity in marriage.

Tillich emigrated from Germany to the United States in 1933 when he was invited to teach at Union Theological Seminary in New York. He also taught at Harvard and the University of Chicago. He wrote many influential books and trained many pastors in theology. His books continue to be reprinted and widely read in spite of the revelations concerning his private life. One of his most widely read works is *Courage to Be,* a brilliant analysis of Stoic philosophy along with the contributions of psychoanalysis for Christian thought. He picks up the Stoic notion of courage for overcoming fear and offers a new explanation for the way Christian faith makes courage available to everyone.

Using contemporary psychology, he analyzes anxiety and shows how Christian faith addresses the basis of all anxieties, dread. He shows with rare insight that dread is the fear of all fears, the fear of our not being whole persons because of a lack of certainty that we have an eternal relationship with God and others. The felt loss of this eternal relationship implies that we too will not exist forever.

Unfortunately, Tillich offers a new kind of Stoic answer which he baptizes as Christian. His god, as I pointed out, is not a person; his god does not reward us with individual immortality, does not guarantee the continuation of human relationships beyond this world, cannot act personally in the affairs of this life, nor relate to us as a divine person in fellowship with the body of the risen Christ (the church).

For him, God is the Symbol of all symbols, the Whole of all the parts of the world, the Spirit and Soul of the world who knows himself (itself?) only as we know him since he is not a specific person with knowledge about himself and his world.[7] God is "he" only in a restricted and symbolic sense.[8]

Yet the whole point of Tillich's theology is to show how we can be liberated from the anxiety of a meaningless existence in the midst of a meaningless world. For him, courage is faith to accept ourselves even though there is no one present "out there" in the universe to accept us. For him, Jesus Christ is only the symbol of that courage.

I have read with care almost all of Tillich's writings. His comprehension of theology is remarkable and his treatment of it exhaustive. I am convinced also that if Tillich had made just one slight adjustment in his thinking, he could have been the champion of orthodox belief. If he had included God in his insights about the meaning of the personal, his writings would have been a marvelous exposition of Christian faith.

But that is exactly the disappointment awaiting you when you finish reading him. A personal God, he says, "disappears" in the anxiety of doubt and he is replaced with a nonpersonal god that is the soul of the universe.[9] "The traditional symbols," he says, "have lost their power" to convince contemporary minds.[10] The need of the times is to offer people release from the anxiety of emptiness and meaninglessness without belief in a transcendent God.

In other words, people want peace. He says they aren't looking for an eternal life beyond the grave; they don't worry about a future judgment; they don't long for a father-figure to tell them how to order their lives. Rather, Tillich says, each one wants to live out his life authentically by being his own person. This goal can be achieved by making peace with the limited possibilities which the world offers.

I will tell you later why I think Tillich's rejection of a personal God may have been rooted in his feelings about his own father. But if our relationships are faulty (and whose are not?), we can be sure that our perceptions of others will be faulty, and our perception of God will be faulty. That is why God's revelation of himself in Scripture, which was committed to the Christian community, is the only way our perceptions of him can be authentic. If we rely on our own ideas, we will in every instance have an idol rather than the true God.

Tillich's *Courage to Be* is a helpful discussion of this anxiety from which he appears to have suffered. His desire for meaning in a world without a personal God, however, cannot be satisfied with a Stoic's courage. The place to look for healing from this affliction of anxiety is the peace which we have with a personal God through Jesus Christ (Rom. 5:1).

THE LACK OF PEACE IN
A FATHER-ABSENT WORLD

One of Tillich's insights is that our age is experiencing the anxiety of emptiness and meaninglessness unlike any previous period of time. Tillich shows that this increasing anxiety is a result of a loss of faith in a personal God.[11] But he thinks we can have courage in spite of the loss.

An obvious reason for the declining sense of peace and the corresponding loss of faith in a personal God is the increasing tensions and complications of having to live in our fast-paced and highly competitive world. Mothers and fathers have little time left in their daily activities to spend building important family relationships. This loss of relationship with parents has more to do with the loss of faith in a personal God than anything else. God is the Father of peace. Throughout Scripture our capacity for peace is dependent upon our relationship to God as our Father (1 Tim. 1:2). Personal peace is the spiritual quality of those who have experienced an inner acceptance of who they are because of whose they are.

Psychosocial studies reveal just how closely connected are the development of our own personal identity and our relationship to our earthly fathers. When this relationship is inadequate, the resulting inner rage is often acted out publicly in destructive ways. The spiritual implications of these professional studies are vitally important.[12] What is true about the physical is just as true about the spiritual. Unless we have an adequate relationship with our earthly fathers we will have difficulty in our relationship with our heavenly Father.

When our first parents were separated from their heavenly Father, the pain of the disunion was immediately disastrous for their human relationships. *Wickedness* is the word the Bible uses to describe this state of broken human relationships. So disruptive and irresponsible for these relationships were the violence and sexual promiscuity that God regretted his creation of the race. The only alternative seemed to be their destruction—except that Noah's faithfulness had to be considered. Genesis shows that the lack of peace in the world was a direct consequence of the failure of our relationship with God as our heavenly Father.

Professional studies on the social and personality development of children brought up in father-absent homes confirm that fathers are the more significant parent for a child's development of self-awareness and personal identity. The focus was not upon the general problems of children from divorced homes, but pointedly upon the effects on children of long-term absences of fathers, whatever the reason.

The effects of father-absence were more serious in male children when the father left home during preschool years. Among female children the effects became more obvious during adolescent years. To be sure, the degree of seriousness depended on other variables in the family situation such as whether or not the mother was emotionally stable and loving, the economic situation, and the presence of male siblings.

Showing up in these studies is the close link between the presence of the father and the sex typing of children. Sex typing is the process whereby children learn to behave in ways appropriate to their gender. It is usually assumed that a connection exists between the masculinity of male children and a healthful relationship with their father; it is now known from the results of these studies that the presence of the father in the home is vital to the femininity of female children and their capacity to engage in appropriate heterosexual relationships.

One study revealed that boys are more likely to exhibit homosexual tendencies if they come from father-absent homes, especially if father-absence occurs during the first five years of life. Another study showed that excessive masculine behavior and toughness, such as membership in street gangs, were often typical among teenagers from lower economic groups with a high incidence of father-absence. This study pointed out that exaggerated masculinity expressed in the form of delinquent behavior is a means of compensating for the feminine sex typing to which they have been subjected due to that absence.

Another study showed that father-absent boys were more impulsive and less able to delay immediate gratification of their needs than father-present boys. One study showed that a strong relationship exists between father-present boys and a well internalized sense of moral values. Father-absent boys developed their moral values based largely on the probability of their getting caught and punished. Father-absent boys were unwilling to accept blame for their own misbehavior and evidenced little sense of guilt.

Another study of first year law and medical students who were without their fathers for significant periods of time during early life scored high on their self-reported antisocial behavior, such as disobedience, disrespect, vandalism, and drinking. One study showed that Peace Corps volunteers who had lived without their fathers for at least five years before the fifteenth birthday tended, because of adjustment and conduct problems, to return home before their terms were up.

Numerous studies reveal the decisive importance of a father's relationship to his daughter for the adequate development of her feminine identity. A healthful father-daughter relationship facilitates the daughter's ability to define for herself her own identity and the uniquely feminine role she plays in social relationships. The significance of this was brought to light in the early 1970s when studies showed that father-absent daughters experienced a higher incidence of social maladjustment in their adolescent years. Their inappropriate patterns of behavior were expressed, not in terms of vandalism and aggressive behavior, but in poor male-female relationships.

One study showed that two marked disturbances involving heterosexual behavior were often characteristic of father-absent daughters. One deviation expressed itself in terms of severe sexual anxiety, such as shyness and discomfort around males. The other and more frequent deviation involved promiscuous and assertive behavior toward males. Several studies show that father-absent daughters are less likely to become juvenile delinquents than are father-absent boys. Delinquency among girls is usually associated with sexual misconduct.

Further results from studies on father-absent children reveal that children who experience father-absence during preschool years are apt to be underachievers. Father-absent boys were found to be cognitively deficient in adulthood as well.

These studies show that children cannot have peace in their lives unless they have peace with their fathers, for self-esteem and personal identity are learned in father-present homes. If one's relationship with his earthly father is interwoven with his relationship with his heavenly Father, as the Scriptures assume, it is no wonder that so many people in our stressed-out world don't have peace with God. Few fathers today seem to have time for their children.

THE HOLY SPIRIT IS GOD'S GIFT OF PEACE

Our heavenly Father didn't abandon us as orphans. We are not spiritually the product of a father-absent world. God is here and his presence has been made known in the history of salvation. This is why Paul speaks of the special standing which we have as persons because in Christ we have "peace with God" (Rom. 5:1–2). Further, Paul shows that inwardly we are released from the anxieties of a troubled life and enabled to live out "whatever is true, whatever is honorable, whatever is just, whatever is pure, whatever is lovely, whatever is gracious" because we have the "peace of God" (Phil. 4:6–8).

This is a peace which the Stoics desired but which comes only through development of meaningful relationships within the body of Christ. The Stoics thought only in terms of a private intellectual peace with an impersonal spirit of the universe. Paul writes about a peace which surpasses human understanding and which "will keep your hearts and your minds in Christ Jesus" (4:7).

This offer of peace comes to us at a great price on the part of God. In an earlier chapter, we traced the history of God's coming to us through ancient Israel and later in the suffering Son of God. God so identified with us that in Jesus he internalized our anxieties that we might have his peace in our minds and hearts. Even the Old Testament prophets foresaw that this peace would come only in the new kingdom. Ancient Israel had hoped for peace in Canaan where the kingdom of David would last forever. But, alas, the kingdom fell apart and the people were taken captive and removed from the land.

Isaiah prophesied that there would be a new Conquest when the kingdom of David would be restored. This time peace would follow because the people would be delivered from fear and would focus their minds on God. "Thou dost keep him in perfect peace, whose mind is stayed on thee" (Isa. 26:3). Isaiah says that this song of perfect peace will be sung when Israel is restored to Canaan. The kingdom of Christ was the fulfillment of Isaiah's expectation of this coming kingdom.

That is why at the birth of Jesus the angels sang about "peace on earth" (Luke 2:14), why Paul said that Jesus is God's Messiah who brings peace to all the peoples of the earth (Eph. 2:17; 6:15), and why Peter said to Cornelius, "You know the word which he sent to Israel, preaching the good news of peace by Jesus Christ (he is Lord of all)" (Acts 10:36). Jesus promised peace to his disciples when the Holy Spirit would be given at Pentecost. "Peace I leave with you; my peace I give to you; not as the world gives do I give to you. Let not your hearts be troubled, neither let them be afraid" (John 14:27).

A REST FOR THE PEOPLE OF GOD

The writer of Hebrews gives us a concrete illustration of this peace which was promised in God's history with Israel and fulfilled in Jesus Christ. He defines this peace as "a sabbath rest for the people of God" (4:9). This writer is describing the same experience of the peace of God which Paul talked about (Phil. 4:7). Some have assumed that this rest refers to our life with God in the hereafter. But I agree with John Calvin and John Wesley that the writer had in mind the experience of faith for this life. John Calvin, as well as his contemporary representative in Karl Barth, believed that this level of rest referred to the perfection of the Christian life which we strive for now even if we don't experience it in this life.[13]

John Wesley believed that the "rest of faith" referred to the purity of our love for God which is available for all believers today. I agree with Wesley. The offer of perfect peace is for real in this life. To think we have to postpone this experience of peace for the future life is to turn it into an idea which we can only imagine we have. But we don't have to be like the Stoics; this rest is available now through the Holy Spirit who is our "Comforter" (John 14:16, 26, KJV). It is a peace which comes from our relationship to God in Christ through his Spirit. Our standing with God in Christ is not merely formal but personal and real (Rom. 5:1–5).

This rest is the fulfillment of the rest which the Israelites were supposed to have enjoyed in Canaan. One of the privileges of living in Canaan was peace and release from fear: "I will give peace in the land . . . and none shall make you afraid" (Lev. 26:6). But rest did not come permanently to the Israelites in Canaan because they failed to live in the light of God's countenance (Num. 6:24–26); and they failed to have a perfect love for God (Deut. 30:1–6).

The writer of Hebrews says that this rest is available today for those who live in Christ. He quotes Psalm 95:7–11 where the word *rest* is substituted for the word *land*. He is thinking of the kingdom of Christ as the fulfillment of the kingdom in Canaan. Just as Canaan symbolized rest from the anxieties of wandering in the wilderness, so does our life in Christ mean a rest "from our labors" and the barrenness of half-hearted commitment. Like the ancient Israelites, many believers lack a wholehearted relationship with Christ. They have made their exodus from the bondage of Egypt, but they haven't crossed over into the rest of Canaan. This is why the writer says that we must "strive" to enter this rest of faith (4:11).

"Let us strive to enter that rest" is a restatement of Joshua 4:10, when "the people passed over in haste." The Old Testament word for *striving* means the same as the New Testament word. It means to strive with eagerness and to do something in "haste." Phillips translates the passage this way: "Let us then be eager to know this rest for ourselves." The writer is urging us to make haste and not to waste any time in accepting the rest which God has promised us. The writer encourages us "today" to experience this rest (Heb. 3:7, 15; 4:7). He uses the present tense in speaking of our entering this rest (4:1, 3, 6, 9–10). Nowhere does he say that we enter it by death. He shows that the rest spoken of is for the people of God, not for those on the outside of faith.

The writer is not engaging in fanciful allegory when he sees the rest initially secured by Joshua as a foretaste of the rest of faith which the exalted Christ gives (4:8). We have seen earlier that the history of the Old Testament was centered in the Exodus and Conquest. These two events brought into being the kingdom of Israel; we also saw how these events prefigured the resurrection of Jesus as the new Exodus and the reception of the Holy Spirit on the day of Pentecost as the new Conquest.

This is precisely the point which the writer to the Hebrews is making. Canaan is a type of spiritual rest which Christ offers us. Just as rest (peace) was a product of living in the kingdom in Canaan, so peace is the kingdom-quality of those who live in Christ.

This peace is a privilege of every believer. There is no need for anyone to wander about in the fears and troubles of spiritual barrenness, for we are offered a rest through faith in the love of God. This does not mean that those who fail to enter this perfect rest are lost. Certainly Moses and the thousands of other Israelites who wandered in the wilderness because they failed to achieve this perfect rest are not a type of those who are eternally lost. This would be an awful thought! After all, only Joshua and Caleb entered the Promised Land out of the entire number of those who were delivered from Egypt.

The wilderness does not represent the bondage of sin in Egypt. It represents a release from bondage, but the wilderness experience symbolizes a barren spiritual life that is still plagued with doubts and fears. Charles Wesley caught the meaning when he wrote:

> Lord, I believe a rest remains
> To all thy people known;
> A rest where pure enjoyment reigns,
> And thou art loved alone.
>
> A rest where all our soul's desire
> Is fixed on things above;
> Where fear, and sin, and grief expire,
> Cast out by perfect love.
>
> From every evil motion freed
> (The Son hath made us free),
> On all the powers of hell we tread
> In glorious liberty.

Safe in the way of life, above
　　Death, earth, and hell we rise;
We find, when perfected in love,
　　Our long-sought paradise.

O that I now the rest might know,
　　Believe and enter in!
Now, Savior, now the power bestow,
　　And let me cease from sin.

Remove this hardness from my heart,
　　This unbelief remove;
To me the rest of faith impart,
　　The Sabbath of thy love.

Come, O my Saviour, come away!
　　Into my soul descend;
No longer from thy creature stay,
　　My Author and my End.

The bliss thou hast for me prepared
　　No longer be delay'd;
Come, my exceeding great reward,
　　For whom I first was made.

Come, Father, Son, and Holy Ghost,
　　And seal me thine abode!
Let all I am in thee be lost;
　　Let all be lost in God.

We don't receive this peace through singing happy songs about smiling our troubles away with a good attitude nor through a wise ordering of our lives as Stoics might have reasoned. Peace is a gift of God's love indwelling us through the power of the Holy Spirit. If separation from God's presence produced fear in the hearts of our first parents, then our reconciliation to God generates a peace which calms our fears and releases us to be truly loving in our relationships to God and others. We don't live in a Father-absent world, for the church is a Father-present family. And peace is the gift of our Father to his children (1 Tim. 1:2).

11

THE SPIRIT OF ASSURANCE

God has sent the Spirit of his Son into our hearts, crying, "Abba! Father!"

Galatians 4:6

I had been sitting in a hard church pew for nearly an hour while attending a Methodist camp meeting. Fourteen years of age, trembling and unsure about the meaning of my life, I was thinking about the future. The evangelist spoke warmly of the love of God as our heavenly Father who wanted us to make a place for him in our hearts. We were now standing and singing the hymn of invitation, "Just As I Am." I felt drawn to the altar of confession to accept God's offer to be my personal heavenly Father. As I knelt silently in prayer, the evangelist spoke these words, "If you will open your hearts to Christ, the Holy Spirit will give you the inner assurance of God's acceptance of you as his child." And I did experience a warm feeling of divine acceptance.

I could hardly have rejected God as my personal heavenly Father that day anymore than I could have rejected my earthly father. For his faith in God had already helped to form my thinking, and the compassionate quality of his life as a father had won my affection for him and all that he believed. So how could I reject his God? The importance of that moment was that

I personally internalized this reality for myself. I left that service with an assurance about the purpose of my life.

I have come to believe that our perceptions of truth are largely developed through daily conversations with other meaningful persons in our lives. This means that our values and convictions about the meaning of life are not something which we learn in the classroom, but which become a part of us through life experiences and significant relationships which we form from early childhood and throughout adult life.[1]

If this is so, then truth is more of a resolution of the mind and heart than it is a conclusion of logic. Of course we can't believe something just because we choose to do so; we must have good reasons for our beliefs. But one can be well informed and even possess a brilliant intellect and still not have good insight and perception. For our knowledge of the meaning of life is primarily formed through personal experience.

WE KNOW GOD BECAUSE GOD KNOWS US

In the Old Testament, the function of God's Spirit was to bring enlightenment, wisdom, and insight (Ex. 31:3; Dan. 5:14). In the New Testament, the Spirit of God came in a new dimension as the indwelling Spirit of Christ. Without the inner witness of the Holy Spirit, no one is able to say, "Jesus is Lord" (1 Cor. 12:3). Paul says that it is the indwelling Spirit who is the "demonstration" that Jesus is the Son of God. For the Spirit will show you that your faith does "not rest in the wisdom of men but in the power of God" (1 Cor. 2:3–5).

What sort of demonstration does the Holy Spirit give us? Paul's explanation is a powerful one. How can you know your own thoughts? Because you yourself are the spirit who knows them! Likewise no one knows God's true thoughts except God. We have received the Spirit of God into our spirits; therefore, we know God because he is knowing himself through his own Spirit in our hearts. We know God because he knows us.

This also means our self-certainty and self-assurance depend upon God's knowledge of himself. This is the basis of spiritual discernment and it is the evidence of God's truth which has been revealed in the history of salvation. Paul is not saying that we can bypass this history of salvation and have an immediate private revelation of God. He asserts that we have the inner witness of its truth through the Spirit. And the certainty of this truth supersedes all human wisdom (1 Cor. 2:10–16).

How then do we know that God is a personal Father? Because he has sent the Spirit of his Son into our hearts, "crying, 'Abba Father,'" and the Spirit reassures us that God is our personal Father. *Abba* is an Aramaic word used as a title of affection for one's earthly father much like our word *daddy*. What intimacy! The Spirit is the inner witness that we have a warm and personal relationship with God. This intimacy makes us feel infinitely secure (Rom. 8:26–39).

Paul says, "I am not ashamed" of the gospel, "for I know whom I have believed" (2 Tim. 1:12). He then warns Timothy, "Guard the truth that has been entrusted to you by the Holy Spirit who dwells within us" (2 Tim. 1:14). This is the final proof of faith—the indwelling Spirit.

This feeling of personal assurance is the meaning of Paul's statement in Romans 8:16, that "the Spirit himself bears witness with our spirit that we are children of God." The apostle is talking about the intellectual certainty of God's truth revealed in salvation history. We know because we have received the Holy Spirit who enables us to understand and see what we could not recognize through human wisdom (1 Cor. 2:12). Our hearts must be prepared by the Holy Spirit to see God's truth with our minds (1 Cor. 2:9–10).

The witness of the Spirit is a more important reason for believing in the gospel than any appeal to human wisdom or knowledge. This is not at all to minimize the importance of human reason, but to put it in its proper place as a support to faith. Sometimes tension will exist between what we understand with our minds and what feel in our hearts. But because we have received the Holy Spirit, we can always trust the inner certainty which he offers us in spite of intellectual uncertainties.

This doctrine of assurance was largely missing in the Christian tradition until John Wesley rediscovered its impor-

tance in the eighteenth century. Though Martin Luther rediscovered the doctrine of justification by faith in the sixteenth
century, he largely bypassed the truth of spiritual assurance.
John Calvin stressed the importance of the inner witness of the
Holy Spirit for certainty of the truth of the Bible, but it was
John Wesley who gave prominence to Paul's teaching of a
personal assurance of our acceptance with God through the
inner witness of the Holy Spirit (Rom. 8:15–16). It became a
distinctive doctrine of Methodism and the revival movements
in America in the nineteenth century.

In his sermon "The Witness of the Spirit," Wesley says,
"The testimony of the Spirit is an inward impression on the
soul, whereby the Spirit of God directly witnesses to my spirit,
that I am a child of God; that Jesus Christ hath loved me, and
given himself for me; and that all my sins are blotted out, and I,
even I, am reconciled to God."

He is careful to preserve this doctrine from abuse by those
who "have mistaken the voice of their own imagination for this
witness of the Spirit of God."[2] He does this by showing that
our beliefs and experiences with God are always subject to the
authority of Scripture. Yet the authority of Scripture loses its
vitality without this inner dynamic. If God's Spirit dwells
within us, then we have the experiential basis for understanding
his Word.

The doctrine of assurance has often been used by some in
our evangelical tradition to mean that we don't have to take
theology too seriously. Supposedly it's what we feel that
matters, not what we think. Tillich zeroed in on this weakness
when he spoke of evangelical beliefs in unflattering terms,
especially its "revivalistic" doctrine of the inner assurance of
faith in a personal God.[3]

I will not dispute the fact that evangelical Christians have
often not paid enough attention to current trends in philosophy
and science. Tillich's evaluation of our weaknesses in this area is
largely correct. But a greater weakness develops when we
neglect or reject biblical teaching on the role of the Holy Spirit
as the one who confirms within us the truth of salvation history
and our personal acceptance in Christ.

Neglect of the Holy Spirit is widespread even among orthodox Christians. Some seem to think that faith is largely an intellectual acceptance of doctrines rather than a vibrant and personal relationship with Christ. More seriously, there are those in the church who lack the certainty that a personal God has even revealed himself in the history of salvation. Tillich represents this kind of liberal thinking which is present in many mainline churches and taught in a number of seminaries.

GOD'S SELF-CERTAINTY IS NOT DEPENDENT UPON US

Tillich wrote an important volume on life in the Spirit. His opening chapter is on the ambiguities of life.[4] He tells us that the need for certainty will never be satisfied. Remember, he didn't believe in a personal God, that Jesus is the embodiment of God, that the Holy Spirit is the agent of God in the world, nor that the history of salvation as recorded in the Bible is a reliable account of God's engagement with us in the world.

Yet, as we have seen, Tillich believed in a God who is himself in the process of being developed.[5] God, he believed, has to struggle also with insecure feelings about who he is. But Tillich's God knows himself only because we know him.[6] Otherwise, he has no specific awareness of his emotions and thoughts.[7]

Despite his view of an impersonal God and his rejection of supranaturalism, Tillich (d. 1965) was an influential theologian, and his writings continue to be widely read and influential. He reinterpreted belief in the Holy Spirit to mean an impersonal "spiritual presence."[8] The Spirit for him is really more like an attitude than a person. Instead of the inner witness of the Holy Spirit reassuring us of acceptance by our heavenly Father, we must have "courage to be" in spite of the uncertainties and anxieties of life. There is no escape from an ultimate despair. In the end, we will cease to be. He believed that a mature person is one who doesn't demand any final security or certainty.[9]

It would perhaps be easy enough simply to ignore this theological trend since it is so evidently contrary to the

Scriptures, but it is still held by a number of theologians in my own denomination as well as others. We could simply denounce it by labeling it one of the "destructive heresies" which Peter warned about. He had said that "the way of truth" would be "reviled" and that some would "exploit you with false words." Peter's commitment to truth was focused in the Scriptures which were written by those who were "moved by the Holy Spirit" (2 Peter 1:20–2:3). Anything else as the final authority for belief was to be rejected.

Though Peter's inspired words are right on target, we should examine the concerns of those who struggle with uncertainty in believing. For even sound evangelical Christians sometimes find it difficult to believe and are unsure about their salvation. I suspect that many struggle with doubts about their faith even though they never consciously admit it to themselves.

OUR CAPACITY FOR SPIRITUAL CERTAINTY SHAPED THROUGH A SECURE RELATIONSHIP WITH OUR EARTHLY FATHERS

Karl Jung reported in his autobiography that one of the first things that caused him to doubt the doctrines of Christianity was that his father, who was a minister, seemed inwardly uncomfortable with the beliefs which he professed to believe and which he preached from his pulpit. Jung unconsciously picked up the doubts with which his father struggled.[10] Jung's rejection of Christianity was rooted originally in this relationship with his father. Insecure feelings and faulty relationships can easily sabotage our faith.

Tillich's life and thought illustrate the tensions which exist between belief and life experience. One of the things which he emphasized was the importance of doing theology from the perspective of one's situation.[11] He often said that our theories are reflections of our experiences. Why did his experiences make it difficult for him to believe in a personal God?

Tillich was brought up in the tradition of Christian orthodoxy. His father was a prominent Lutheran pastor and a superintendent; his mother was a Calvinist. Tillich's relationship with his father was strained because of the elder's authoritarian and autocratic manner, making communication with him difficult.[12] "The most happy instances of a positive relation to my father," he wrote, "[occurred in] the long philosophical discussions which developed." Tillich felt his father stifled his own developing sense of independence. He said that he was able to make a "break-through to autonomy" by developing competence in philosophy.[13] This ability delivered him from dependence upon his overbearing father. Tillich reported that in this way he forced his way out of an emotionally depersonalizing situation.

The trauma of his breakout from dependence upon his parent was so great that he determined never again to allow himself to enter into a similar relationship. He wrote, "It is this difficult and painful break-through to autonomy which has made me immune against any system of thought or life which demands the surrender of this autonomy."[14]

His mother's Calvinism forced upon him a set of "rigid morals." He felt from her "a restrictive pressure in thought as well as in action," but Tillich idolized her as a warm and loving mother.[15] Her untimely death when he was seventeen left him emotionally devastated. His biographers speak of him as having repressed his grief so successfully that he never spoke to anyone about her.

In a recent book on Tillich, Mark Kline Taylor describes Tillich's "life journey" as "Tillich's greatest teacher."[16] Certainly his life's journey didn't begin very well, for he barely survived the trauma of birth. His life was often filled with trouble and controversy. He lived through two world wars in both of which his own nation was defeated. He was dismissed by Hitler from his university position and was compelled to leave the country. His difficulties in personal relationships were publicly revealed after his death when his widow and friends openly discussed and published accounts of his extramarital sexual affairs.

Early in his education he rejected the traditional beliefs of the church. Even during early youth he said he experienced a "conflict" between his secular education which he received in the classroom and the Christian faith which was taught in his home and church.[17] His formal theological studies occurred during the heyday of liberal theology in Germany, when the climate of opinion was clearly against traditional beliefs.

Tillich became one of the most influential people of this century. Few scholars have ever attained the breadth and depth of his knowledge. His influence reached Americans in the pews through pastors who learned their theology from him. Tillich demolished their confidence in conservative Christianity with his penetrating criticisms which often were so right! Many young men coming from evangelical homes were pressured into a type of Christianity which left them empty and disillusioned.

A United Methodist bishop once told me that as a seminary student he was enamored of Tillich's thought because of the beauty of its organization and the splendor of his ideas. "However," the bishop said, "I lost interest after I preached my first funeral. Tillich's message just won't preach." Many others never freed themselves from his theology.

I became acquainted with Tillich's writing during post-graduate studies under professors whose theological training took place largely under Tillich. I have also carefully read his books. His vigorous denial of the personal character of God made me sad. But his arguments seem to be more personal than logical. For example, in most instances when he argues against God as personal, as a supranatural being, he associates it with authoritarianism, interference, and a childish need for security and certainty. In one paragraph when he discusses his rejection of God as a person, he uses the word *interference* no less than nine times to make his point.[18]

His rejection of the notion of a personal God reminds us of his decision never to allow himself to enter into any relationship which made him feel dependent and which demanded "the surrender of this autonomy." Incidentally, Tillich's appreciation for Nietzsche focuses on his denial of a personal God. If God is personal, then one must submit to him, and Tillich complains that submission means emotional pain and hurt: "The submissive self is the opposite of the self-affirming self, even if it is submissive to a God. It wants to escape the pain of hurting and being hurt."[19]

When I first read about Tillich's rejection of a personal God, I thought of C. S. Lewis' *Surprised by Joy*. Lewis says that one of the nice things he found about atheism was that he no longer worried about God interfering in his life as parents do.[20] He experienced a real "peace" when one of his teachers convinced him that there is no personal God.[21] Nor did Lewis have to worry about establishing an intimate relationship with God inasmuch as such a being does not exist.

Lewis' pilgrimage and conversion are now well known. Though reluctant at first, he opened himself to God and experienced a peace and freedom which he never before knew. Lewis' early life lacked intimacy following his mother's death, yet he craved the "joy" of relationships.[22] The intimacy and "interference" which he had dreaded so much now brought him the longed-for joy which only peace with God could bring.[23]

His approach to Christianity was largely intellectual. Even so, he acknowledged that most of our doubts are rooted in our emotions, not in our ability to be logical and intellectual.[24] The loss of his mother when he was eight and the failure of God to heal his mother in response to his desperate prayer emotionally preconditioned him to become a nonbeliever in his youth. Other painful experiences added to his decision to deny God's existence.[25] I suspect that his failure to experience emotional warmth or intimate relationships in his early life caused anxiety when he confronted the notion of intimacy with God.[26] So of course he was relieved when he was persuaded by logic (!) that God does not exist. Providentially, Lewis found his way back to faith in a personal God.

Many prominent psychologists, philosophers, and theologians who have been brought up in the church and trained in the biblical faith never found their way back home. Their insightful writings about the nature of the personal meaning of life have been borrowed from their Judeo-Christian heritage even though they rejected the notion of God's personhood.

Why? What generates feelings of uncertainty about the

existence of a personal God? Why do so many, inside and outside the church, struggle with doubts in this regard? Kierkegaard gives us a precise answer. He lived in the last part of the nineteenth century, but hardly anyone knew of him because relatively few outside Denmark read Danish in which, of course, he wrote. By the early part of this century his books were beginning to be known.

Tillich had almost given up hope of finding any Christian solution to the meaning of human life when as a university student he happened across a private translation of Kierkegaard's writings.[27] He immediately devoured the Dane's thoughts, and used his ideas to reinterpret Christian belief. Tillich did this in a way that left out Kierkegaard's evangelical pietism. And, more importantly, Tillich omitted Kierkegaard's personal God.

OUR SPIRITUAL PERCEPTIONS ARE FILTERED THROUGH THE EYES OF OUR PARENTS

The most valuable insight in Kierkegaard's writings is that our perceptions of truth are always filtered through human relationships. Because these relationships are generally faulty, we experience insecure feelings about the meaning of life. Our intellectual doubts about God, our psychological fears about ourselves, and our emotional uncertainties about our acceptance with others result largely from our broken relationships in a fallen world. In fact, Adam's fall was a fall away from a relationship with God; it was a detachment and a retreat away from the personal nature of God.

That is why Kierkegaard says that the fundamental problem with human relationships is dread, a feeling of "horrible unreality."[28] For dread is the fear of our possible not-being, and that which makes us feel the loss of our being is the loss of relationships with God and others. This is why Adam and Eve were afraid. Fear gripped them because of the brokenness of their relationship with God. Fear in its most fundamental meaning is just this—fear of our possible not-being because we fear the loss of being-with-others.

This disrelationship, as Kierkegaard called it, is the foundation of all human fears and conflicts. It is an experience handed down from one set of parents to another through the children. It is the origin of doubt about one's own existence as well as doubt about the being of God. He shows with a degree of genius never before seen that truth is a paradox because human relationships are a paradox. Kierkegaard showed that we are born in a state of innocence.[29] This means that we are not yet aware of our individuality. But just as soon as we begin as small children to be aware of ourselves we become aware of our responsibilities to others. No longer then are we simply innocent infants.

When we begin to develop our sense of responsibility to others, we are thrown into a state of panic because of the uncertainty we feel about entering into a relationship with another. All of this happens intuitively with children even though they are hardly aware of it. But a child finds himself in the paradoxical situation of being an *I* over against another *I*. How do I live in my own world and in the world of another person at the same time? Our perceptions of truth are always formed out of this give-and-take relationship of living in both worlds at once.

Kierkegaard spent a lot of time attacking pantheism because it denied this paradox.[30] Pantheism represents an attachment to mother nature which means that there is no relationship between the individual and a personal God. Pantheism implies the end of all human relationships because it assumes that we are simply the same as mother nature. We no longer have individuality of our own. Actually, the dominant philosophies of his day, he believed, offered people only ideas to store in their heads instead of genuine relationship with the eternal God. This is why he believed for the most part that human philosophy was basically pantheistic even if philosophers didn't admit it.[31]

On the other hand, he showed that Christian belief was not a philosophy but a personal communication of God with real people in the real world in the history of salvation. His contrasts between Socrates and Jesus in *Philosophical Fragments* is classic because he shows that God is revealed through a dialogue with the human race which is more than a sharing of ideas and thoughts; God is revealed in the paradoxical relationship of Jesus as God and man. God really gave himself to us; he didn't simply offer us a block of impersonal and abstract ideas.

Kierkegaard showed that we don't develop our opinions about life simply by reasoning in the abstract. *The people whom we trust and the relationships we develop are much more important for the formation of our ideas than are mere logic or reason.* If these relationships are dominated by fear and insecurity, we tend to create a world of ideas and protective beliefs which we unconsciously think will shelter us from hurt and preserve our struggling self-esteem.

Kierkegaard shows that dread, the fear of all fears, emerges when the awareness of our freedom to be our own person is forced upon us. Psychological studies show that if this freedom is not forced upon a child before he is capable of handling it, he may not experience this dread.[32] Such freedom is forced upon a child when he suffers an early and prolonged separation from his mother or other source person. The absence of the source person for the child becomes intolerable and makes him feel spiritless and detached not only from the source person but also the outside world. This makes the infant "feel" that he has lost his own being. This feeling of separation may prevent the child from developing his own "I-my-self," and he may grow up to suffer from feelings of separation-anxiety for the rest of his life.

This sense of dread is driven underground because it is intolerable to the conscious mind. Dread is the insecure feeling of living in an isolated world where you are the only object. In the hysterical-emotional person, this fear causes the person to cling to others; in the retreating-intellectual person, the fear causes people to detach themselves from others.

This analysis of insecurity was written out of Kierkegaard's own experience. His relationship with his father and mother was strained. He talks about how his relationship with his father distorted his view of God as heavenly Father. In spite of this, he writes about his need to grow up, to accept the freedom which was *forced* upon him and to become responsible for himself.[33]

He recognized that it doesn't solve anything simply to grieve over failed relationships and nourish the hurt. He saw that he must decide to take charge of his own life and become a morally responsible person. But Kierkegaard also saw that this decision was not one that a human being can make by himself. He can decide only through a relationship with Christ. Faith is the gift of God, not an act of human choice.[34] Our capacity to decide is measured in terms of the relational. Faith is not a blind leap of the will. Faith is our response to God's initiative. He comes to us and empowers us to become fully restored to himself. Then our lives are no longer driven by deep feelings of insecurity but by the love of God.

Kierkegaard's insight into the importance of relationships for making decisions and becoming morally responsible persons has enormous implications for understanding how we develop the ideas which we hold about ourselves, the world, and God. He has helped us to see how early family relationships are more important for the way we develop our beliefs than critical scholarship, though he was of course a brilliant thinker.

His original insights concerning early family relationships have been amply confirmed by clinical studies in the subsequent development of human psychology, particularly his analysis of dread and its development in an infant. For many years medical science had assumed that the nervous system of a baby was too undeveloped for memories of birth and of the earliest months of life to be recorded in the brain. But since the 1950s, the psychiatric use of abreactive drug therapy has shown just how vividly the earliest events of life are imprinted on the mind.[35] Patients literally were able to relive the trauma of birth and any damaging experience of physical and mental pain as they were pushed through the birth canal.

Autism sometimes results from this trauma. Life's first impression for some infants is so harsh, cold, and cruel that the infant protects himself from feelings of rejection by retreating into himself and away from the outside.[36] Based on the results of Wilder Penfield's brain surgery, we know that no experience is ever forgotten.[37]

Clinical studies do not confirm Kierkegaard's opinion that everybody feels this excessive sense of insecurity about life, though it may be the experience of most people.[38] Infants who haven't experienced severe trauma during the earliest moments of life and have been assured of their welcome into the world and been made to feel secure about their own being will probably never be afflicted with dread.

But Kierkegaard's life and writings reflect this affliction. Sometimes we have too easily dismissed him as an eccentric who glorified paradox and who interpreted life as an absurdity. But this is to miss his enduring insight—that most people successfully push their feelings of absurdity and dread below the surface of conscious thought.

He shows in particular that scholars are guilty of this. They talk about their knowledge of truth and their philosophy of reason, which they imagine give them a firm handle on the meaning of life. The problem is that their ideas succeed only in hiding from them their true opinions and feelings. This is especially true, he believed, when philosophers and theologians turn the personal God of the Bible into a pantheistic god. He didn't hesitate to point out that many scholars live in a world of fantasy.[39] The driving force behind these notions about God was dread, not reason.

Pantheism emerged, Kierkegaard says, out of the dis-relationship with God and out of the fear of not being.[40] Pantheism is compensation for the fear that we have lost our individual significance because we are unsure of the relationships we have with our parents and with others. The only way to find the truth about God and to experience freedom from dread is to receive the offer of a relationship to God through faith in Jesus Christ.

This makes Kierkegaard a powerful defender of the faith. He saw with penetrating insight the implication of faith as the relational basis for development of a mature and responsible belief. Our capacity to trust in a personal God is learned from trusting our parents or other source persons. All our ideas are extensions of our relationships in life, especially early-life experience. The Scriptures certainly emphasize this relationship between what we learn from our parents and what we believe about God. If parents love God with all their hearts and practice their faith in the home, then their children will learn to do so as well:

> "Hear, O Israel: The LORD our God is one LORD; and you shall love the LORD your God with all your heart, and with all your soul, and with all your might. And these words which I command you this day shall be upon your heart; and you shall teach them diligently to your children, and shall talk of them when you sit in your house, and when you walk by the way, and when you lie down, and when you rise. And you shall bind them as a sign upon your hand, and they shall be as frontlets between your eyes. And you shall write them on the doorposts of your house and on your gates" (Deut. 6:4–9).

It is not a mark of maturity for adults to think that they must discard what they have learned from their parents. Immaturity in adults is the result of their never having learned as children to feel secure in themselves; then in adulthood they still, to a greater or lesser degree, think and act like children and are unable to make responsible decisions for themselves.

But if relationships at home have been developed in an appropriate fashion, the foundation for the development of one's own ideas and beliefs has been laid. But when this foundation has been cracked by poor relationships, the child learns to relate either by clinging to others or by detaching himself from others. Clinging to others is a hysterical reaction, the attempt to find oneself. Undoubtedly many people have a clinging and panic-driven relationship to God. They often speak of their relationship to God in emotional and affective terms. They may even give the appearance of being superspiritual, which is usually compensation for feelings of insecurity.

Detaching oneself from others is a commitment-anxiety disorder; it is the attempt to protect ourselves from being hurt by creating distance from others. The affliction of dread is seen particularly in intellectual people, as clinical studies in general show, and the special difficulty of someone suffering from anxiety-commitment is failure to feel the presence and love of God as a caring heavenly Father. He finds it difficult to *feel* because he is locked into a world of *reason*.

Frank Lake had extensive clinical experience with patients of every conceivable anxiety disorder. His work in this area is the most reliable and the most competent of anyone who is both a highly trained psychoanalyst and a Christian theologian. His insights, especially into the problems of feelings of detachment, are most helpful. He has also shown that the more the affliction of dread rises to consciousness the less likely it is that one will be able to believe in the goodness of God, or even in his existence.

He worked with many in Britain who came out of the Christian tradition and who suffered from a sense of detachment. He concluded that their anxiety caused them to reject the historical foundation of faith and turn it into subjective ideas which merely symbolize human values. Lake believes that some theologians who deny the biblical revelation of a personal God suffer from a sense of detachment. They prefer their own ideas of reality rather than those communicated through other persons. They can't trust in the "out there" because they have no early memory of a secure world centered in a source person who came to answer them in their time of need.[41]

Very early in life they began to develop a trusting relationship, but the prolonged absence of their mother or source person split their being from top to bottom and now they have only the appearance of trust. Their spirit was allowed to exist in "godless chaos." Consequently, nature-mysticism and pantheism (in its various forms) offers them no object out there for them to have to trust. Besides, they tend to be contemptuous of those who do believe in the "out there."

Their hope is to sink down into a subpersonal "ground of being" below the chaos. Pantheism is the desire of the adult to reexperience the security he once knew during the earliest weeks of life in mother's womb. There he enjoyed the feeling of total oneness with nature and was not burdened with being a morally responsible person. Pantheism is union with the spirit of the universe where one loses his individuality just as a drop of water loses its being when it is dropped into the ocean. Mother's womb symbolizes our oneness with the mother-god of the universe.

Lake shows that nature-mysticism (pantheism) is rooted in faulty parental relationships. Inadequate mothering deprives the infant of its feelings of personal well-being, and inadequate fathering deprives it of its feelings of personal identification with other people. Without adequate mothering and fathering, an infant's world is depersonalized; and the foundation for a pantheistic (impersonal) view of the world is begun. Consequently, a poor parent/child relationship makes it difficult to have a warm and personal relationship with our heavenly Father.[42] Kirkegaard found this true in his own life, and his conversion to God as a young man came as a result of his reconciliation to his father.[43]

I don't know whether these dynamics influenced the inner life of Paul Tillich who so strongly protested the view of God as a personal Being. We can't be sure about the motives of other people. But Tillich has told us about his poor relationship with his father and his determination to allow no further interference in his hard-earned sense of independence. His struggle for survival in the hours following his birth may have been enough to afflict him with a profound sense of insecurity regarding the meaning of life. The word *ambiguity* was so often repeated in his writings that it seemed that insecure feelings were almost an obsession with him. He reports in *Courage to Be* that looking into the "abyss of nothingness" was an experience which someone could tolerate for only a moment without becoming severely disturbed. His acute description of this "naked anxiety," which he believes everyone shares in, indicates that he himself suffered from it.[44]

It is also a well-known psychological fact that people afflicted with excessive fear of relationships suffer from anxiety-commitment, and they are especially prone toward promiscuity because it permits them to have a degree of intimacy without the bonding that normally goes with commitment. It may well be that Tillich suffered from deep feelings of dread which exceed the experience of most people. Recent biographers believe that his erotic lifestyle is traceable to the deeply felt loss of his mother.[45]

Kierkegaard has shown that it is not easy for one whose life is afflicted with dread to believe in the goodness of a personal God. As I said, Tillich never recovered from grief over the death of his mother. His relationship with his father was stormy. I can't help but believe that these depersonalizing events helped to shape his thinking and made it difficult for him to believe in a personal God.

One of the things which Tillich strongly emphasizes in his theology is the influence which our life situation has upon the development of our ideas. In fact, this point is carried to the extreme because he rejects the authority of Scripture as the final and normal standard of belief. Our present understanding of the world, he says, is the reason for reinterpretation of the Bible so that it will speak meaningfully to us today.[46] He believed that psychoanalysis helps us enormously in our understanding of the world, for many irrational forces are at work in our lives. Psychoanalysis offers us the categories to help us deal with these influences.[47]

His theology of the Holy Spirit is developed in the third volume of *Systematic Theology,* and it is largely a restatement of Christian faith in psychoanalytic concepts. In *Courage to Be,* Tillich makes effective use of psychoanalysis in his attempt to redefine the meaning of Christian faith for today. The softening of his attitude as he grew older toward the possibility of life after death illustrates how his experiences influenced his thinking. In *My Search for Absolutes,* he tones down his harshness toward the concept of immortality and even gives it a favorable hearing.[48]

It is sad that there was no softening of his attitude about the God of Abraham, Isaac, and Jacob, and the God and Father of our Lord Jesus Christ. He clung tenaciously to a belief in an impersonal spirit as his god. But there is no inner assurance about the meaning of life unless God is a personal being. Ambiguity is not a good feeling to have in the last moments of life. This is why we are offered a secure relationship to God through his Spirit. The inner witness makes it possible for us to speak to God in personal terms of affection: "Abba, Father." That's how intimate he wants to be with us. Such intimacy reassures us of our own worth as God's children.

OUR NEED FOR SPIRITUAL ASSURANCE

I remember when I was a seminary student that it was often considered a sign of personal weakness and immaturity to talk about the need for inner assurance. About that time an editorial comparing the gospel song "Blessed Assurance, Jesus is Mine" with the immature practice of autoeroticism appeared in a campus newsletter from a liberal seminary. Supposedly, to believe in a deeply personal relationship with Christ which provides us with an emotionally satisfying experience of inner assurance was childish.

I admit that much of our evangelical pietism sometimes tends to be mushy and self-centered. I am also aware that we may repress our insecurities beneath a pretense of spiritual certainty. But I also believe that the Spirit of God offers us a relationship with Christ which reassures us of our acceptance with God and which brings healing over a period of time for those insecurities and fears.

John Wesley's life and theology illustrate the tension between the assurance of our acceptance with God and our struggles with insecurity and dread. The story of his life is an open book because of his Journal, the preservation of his voluminous correspondence, and his lifelong habit of extensive note taking. If someone were interested in studying the inner dynamics of his life from a psychiatric perspective much like Erik Erikson did of Martin Luther,[49] plenty of data would be available.

Whatever may be concluded about Wesley's emotional makeup and motives, one thing that emerges clearly is the portrait of a man deeply devoted to God and his fellow human beings. But this does not mean that Wesley was free from faults and anxieties. Though he lived a holy life and possessed a contagious Christian witness, he certainly was not immune to discouragement and uncertainties.

May 24, 1738, was a memorable event in Wesley's life as well as for the subsequent rise and development of the evangelical movements in England and America. This was the date of his evangelical conversion when he "felt [his] heart strangely warmed" with an inner assurance that Christ had taken away his sins and saved him "from the law of sin and death."[50]

This inner certainty came after many years of self-doubt and inner struggles. Up to this point he had been an influential Christian leader, a lecturer in Greek, philosophy, and logic at Oxford. He was ordained an Anglican priest in 1728, and in 1735 went to Georgia with General Oglethorpe as chaplain to the English settlers and missionary to the Indians. But he had never felt assured of his salvation in Christ. While on board a ship to Savannah, a storm erupted which threatened to sink the vessel. Wesley became deeply anxious over the possible loss of his life, but he was impressed with a group of Moravians who calmly faced their pending doom.[51] He learned from them what the inner assurance of faith means for one's relationship to Christ.

Wesley desired this kind of security in Christ, and some months later as he listened to another read from the preface to Luther's commentary on Romans, he experienced this assurance. His preaching from that moment on stressed the security which the believer has in Christ through the inner testimony of the Holy Spirit.

Yet Wesley's life was not completely free from moments of dread and troublesome anxiety. In 1766 he wrote to his brother Charles about feelings of self-doubt which were plaguing him during a time of pressure caused by his evangelistic work. This letter is remarkable because it shows how stress caused dejection, yet in spite of that Wesley shows his determination not to let up in his work for the Lord. In another letter he wrote of being plagued by fear, but it was not the "fear of hell." Rather, he said, it was the fear of "falling into nothing."[52] This dread of nothingness often accompanies the struggle with feelings of uncertainty. It may well be that Wesley had an unusually strong need for a sense of security, and this may have influenced his spiritual pilgrimage which led to his evangelical conversion at Aldersgate. At any rate, Wesley's personal struggles and pilgrimage helped him to recognize the importance of Paul's teaching concerning the inner testimony of the Holy Spirit.

The events of his early life are well documented and widely known. His early home life was troublesome. He was the fifteenth child and three more were born after him. His father and mother were devout believers, but they often experienced severe differences of opinion which led to separation on occasion. Wesley was himself the product of one of their times of reconciliation. Yet it seems that he enjoyed a good relationship with his parents in spite of the family size and their marital conflicts.

But conflict was the cradle which often rocked the Wesley home. His father was imprisoned at one time for indebtedness, and the older Wesley also was an unpopular rector of the Anglican Church in Epworth. The people stabbed his cattle, maimed his sheep, and on one occasion burned his house. John, at the age of five, was miraculously rescued from the flames as they almost engulfed him, a terrifying experience which he never forgot.

Throughout his life, Wesley's life was torn with conflict: with the authorities when he was in Georgia, with fellow Anglican clergymen who opposed his evangelistic efforts, with members of the Methodist movement which lead to a split between Calvinistic Methodists and Arminian Methodists, over the issue of whether and whom to marry, with his wife in a marriage doomed to failure, with his church and the news media.

He endured a great deal of hardship as he traveled over a million miles on horseback in all kinds of weather and preached more than 40,000 sermons under all kinds of circumstances. Often he was attacked by mobs. Yet in spite of his exhausting work as an untiring evangelist, Wesley remained true to his divine calling and witnessed the spread of the Methodist movement across the British Isles and into America.

His heartwarming experience on Aldersgate Street, which gave him the abiding witness of his salvation, sustained him to the very end. The day before he died, he sat up in his bed and sang Isaac Watts' hymn "I'll Praise My Maker While I've Breath." Before going to sleep that evening, he cried out, "The best of all is, God is with us." On several occasions during the night, he whispered, "I'll praise, I'll praise." At ten o'clock the next day, March 2, 1791, he died peacefully.[53]

Most of us suffer from the grand illusion that we are the product simply of our rational choices. The idea that the personal relationships which we have formed and the external circumstances of our lives from early childhood to the present moment somehow are the dominant influences which form our character is often not well received. Not only do social and psychological studies support this view, but it is assumed in Scriptures. That is why we are told to guard carefully what we allow to enter our hearts and minds (Prov. 4:23). That is why Paul says to form friendships especially with those whose life and behavior are in accord with the teaching of Christ (2 Cor. 6:14), and why James says to keep ourselves unspotted from the world (James 1:27).

For this reason, Paul stresses the importance of the indwelling Spirit. He cautioned the Galatians not to allow themselves to be influenced by those whose teachings depart from the gospel. "Who hindered you from obeying the truth?" he asks them. "This persuasion is not from him who called you. A little yeast leavens the whole lump" (Gal. 5:7–9). Paul's point is that truth can be easily subverted when we develop deeply personal and "unsettling" (Gal. 5:12) relationships with those whose life and beliefs are contrary to the gospel. Rather, the truth of Christ is proved by the way we relate to God and others (Gal. 5:13). This proof is the fruit of the Spirit. How do we know that God is revealed in Jesus Christ? By the inner witness of the Spirit that we are his children (Gal. 4:6) and by the fruit of the indwelling Spirit (Gal. 5:22–23). This spiritual assurance will give us the peace of mind and heart to keep us throughout the stresses of life.

"By this we know that we abide in him and he in us, because he has given us of his own Spirit" (1 John 4:13).

12

RECEIVING THE HOLY SPIRIT

Did you receive the Holy Spirit when you believed?

Acts 19:2

To receive is to accept something given to us by another and which we make a part of ourselves. We may receive a letter in the mail; we may receive our weekly paycheck; we may receive a guest into our home; or we may receive advice from a friend. Receiving has a deeply personal meaning. It implies that someone has offered us something that he expects us to embrace completely in a personal way. If we accept something with reservations, we say something such as, "We didn't receive it very well."

Receiving also implies that we are doing something self-consciously. For example, receiving a gift at Christmas is a self-conscious act of accepting a present from a friend or loved one. Rarely do we ever use the word *receive* without intending to say that we are doing something personally, completely, and self-consciously. Without this kind of personal involvement there can be no real receiving. For example, to "receive the word of God" (Acts 2:41; 8:14) is to embrace God's word in a personal way without reservation.

To "receive the Holy Spirit" (Acts 19:2) is to embrace God fully and completely. This is the meaning of Pentecost. For

197

God as Father, Son, and Holy Spirit is now made known to us in the history of salvation.

New Testament scholarship generally doesn't distinguish between "receiving the Spirit" (Acts 19:2), the baptism with the Spirit (Matt. 3:11; Mark 1:8; Luke 3:16; John 1:33; Acts 1:5; Acts 11:15–16), the Spirit "falling upon" (Acts 8:16; 10:44; 11:15), the Spirit "coming upon" (Acts 1:8; 19:6), and "filled with the Spirit" (Acts 2:4; 4:8, 31; 9:17).[1] In every instance when "receive the Holy Spirit" is used, it always refers to the giving of the Holy Spirit on the day of Pentecost. As you would also expect from its ordinary usage, to receive implies "to receive the fullness" of the Holy Spirit in a personal and self-conscious moment.

A quick reading of the twelve instances where this phrase appears in the New Testament will demonstrate its *technical* designation of Pentecostal fullness:

> This he said about the Spirit, which those who believed in him were to receive; for as yet the Spirit had not been given, because Jesus was not yet glorified (John 7:39).
>
> I will pray the Father, and he will give you another Counselor, to be with you for ever, even the Spirit of truth, whom the world cannot receive, because it neither sees him nor knows him; you know him, for he dwells with you, and will be in you (John 14:16–17).
>
> He breathed on them, and said to them, "Receive the Holy Spirit" (John 20:22).
>
> You shall receive power when the Holy Spirit has come upon you (Acts 1:8).
>
> Peter said to them, "Repent, and be baptized every one of you in the name of Jesus Christ for the forgiveness of your sins; and you shall receive the gift of the Holy Spirit" (Acts 2:38).
>
> When the apostles at Jerusalem heard that Samaria had received the word of God, they sent to them Peter and John, who came down and prayed for them that they might receive the Holy Spirit (Acts 8:14–15).
>
> They laid their hands on them and they received the Holy Spirit (Acts 8:17).

> Give me also this power, that any one on whom I lay my hands may receive the Holy Spirit (Acts 8:19).
>
> Can any one forbid water for baptizing these people who have received the Holy Spirit? (Acts 10:47)
>
> Did you receive the Holy Spirit when you believed? (Acts 19:2)
>
> Did you receive the Spirit? (Gal. 3:2)
>
> That we might receive the promise of the Spirit through faith (Gal. 3:14).

Some preachers and evangelists distinguish between the baptism with the Spirit and being filled with the Spirit. J. B. Atkinson, for example, in *The Beauty of Holiness* believes that every Christian is baptized with the Spirit at conversion but that not everyone is filled with the Spirit.[2] Billy Graham takes this position in *The Holy Spirit*.[3] Their concern is to show that every Christian is regenerated by the Holy Spirit and possesses the Holy Spirit even though not every believer is filled with the power and love of the Spirit.

This is an important point. Every believer has the Spirit in some degree. Even Abraham whose knowledge of God was not so advanced as the New Testament revelation possessed some degree of the Spirit. Before Pentecost the disciples of our Lord had been regenerated by the Spirit and possessed the Spirit, but they had not *received* the Spirit in Pentecostal fullness. New Testament scholarship, while recognizing this important point, generally assumes that the various Pentecost phrases, such as "receive the Spirit," and "be filled with the Spirit," intend to imply a Pentecostal fullness, not the more general meaning of the Spirit simply being a part of our lives

THE WITNESS OF THE EPHESIAN BELIEVERS

Notice the specific way that Paul phrases his question to the Ephesians: "Did you receive the Holy Spirit when you believed?" (Acts 19:2) He assumes that some may be disciples and believers of our Lord and still not have received the Pentecostal fullness. Without any hesitation, Luke says that these Ephesians were disciples.

One of the most respected contemporary New Testament scholars is F. F. Bruce. He comments on this passage, "When Luke uses the term 'disciples' without qualification, as he does of these men, he elsewhere means disciples of Jesus; and Paul appears to have recognized them as Christian believers."[4] The King James Version translates this question just as correctly: "Have ye received the Holy Ghost since ye believed?" This phrasing suits the theology of the Church of England. As we shall see, the Anglican Church used this passage, along with the one about the Samaritans receiving the Spirit in Acts 8, as the basis for their ritual of confirmation. Since the Greek New Testament allows for and even implies a distinction between *believing* and a later *receiving* of the Holy Spirit, it was natural for the translators to render it "Have ye received the Holy Ghost since ye believed?"

Regardless of how you translate it, the result is the same. *The Ephesians were believers but had not received the Spirit of Pentecost.* Attempts to explain away this obvious point go against the natural reading of the text, and to think that their two-stage experience of becoming believers and later receiving the Spirit's fullness was unique to them alone is also not a natural inference from the text.

THE WITNESS OF JEREMY TAYLOR

Take a look at our evangelical heritage which prepared the way for the contemporary emphasis on the Spirit-filled life. An understanding of our history will help to put things in focus for us. A review will show that the emphasis on the indwelling of the Holy Spirit in our day is not a new theology. Let's begin with Jeremy Taylor, an English bishop (1613–67) whose devotional writings including *Holy Living* and *Holy Dying* continue to be read by Christians from many different denominational backgrounds. Taylor was not just an ordinary bishop concerned about the daily administration of the church. He was involved in the spiritual life of his people. He wanted each one to be more than a mere member and to exemplify a life of love and holiness.

In the essay "A Discourse on Confirmation," he wrote of his concern that the evangelical meaning of confirmation be properly understood.[5] The Anglican Church, like the Greek Orthodox and Roman Catholic churches, had a more sacramentarian view of grace than most Protestants. The formal rituals of water baptism and confirmation were especially significant. Water baptism was the sacrament of Easter; it represented regeneration and the new life in Christ and was the rite of initiation into the church. Confirmation was the sacrament of the Spirit, the sacrament of Pentecost; it represented the sanctification of the believer and reception of the fullness of the Holy Spirit; it was the final moment of initiation into the church. Afterward, the confirmed member was permitted to partake of the sacrament of Holy Communion and exercise his rights as a full member.

Like a good Anglican, the bishop regarded confirmation as a rite patterned on the experience of the Spirit which the Samaritans and the Ephesians had in Acts 8 and 19. It was not enough for them to be regenerated and baptized with water; so the apostles sent John to them that they might receive the Spirit of Pentecost through the laying on of hands. This deeper experience with the Spirit of Pentecost makes believers strong and mature, and so Taylor believed that the laying on of hands in confirmation was the anointing of the Holy Spirit and represented an important stage of spiritual growth. In instructions to his ministers, he insisted that confirmation be more than a ritual; to be a valid ordinance in the church it must be met with genuine faith.[6] Taylor wanted the meaning of these rituals to be deeply internalized. If we are to "receive perfective graces," we must experience "the overflowings of the Spirit" for ourselves, he said. Unless we really "receive the Spirit of . . . confirmation, we are but babes in Christ."[7]

As I examined Taylor's evangelical understanding of the holy life, I began to realize the genuine spiritual genius of John Wesley who followed him a century later. We know that Wesley was influenced by a number of writers who stressed a devotional life with Christ. A major influence was Jeremy Taylor. We also know that Wesley was a loyal Anglican and was part of the same tradition as Taylor and that Wesley understood Christian experience in an evangelical rather than a ritualistic sense. The important thing is not water baptism but the resurrected life of Jesus; not the laying on of the bishop's hands in confirmation but the personal sanctifying presence of the Holy Spirit.

THE WITNESS OF JOHN FLETCHER

One of the most compelling expositions of the Spirit-filled life is given by John Wesley's closest friend and intimate preaching companion, John Fletcher. He was a well-educated Anglican priest, and his participation in the early Methodist movement in England earned him a reputation as the first systematic theologian in Methodism. He came from Geneva, Switzerland, where he was formally educated and trained for the ministry, and had moved to England in his early twenties. There he met John Wesley and looked upon him as his spiritual guide.

In his biography of Fletcher, Wesley reported that his friend's "favourite subject" was "the promise of the Father, the gift of the Holy Ghost." "We must be filled with the Spirit," was the theme of Fletcher's writings and preaching.[8] He described this experience as "union with the Father and the Son, mentioned in the seventeenth chapter of St. John." The evidence of the Spirit-filled life is "the sweetness of the drawings of the Father, all the love of the Son, all the rich effusions of peace and joy in the Holy Ghost—more than ever can be expressed."[9]

Fletcher preached and taught that the growth of our spiritual life requires that we personally share in the same events of salvation history that are recorded in the Bible. God was revealed progressively in history as Father, Son, and Holy Spirit. We, too, progressively come to know God as Father, Son, and Holy Spirit in our own spiritual history and pilgrimage. So different people have varying degrees of the knowledge of God.[10]

Everyone who knows God as Father has at least a limited

relationship with the Son and the Spirit because God is a unity; but not everybody takes advantage of the privileges of New Testament revelation. We are offered a deeper relationship with God than merely the knowledge of him as Father; we can know him more intimately through acceptance of Jesus as the Son of God who offers us forgiveness of sins and newness of life. We can know him most intimately through the fullness of the Spirit of Christ.

Fletcher drew an interesting parallel between God as a trinity of persons and the three stages of the believer's faith. As we worship God, devotionally speaking, we feel no difference between Christ and the Holy Spirit, for the Spirit is the exalted Christ (Acts 2:33; 2 Cor. 3:18). But in a more precise sense, we recognize a distinction among the Father, Son, and the Holy Spirit, but it is a distinction-within-unity. For the three divine persons all share the same functions together. God the Father is Creator, yet the Son and the Holy Spirit are involved in creating; God the Son is redeemer, yet the Father and the Spirit are involved in redeeming; God the Spirit sanctifies, yet the Father and the Son are involved in the process of sanctifying. Each of the divine persons has his own special function, yet all three of the divine persons are involved in the special ministries of the others.[11]

So when we speak of the trinity of persons, we do not mean that God has three independent centers of consciousness as if the Father, Son, and the Holy Spirit could all be off at different places without the presence of each other. God is One, yet possesses three personal distinctions. God is Mystery and beyond our ability to explain. But there are some things we believe because that's the way God revealed himself. God is much too "real" for us to understand with our finite minds. Who he is (I AM) we can never comprehend.

There is one more point which Fletcher helps us to understand. All who trust in God have the same kind of faith even though they may have different degrees of this one faith.[12] All believers have at least limited awareness of the work of the Holy Spirit in their lives. When he explained that there were progressive stages of Christian experience, he did not mean that we have the Son without the Spirit, as if the Christian life were made up of disjointed events. There may be gradual stages in our spiritual growth, but they are not disconnected from each other. So we can speak of the deeper Christian life as the fullness of the Spirit without depreciating the reception of Christ in conversion; we can speak of the unique coming of the Spirit on the day of Pentecost as a deeper revelation of God without depreciating the person of Jesus in his earthly ministry. So the stages of God's revelation are connected even as the different stages of our personal experiences with God are all interrelated.

Fletcher's influence extends beyond Anglican and Methodist traditions. No other writer before him placed a more balanced and clearer understanding of the relevance of the Holy Spirit in the life of the Christian. Wesley recognized this: "I believe that difficult subject was never placed in so clear a light before."[13] Fletcher did not simply theorize about the meaning of the Spirit-filled life; it was a personal experience for him. Wesley recorded Fletcher's personal testimony of August 24, 1781. The opening words express the essence of his experience: "My dear brethren and sisters, God is here! I feel him in this place."[14]

The infilling of the Spirit involves this awareness of God's presence. Notice that true self-awareness is God-awareness. This experience fulfills the promise of God to Abraham: "I will be their God and they shall be my people." The promise, "I will be their God," is God-awareness; "they will be my people" is self-awareness. There can be no true self-awareness without divine awareness. Fletcher's words, "I feel him in this place," is a personal expression of this truth. When we receive the fullness of the Spirit, we too feel that God is wherever we are. His presence transforms and sanctifies the meaning of our existence.

John Wesley, his brother Charles, and Fletcher led the Methodist movement.[15] The particular contribution of John Fletcher to the Methodists was his help in clarifying the doctrines which they preached. The most important teaching which he helped to make clear was that the invitation of Christ for us to love him perfectly is available through the infilling of the Holy Spirit. Contrary to Anglican emphasis upon confirmation as the means of the imparting of the Spirit, Fletcher showed from Scripture that the Spirit's coming is primarily a personal experience.[16] Fletcher agreed with the observation that in the book of Acts the experience usually occurred within the congregation of believers at worship, but to him a formal ritual was not necessary.

The importance of Fletcher for us today is that he rediscovered the evangelical preaching of the Spirit-filled life which enables believers to love God with their heart, mind, and soul. Wesley agreed. "It seems that God has raised him up for this very thing," Wesley wrote in a letter to a friend along with a recommendation that she read Fletcher's description of the various stages of the Christian life.[17] Wesley usually referred to this deeper Christian experience in terms of perfect love; Fletcher usually talked about it in terms of the Spirit-filled life. Yet both of them used the terms *perfect love* and *the fullness of the Spirit* to speak of one and the same reality.[18] Some have suspected that Fletcher and Wesley were not in agreement because of their different ways of talking about the holy life, but they both insisted that they were in agreement. Fletcher made it a point to quote from Wesley's sermons to show that they agreed,[19] and Wesley edited and published Fletcher's writings. Wesley specifically said, "There is no difference between us."[20]

The significance of their "discovery" is truly a milestone similar to the significance of Luther's rediscovery of Paul's teaching on justification by faith. Our distance from the eighteenth century may make it difficult to appreciate the significance of their insights. Fletcher's "rediscovery of the Holy Spirit" made a lasting impression on Methodist preachers in his day, and it continued to gain momentum throughout the nineteenth century in America until it has now reached a crescendo in evangelical churches scattered throughout the world. My colleague Dr. Melvin Dieter owns a personal copy of the original American Edition of Fletcher's writings (published by Joseph Crukshank in Philadelphia, 1791–1796). From the time when Methodism was first planted in America, Fletcher's dynamic understanding of holiness as the fullness of the Spirit was an essential part of Methodist preaching. But this "new doctrine" was not really new.

Somehow it had been lost under the rubble of time, though it was still preserved in the formal rituals of the church. Luther released the personal meaning of the doctrine of justification by faith (the Easter experience) from its imprisonment in the formal rite of water baptism in the Roman Catholic Church. The Wesleys and John Fletcher released the personal meaning of the doctrine of sanctification (the Pentecost experience) from its imprisonment in the formal rite of confirmation in the Anglican Church. Though Methodists did not reject the sacraments of the church, they emphasized their evangelical meaning.

It is difficult to exaggerate the importance of these three Anglican priests. Charles Wesley's hymns so heavily emphasize the Holy Spirit, and they are found in the hymnals of most churches. John Wesley's sermons and general writings on the holy life continue to be read beyond the Methodist denominations which later emerged. And certainly the distinctive emphasis of John Fletcher on the personal meaning of Pentecost provided the original momentum for our contemporary renewal movements which are calling us to a deeper experience with God through his Spirit. Nothing like their hymns, their preaching, and their evangelical doctrines can be found in the pages of history before the eighteenth century and since the days of the apostles.

Harold J. Ockenga preached a sermon which is included in the book *Great Preaching: Evangelical Messages by Contemporary Christians,* first published by the Billy Graham Evangelistic Association in 1963 and again in 1971. The title of that sermon is "The Third He." This sermon could not have been preached before the Wesleyan evangelical revival. Instead, Dr. Ockenga could have written on the general nature of the holy life and possibly a homily on the meaning of confirmation. But that is not what he does in this sermon. He specifically appeals to his congregation to receive into their lives the fullness of the Holy Spirit, and he makes no reference to the rituals and sacraments of the church. "The Third He" is, of course, the Holy Spirit who came in fullness subsequent to the coming of Jesus. Dr. Ockenga shows that the average Christian knows about Jesus but little about the person of the Holy Spirit. This sermon makes the same emphasis found in the preaching and writings of John Fletcher.

Dr. Ockenga was not an Anglican or a Methodist. For thirty-two years he pastored Park Street Congregational Church in Boston, later becoming president of Gordon College and Gordon-Conwell Theological Seminary. He was the first president of the National Association of Evangelicals and served for a time as president of the board of Christianity Today, Inc. I am not sure how much he might have been directly influenced by Fletcher; perhaps not at all. But that's not the point.

Fletcher's role in the contemporary renewal movement may not be known by everyone, but no one before him wrote and preached so pointedly about the necessity of a personal and evangelical experience of the Spirit. Some of the Anglican priests were saying that Wesley's teaching on the perfection of love was a new doctrine, but Fletcher reminded them that the Methodists were only encouraging others to make real in their lives what the bishops had said ought to be true for them in the ritual of confirmation.[21] This was Jeremy Taylor's same point in his essay on confirmation—except that Fletcher made it stronger. Father Karl Rahner points out that the Spirit-filled movements throughout the church today are personal expressions of the sacrament of confirmation.[22] The ordinance of confirmation has preserved the meaning of Pentecost for us.

Wesley chose Fletcher to succeed him as the leader of the Methodists. But he died, probably from tuberculosis, in 1785, nearly six years before Wesley's death. Wesley remarked about his friend's untimely death:

> I was intimately acquainted with him for thirty years. I conversed with him morning, noon, and night, without the least reserve, during a journey of many hundred miles; and in all that time I never heard him speak an improper word, or saw him do an improper action. To conclude: within fourscore years, I have known many excellent men, holy in heart and life: but one equal to him I have not known; one so uniformly and deeply devoted

to God. So unblameable a man, in every respect, I have not found either in Europe or America. Nor do I expect to find another such on this side eternity.[23]

A list of Spirit-filled Christians throughout the history of the church would be almost endless. A review of twenty people within the last hundred years is contained in a book by V. Raymond Edman, the former president of Wheaton College. Entitled *They Found the Secret,* it contains the testimonies of several Christians from various doctrinal backgrounds.[24] Writings of five witnesses to the Spirit-filled life have had a special influence upon me. They are Daniel Steele, Andrew Murray, E. Stanley Jones, Karl Rahner, and Karl Barth.

THE WITNESS OF DANIEL STEELE

Daniel Steele, a theology professor at Boston University, was an influential Methodist preacher in Massachusetts whose writings were widely read and appreciated. He was also one of the significant Greek scholars in his day. Professor Steele's testimony of the Spirit-filled life was given in a sermon he preached before the Boston University School of Theology, May 30, 1871. The dignity and yet the personal nature of his experience is compelling:

> On the subject of the fullness of the Holy Spirit as a possible and sudden attainment in modern times, I am not here to theorize, to philosophize, to dogmatize, but to testify. Let me turn my pulpit into a witness-stand for one moment. Although this school may teach that testimony in the pulpit should be of an indefinite and impersonal sort, I must speak for myself. Six months ago I made the discovery that I was living in the pre-pentecostal state of religious experience, admiring Christ's character, obeying his law, and in a degree loving his person, but without the conscious blessing of the Comforter. I settled the question of privilege by a study of St. John's Gospel and St. Paul's Epistles, and earnestly sought for the Comforter. I prayed, consecrated, confessed my state, and believed Christ's word. Very suddenly, after about three weeks' diligent search, the Comforter came with power and great joy to my heart. He took my feet out of the realm of

doubt and weakness, and planted them forever on the Rock of assurance and strength.[25]

Professor Steele's sermon was entitled "The Qualities of a Successful Ministry." His point was that a formal theological education is not adequate to do the work of a minister; the infilling of the Spirit is the experience which qualifies one to preach the gospel because the Spirit is the indwelling Christ who makes God real to us in the depths of our emotions and feelings. Christian ministers must feel with deep conviction the presence of God in their lives before their words can have persuasive power with their hearers.

Though a scholar and educator, Professor Steele challenged his denomination and its ministers to be spiritually alive to God through the Spirit. His emphasis was upon the reception of the perfect love of Christ which comes through the infilling of the Spirit. He was careful to dissociate himself from emotional excesses and calmly preached the privilege of a life transformed by the infused love of the Spirit.

THE WITNESS OF ANDREW MURRAY

Andrew Murray was a Dutch Reformed minister of South Africa. He is remembered as the author of many devotional books which continue to be published and read. One is titled *Abide in Christ,* which suggests the general theme of his preaching and life. The Spirit-filled life is one of total trust in Christ and a consecration to the will of God. His personal testimony was given at the English Keswick Convention around 1870:

> Some of you have heard how I have pressed upon you the two stages in the Christian life, and the step from the one to the other. The first ten years of my spiritual life were manifestly spent on the lower stage. I was a minister, I may say, as zealous and as earnest and as happy in my work as anyone, as far as love of the work was concerned. Yet, all the time, there was burning in my heart a dissatisfaction and restlessness inexpressible. What was the reason? I had never learnt with all my theology that

obedience was possible. My justification was as clear as noonday. I knew the hour in which I received from God the joy of pardon. I remember in my little room at Bloemfontein how I used to sit and think, What is the matter? Here I am, knowing that God has justified me in the blood of Christ, but I have no power for service. My thoughts, my words, my actions, my unfaithfulness—everything troubled me. Though all around thought me one of the most earnest of men, my life was one of deep dissatisfaction. I struggled and prayed as best I could.[26]

Murray then described his experience with the Spirit as a progressive realization that God had filled him with his presence. He reported that he could not remember a specific occasion when this happened to him, for it gradually dawned upon him that he was now living out the meaning of the Spirit's fullness. "What I think God has given me now, in contrast to the first ten years of my Christian life [is a] blessed assurance that He, as the everlasting God, has guaranteed His work in me." He adds,

With the deepest feeling of my soul I can say that I am satisfied with Jesus now; but there is also the consciousness of how much fuller the revelation can be of the exceeding abundance of His grace. Let us never hesitate to say, This is only the beginning. When we are brought into the holiest of all, we are only beginning to take our right position with the Father.[27]

As a high school senior, I was introduced to Murray through his devotional book *Absolute Surrender*. The experience which he described as an absolute trust in the merits of Christ's death-resurrection comes from the abandonment of our wills to the will of God. The Spirit-filled life is the inner guarantee and an inner conviction that we are truly in Christ. I am happy to say that this higher level of consciousness with Christ became a personal experience for me as a first-year college student. I will always be indebted to Murray's devotional books which put me on the track to this higher Christian life.

THE WITNESS OF E. STANLEY JONES

A third example is E. Stanley Jones, a graduate of Asbury College. He was one of the best known missionary leaders in the world until his death in 1973. Though a Methodist, he was asked to address audiences from various denominational and religious backgrounds and was highly respected in other countries among even non-Christian communities. His impact among Hindu leaders was widely known and publicized. He often deeply involved himself in political situations with the governments of the world, for he believed that Christians could and should make a difference in social and political issues.[28]

His devotional writings, like Murray's, continue to be published and read. *Abundant Living* is a classic, but all of his devotional writings teem with spiritual and intellectual insights. A major theme running throughout his works is the Spirit-filled life. He often used the contemporary language of psychology to explain the meaning of life in the Spirit. But at no point did he allow a secular understanding to confuse the supernatural work of the Holy Spirit in the life of the believer. He begins the account of his own experience with a use of psychological terms to explain the meaning of conversion:

> In conversion a new life is introduced into the conscious mind as we consciously accept Christ as Savior and Lord. A new love and a new loyalty flood the conscious mind. The subconscious mind is stunned and subdued by this new dominant loyalty to Christ, introduced into the conscious mind by conversion. Sometimes it lies low for long periods, subdued but not surrendered. It waits for low moments in the conscious mind and then sticks up its head and, when it sees an opportunity, takes over the conscious mind.[29]

Brother Stanley (as he was affectionately called) says this corresponded to his own experience. For about a year after his conversion, he felt much joy in his heart, but then began an inner conflict between his loyalty to Christ and the inner pressure to be self-serving. "I was in a crisis," he said. "I was stymied by this inner conflict." Then he read *The Christian's Secret of a Happy Life,* by Hannah Whithall Smith, a Quaker. "I felt a sense of destiny in reaching for it. A kind of tingle went through me, a tingle of expectancy."

My heart was kindled with desire as I read it. I wasn't reading it; I was eating it. I got to the forty-second page when God spoke to me: "Now is the time to find." I pleaded: "Lord, I don't know what I want. This book is telling me. Let me read the book first and then I can intelligently seek." But the voice was imperious: "Now is the time to find." I tried to read on, but the words were blurred. I saw I was in a controversy with God, so I closed the book, dropped on my knees beside my bed, and said: "Now, Lord, what shall I do?" And he replied: "Will you give me your all?" And after a moment's hesitation I replied: "Yes, Lord, of course I will. I will give you my all, all I know and all I don't know." Then he replied: "Then take my all, take the Holy Spirit." I paused for a moment: my all for his all; my all was myself, his all was himself, the Holy Spirit. I saw as in a flash the offer. I eagerly replied: "I will take the Holy Spirit."[30]

Brother Stanley rose from his knees with no evidence except the promise of Christ; God's Word was the basis of his trust in the promise of receiving the Holy Spirit. "I walked around the room repeating my acceptance," he said. But doubts continued to trouble him.

I did what Abraham did when the birds came to scatter his sacrifice; he shooed them away. I walked around the room pushing away with my hands the menacing doubts. When suddenly I was filled—filled with the Holy Spirit. Wave after wave of the Spirit seemed to be going through me as a cleansing fire. I could only walk the floor with the tears of joy flowing down my cheeks. I could do nothing but praise him—and I did. I knew this was no passing emotion; the Holy Spirit had come to abide with me forever.[31]

E. Stanley Jones was not one to get emotional. His feeling for God was deep, personal, and contagious, but not high strung. In simple but meaningful psychological terms, he describes what happened in that moment of his infilling of the Spirit. "He had been with me, with me in the conscious mind in conversion. Now he was in me, in me in the subconscious. When he was with me in the conscious, it was conversion limited, for the subconscious was not redeemed; cowed and suppressed, but not redeemed. Now the subconscious was redeemed."[32]

Some like Daniel Steele and E. Stanley Jones emphasize the consciousness of a specific occasion when this level of spiritual life is experienced; others like Murray stress the importance of an awareness of the Spirit in daily life rather than a particular moment when the experience happened. The decisive thing is the expectation and the awareness that the Spirit of Christ indwells us in his fullness. This is the secret of living the Christian life; it is the reward of waiting for the Holy Spirit.

THE WITNESS OF FATHER KARL RAHNER

I was delighted recently to read a short book written by one of the most important theologians in our day, Father Karl Rahner. If you know anything about the Roman Catholic Church, you know that his writings and teachings are taken more seriously than anyone else's from that tradition. Father Rahner has a warm relationship with Protestants and is a highly respected scholar among secular philosophers as well. He recognizes the present revival of Spirit-filled Christianity as a valid expression of God's work in the world. The title of his book is *A New Baptism in the Spirit: Confirmation Today,* published in 1965. Catholics believe that the original event of Pentecost is repeated in believers in the rite of confirmation.

To Father Rahner renewal groups in the church represent the internalizing of the formal event of confirmation. At this point, he sounds like a Protestant! He asks, "Why, then, may we not look forward to a new, revitalized understanding of Confirmation, the sacrament of the Spirit, on the basis of these experiences bursting forth everywhere in the Church today?"[33] My Protestant heart replies, "Right on!"

THE WITNESS OF KARL BARTH

Karl Barth (d. 1968), one of the most important and influential theologians in our century, was a professor of theology at Basel University for many years. His studies on the doctrine of sanctification are especially helpful. He showed through his exposition of Scripture the same general perceptions which I have set forth in these pages about the meaning of Easter and Pentecost. He believed that they are "the only two bases" for the Christian life. He explained that water baptism is a sign of the new birth (Easter) and one's beginning walk with the Lord. He showed that the fullness of the Spirit (Pentecost) is the goal of the Christian life, and described Pentecost as the "confirmation" of Easter. He held that the reality of Jesus' resurrection life is not only a truth to be accepted intellectually at conversion, but it is to be branded upon our hearts through the outpouring of the Holy Spirit.[34]

Barth has a thoughtful and helpful exposition of the Bible on this subject, but unfortunately he interprets the ideal of the Spirit-filled life as a goal toward which we are always striving without ever truly experiencing it in this life. This experience is an event which takes place in the mind of God for us, but we can never actually hope to achieve it until the life hereafter.[35] For him the different occasions mentioned in Acts when the church received further infilling of the Spirit imply that believers were getting closer and closer to this level of spiritual consciousness. But they never reached it.[36]

ARE YOU A WITNESS TODAY?

I mention Barth's opinion at this point because many people share his belief. He is a witness to the longing for the Spirit-filled life. His exposition on the meaning of Pentecost clearly demonstrates the scriptural bases for that relationship. But his pessimism reduces our motivation to wait for and expect the coming of God's Spirit. According to the apostle John, who reminds us that God's expectations of us can be truly satisfied through Christ (1 John 5:3), the promises of God are all possible of fulfillment in our lives today. We can know the perfect love of God in our hearts through the Spirit (1 John 4:12–13).

Jesus said to his disciples, "Wait for the promise." Surely

this includes the attitude of expectation. If we are to continue in a personal way the history of the book of Acts, it must mean that we are to love God, through the indwelling of the Holy Spirit, with all the heart, mind, and soul.

A student recently said to me that she did not remember the occasion when she received the fullness of the Spirit, but she believed that it must have happened at her conversion. I reassured her that there was no good reason why she should not have received her Pentecost at the moment of her Easter experience. For the decisive thing is the reality of the Spirit in her life now.

Many of us have not known it this way, however. Just as the historical Easter and Pentecost were two distinct events, so it has happened with us. But more importantly, the reality of Pentecost must be an ongoing and continuously updated experience. All spiritual growth assumes a daily renewal of Pentecost and a further development of its reality in our psychic processes. D. L. Moody once said, "A great many think because they have been filled once, they are going to be full for all time after; but O, my friends, we are leaky vessels, and have to be kept right under the fountain all the time in order to keep full."[37]

Easter and Pentecost happened not only in the past, but they happen as real events for us, and they continue to happen now and forever throughout the course of our spiritual history. In our private devotional moments, in our public worship in the congregation, in celebration of the sacraments, in small fellowship groups, and in our more formal Bible study times, we live again the once-and-for-all events of Easter and Pentecost. It is not enough to have one dramatic initial experience as important as that might be for us.

Nor is it sufficient for us to have merely a private experience with the Spirit. For the Spirit binds us not only to God, but to each other. This is the meaning of the church as the body of Christ. We belong to each other because we belong to Christ through his Spirit. For the same Spirit who came on the day of Pentecost is the same Spirit of Christ who indwells us and binds us together in the fellowship of the church and in the communion of the saints of all ages, beginning with the apostles and continuing through the centuries to the present. Here in the fellowship of the church, we exercise the gifts of the Spirit as he chooses to give them by his sovereign will for the strengthening of the body of Christ.

Paul's question to the Ephesians who had become believers in Christ through the baptism of John the Baptist is still relevant today: "Did you receive [the fullness of] the Holy Spirit when you believed?" (Acts 19:2) They didn't know about the Pentecost event of Acts 2, and they understood nothing about the Holy Spirit.

Unlike the Ephesians, we are aware of that first Christian Pentecost. But have we experienced it for ourselves? Like Andrew Murray, you may not remember the specific occasion, but do you know the spiritual presence of God deep down in your heart now?

Dr. Edman concludes his study of those who had discovered the fullness of the Spirit with these simple observations: First, there must be an awareness of our need; second, there is agony of soul; third, there follows abandonment to the Savior; fourth, there must be an appropriation by faith of the Holy Spirit to fill life with the presence of the Lord Jesus; fifth, there follows an experience of abiding by faith in Christ; sixth, there is a feeling of abundance; and seventh, our life in the Spirit becomes one of constant adventure. Then he adds, "That life can be yours and mine!"[38] Charles Wesley's Pentecost hymn invites the Holy Spirit to be ours in his fullness:

> Love divine, all loves excelling,
>   Joy of heaven, to earth come down;
> Fix in us thy humble dwelling;
>   All thy faithful mercies crown!
> Jesus, thou art all compassion,
>   Pure, unbounded love thou art;
> Visit us with thy salvation;
>   Enter every trembling heart.
>
> Breathe, O breathe thy loving Spirit
>   Into every troubled breast!
> Let us all in thee inherit;
>   Let us find that second rest.

Take away our bent to sinning;
    Alpha and Omega be;
End of faith, as its beginning,
    Set our hearts at liberty.

Come, Almighty to deliver,
    Let us all thy grace receive;
Suddenly return, and never,
    Never more thy temples leave.
Thee we would be always blessing,
    Serve thee as thy hosts above,
Pray and praise thee without ceasing,
    Glory in thy perfect love.

Finish, then, thy new creation;
    Pure and spotless let us be.
Let us see thy great salvation
    Perfectly restored in thee:
Changed from glory into glory,
    Till in heaven we take our place,
Till we cast our crowns before thee,
    Lost in wonder, love, and praise.

NOTES

Chapter 1

1. John Wesley, "The Means of Grace," *The Standard Sermons of John Wesley*, ed. E. H. Sugden (London: Epworth, 1961), I:238–60.
2. Wolfhart Pannenberg, *Jesus—God and Man*, trans. Lewis L. Wilkins and Duane A. Priebe (Philadelphia: Westminster, 1977), 179–80.

Chapter 2

1. The idea of salvation history with its emphasis on the Bible as a record of the mighty acts of God in history has been a prominent theme of biblical theology during the last fifty years. See especially Oscar Cullmann, *Salvation in History*, trans. Sidney G. Sowers (London: SCM, 1967). Also see Gerhard von Rad, *The Problem of the Hexateuch and Other Essays*, trans. E. Dicken (New York: McGraw-Hill, 1966); von Rad, "Typological Interpretation of the Old Testament" in *Essays on Old Testament Hermeneutics*, ed. Claus Westermann, trans. James Luther Mays (Richmond: John Knox, 1964). Also see Werner H. Schmidt, *The Faith of the Old Testament*, trans. John Sturdy (Philadelphia: Westminster, 1983), 30–37. Also, Walther Eichrodt, *Theology of the Old Testament*, vol. I, trans. J. A. Baker (Philadelphia: Westminster, 1961).
More recently, there has been a trend to interpret the Scriptures in terms of a "narrative theology" as Hans W. Frei does in his book *The Eclipse of Biblical Narrative* (New Haven: Yale University, 1974). This new trend is often disappointing because it makes the Bible to be more story than history. An excellent review of recent critical biblical scholarship and its understanding of the narrative intention of the Scriptures is found in David Damrosch, *The Narrative Covenant* (New York: Harper, 1987). For a fine discussion of the importance of a narrative interpretation of theology and faith, see Stanley Hauerwas (with David Burrell and Richard Bondi), *Truthfulness and Tragedy* (Notre Dame, Ind.: University Press, 1977). A survey of recent narrative theology is given in Michael Goldberg, *Theology and Narrative* (Nashville: Abingdon, 1981).

2. Victor Paul Furnish, "The Letter of Paul to the Galatians," *The Interpreter's One-Volume Commentary on the Bible,* ed. Charles M. Layman (Nashville: Abingdon, 1971), 829; Hermann W. Ridderbos, *The Epistle of Paul to the Churches of Galatia, The New International Commentary on the New Testament,* ed. F. F. Bruce (Grand Rapids: Eerdmans, 1953), 128; Donald Guthrie, *Galatians, The Century Bible* (Camden, N. J.: Thomas Nelson, 1969), 104; Georgia Harkness, *The Fellowship of the Holy Spirit* (Nashville: Abingdon, 1966), 68–71; George S. Hendry, *The Holy Spirit in Christian Theology* (Philadelphia: Westminster, 1956), 21–25, 30, 36, 39; Hendrik Berkhof, *The Doctrine of the Trinity* (Richmond: John Knox, 1964), 94.

3. Jürgen Moltmann, *The Trinity and the Kingdom of God* (New York: Harper, 1981), 202–22. See Yves M. J. Congar, OP, *Theologians Today,* ed. Martin Redfern (New York: Sheed and Ward, 1972), 31–32, where he points out that this Trinitarian interpretation of salvation history goes back to the early church fathers and that it continues to be an important way of understanding Christian experience today. Congar and the Catholic tradition which he represents interpret the stages of one's Christian life according to how they personally relate to the development of God's revelation in history as Father, Son, and Holy Spirit. The primary difference between the Catholic tradition and the position which I am representing here is that the former is linked to a highly sacramentarian view of grace. According to the Catholic view, new birth and the reception of the Spirit's fullness occur in baptism and confirmation.

4. John Wesley, *Sermons on Several Occasions* (New York: T. Mason and G. Lane, 1839), II:383. This is the same point made by the Roman Catholic theologian Father Congar, who says that Easter and Pentecost constitute the two distinct stages of the Christian life as experienced in baptism and confirmation. "With the help of the Bible we can (as the early Fathers did) apportion the various parts of God's work among the divine persons of the Blessed Trinity; and we then see what can be called, in human terms, an ever-deepening and closer concern of God with his creatures" (*Theologians Today,* 28–29).

5. Wesley, *Standard Sermons,* II:157. See John Fletcher, *Checks to Antinomianism* (New York: Hunt and Eaton, 1889), I:589.

6. John Wesley, *Explanatory Notes Upon the New Testament* (London: Epworth, 1958), 435.

7. Moltmann, *The Trinity and the Kingdom of God,* 221.

8. A widely respected Catholic New Testament scholar, Father F. X. Durrwell, defends the idea of two distinct stages of Christian experience as first receiving the Son and at a later time receiving the Spirit of Christ on the basis of Paul's comments in Galatians 4:6. "The sending of the personal Spirit indeed presupposes that we have first been integrated into the Son— at least if the most natural rendering of Gal. iv.6 is also the right one: 'Because you are sons, God hath sent the Spirit of his Son into your hearts.' " See his book, *The Resurrection,* trans. Rosemary Sheed (New

York: Sheed and Ward, 1961), 219. Father Durrwell also writes, "According to the Acts, baptism incorporates us into the Church, the expression in the world of that Kingdom of God that was set up when Christ was glorified (ii.41). Administered in the name of Jesus (ii.38; viii.16; x.48), it sets the seal of the Lord's possession upon those who believe; it confers remission of sins (ii.38), and the right to receive the Holy Ghost (ii.38), which are graces that belong to the risen Christ (vv. 31–32). But it seems as though only the right to receive the Spirit is given [at baptism]" (*The Resurrection,* 315). Ernest DeWitt Burton says that sonship is "here spoken of being antecedent to and the ground of the bestowal of the Spirit." He writes of Galatians. 4:6, "The direct affirmation of the sentence is that the sonship is the cause of the experience of the Spirit." See Burton, *A Critical and Exegetical Commentary on the Epistle to the Galatians, The International Critical Commentary* (Edinburgh: T. and T. Clark, 1964), 221.

9. R. K. Harrison, *Introduction to the Old Testament* (Grand Rapids: Eerdmans, 1973), 85–143. Bernard W. Anderson, *Understanding the Old Testament,* fourth ed. (Englewood Cliffs: Prentice-Hall, 1986), 27–41. See especially W. F. Albright, *From the Stone Age to Christianity* (Baltimore: Penguin Books, 1946); also Albright, *The Archaeology of Palestine* (Penguin Books, 1961).

10. Reinhold Niebuhr writes, "A general revelation can only point to the reality of God but not to His particular attributes. A theology which believes only in a general revelation must inevitably culminate in pantheism; because a God who is merely the object of human knowledge and not a subject who communicates with man by His own initiative is something less than God. A knowledge of God which depends only upon a study of the behaviour of the world must inevitably be as flat as the knowledge of any person would be, which depended merely upon the observation of the person's behaviour. The study of human behaviour cannot give a full clue to the meaning of a personality, because there is a depth of freedom in every personality which can only communicate itself in its own 'word'." *Beyond Tragedy* (New York: Scribner, 1965), 15–16.

11. Gerhard von Rad shows the decisive importance of Israel's experience with a personal God which formed the basis of their understanding of history. He writes, "There are only two peoples in antiquity who really wrote history—the Greeks and, long before them, the Israelites." *The Problem of the Hexateuch,* 167. Von Rad also shows that it was Israel's experience of God in history which gave rise to the true meaning of personal existence: "Here alone, in his encounter with God, does mankind become great and interesting, breaking through the enigma of his humanity to discover all the inherent potentialities of his self-conscious existence. He becomes, in the final analysis, a man taken over by God, one who must surrender to God all his rights over his own history and who by the very fact of so

doing is led to new and unsuspected horizons of freedom." *The Problem of the Hexateuch*, 153.

Psychoanalysts have been interested in the origin of the meaning of the personal. Erich Fromm is representative of those who seek to explain the development of what it means to be a person. He says the "seeds" of the meaning of personhood "are to be found in the history of monotheistic religion." He writes, "The development of the human race as far as we have any knowledge of it can be characterized as the emergence of man from nature. . . . He finds his security by going back, or holding on to these primary bonds. He still feels identified with the world of animals and trees, and tries to find unity by remaining one with the natural world." But in the history of the Old Testament, man becomes aware of himself as he becomes aware of his difference from nature and he becomes aware of his transcendence over nature. Fromm shows that Abraham's awareness of God made him aware of his difference from nature and his own responsibility as a person in relationship to God. Fromm frankly acknowledges that belief in God was a necessary stage in human development. See Fromm, *The Art of Loving* (New York: Harper, 1963), 53–69.

In an interesting study on the uniqueness of Israel's experience with God as the Lord of history in comparison with other religions of the Near East, the following authors have shown that a direct consequence of Abraham's experience with God was a self-awareness of his individual responsibility and sense of personal freedom. This personal awareness stood in stark contrast to the mythical peoples of the ancient world who felt themselves to be controlled by the gods of nature (Henri Frankfort, Mrs. H. A. Frankfort, John A. Wilson, Thorkild Jacobsen, *Before Philosophy* (Baltimore: Penguin, 1964), 244–55. The discovery of the meaning of history and the personal are mutually related experiences. This does not mean, of course, that no degree of personal awareness was to be found among the ancient people. Of course they possessed a sense of individuality, but it was marked by fear and a desire to be joined to mother nature through mythical rituals rather than becoming emancipated from the eternal cycle of trying to satisfy the insatiable appetites of the gods of nature. In *Epic of Gilgamesh*, which dates back to 2000 B.C., Gilgamesh seeks for eternal life for himself and mankind which will restore his sense of youth. He discovers the precious plant which will give him eternal life, but it is stolen away by a snake. That is why snakes were said not to die but simply to shed their old bodies and be reborn in youthful vigor. Such concepts of eternal life as merely an extension of the natural world show that the meaning of the personal as possessing a spiritual freedom over the world instead of being immersed in the relativities of nature was lacking in the mythical experiences of the ancient world.

The "image of God" gave man his sense of "dominion" over creation and nature (Gen. 1:26). That we are free (which is the fundamental ingredient of personhood) is an experience derived from our relationship to a transcendent God who created the world from nothing. So long as man thought of himself as merely an extension of nature, he was not truly free to be himself and could not experience his personhood in the fullest sense of the term. The distinction between "nature" and "spirit" is foundational to the meaning of the personal. Reinhold Niebuhr's classical exposition of the Christian view of man has clearly demonstrated that the modern concept of personhood could not have developed without the biblical revelation. "God as will and personality, in concepts of Christian faith, is thus the only possible ground of real individuality. . . . But faith in God as will and personality depends upon faith in His power to reveal Himself. . . . The conviction that man stands too completely outside both nature and reason to understand himself in terms of either without misunderstanding himself belongs to general revelation in the sense that any astute analysis of the human situation must lead to it. But if man lacks a further revelation of the divine he will also misunderstand himself when he seeks to escape the conditions of nature and reason. He will end by seeking absorption in a divine reality which is at once all and nothing. To understand himself truly means to begin with a faith that he is understood from beyond himself, that he is known and loved of God and must find himself in terms of obedience to the divine will." *The Nature and Destiny of Man* (New York: Scribner, 1964), I:15. The one thinker whose thought lies so much in the background to contemporary discussions on the meaning of the personal—whether existentialists, psychoanalysts, or theologians— is Søren Kierkegaard. His book *Fear and Trembling* is particularly important because it shows that Abraham's sense of responsibility to God gave Abraham his sense of freedom and made him aware of his distinct individuality.

12. Vitezslav Gardavsky, a Marxist Czech philosopher, writes, "Not merely the Book of Genesis but the Old Testament as a whole contains something which is exceedingly important for the whole of European thought in particular: this is the first appearance of the idea of transcendence, of a step beyond all that has so far been achieved—although it is revealed here in a pre-scientific and mythological form, it is nonetheless perfectly clear; the dream of a personal identity in the midst of Time begins to show itself here for the first time," *God Is Not Yet Dead,* trans. Vivenne Menkes (Baltimore: Penguin, 1973), 28. Gardavsky is an atheist, but he believes it is atheism which needs to be justified today rather than theism. Hence the title of his book.

13. Typical of this are the Babylonian creation stories. The goddess Tiamat tried to destroy her offspring, but Marduk, the god of the gods, intervened by killing her and creating the world out of her corpse. So both the gods and the world are derived from her divinity. This means that the world of nature is a god as well since it is made out of the essence of the gods. The essence of paganism and all nonbiblical religions is their ignorance of God

as One who is independent of and transcendent over nature. This is what is meant by supernaturalism. Pagan worship thus involved sacrifices (including human sacrifices) which were intended to please the gods. See Yehezkel Kaufmann, *The Religion of Israel,* trans. Moshe Greenberg (Chicago: University Press, 1960), 21–59.

14. For a helpful discussion on this problem of conflictual relationships, see David Augsburger, *Caring Enough to Confront* (Glendale, Calif.: Regal, 1980).

15. Edmond Jacob has shown that God's name as Yahweh (or Jehovah) means that God is defined as He Who Is Present with his people as the eternal one. See *Theology of the Old Testament,* trans. Arthur W. Heathcote and Philip J. Allcock (New York: Harper, 1958), 51–52.

16. Karl Barth's writings have emphasized this theme of God's self-verification: "God's Word is God Himself in His revelation." *Church Dogmatics,* trans. G. T. Thomson (Edinburgh: T. and T. Clark, 1963), vol. I, part 1:339.

17. Emil Fackenheim, *The Presence of God in History* (New York: New York University Press, 1970), 40.

18. Edmond Jacob, *Theology of the Old Testament,* 190–93.

19. Alan Richardson, "Salvation, Savior," *The Interpreter's Dictionary of the Bible,* ed. George A. Buttrick (Nashville: Abingdon, 1962), R–Z:170.

20. Wesley defined circumcision as a symbol of perfection of love. *Standard Sermons,* I:267–68.

21. Kaufmann, *Religion of Israel,* 426.

22. von Rad, *Deuteronomy, A Commentary,* trans. Dorothea Barton (Philadelphia: Westminster, 1966), 183–84.

23. Rudolf Bultmann was not able to see the real connection between the Old and New Testaments because of his philosophical existentialist presuppositions. Consequently, he could see no continuity between God's promise to Abraham and its fulfillment in the historical event of Pentecost with the outpouring of the Spirit of Christ. See Bultmann, *History and Eschatology* (Edinburgh: The University Press, 1957), 36, 121. This negative attitude about the importance of a real history of salvation undermines the meaning of the personal which is so important to Bultmann's theology.

24. von Rad, *The Problem of the Hexateuch,* 95.

25. *Calvin Commentaries of the Epistle of Paul the Apostle to the Hebrews,* trans. John Owen (Grand Rapids: Eerdmans, 1948), 92–101.

Chapter 3

1. Bultmann has shown that the real "sign" of the new kingdom was not merely the external miracles and gifts of prophecy, but Jesus himself: "But what are the signs of the time? He himself! His presence, his deeds, his

message!" *Theology of the New Testament*, trans. Kendrick Grobel (New York: Scribner, 1955), I:6–7. The emphasis is on the person of Jesus, not a sensational preoccupation with physical miracles. Yet Bultmann fails to see the significance of physical miracles altogether, and downplays the importance of the signs which accompanied the coming of Jesus into the world.

2. Barth, *Church Dogmatics*, trans. G. W. Bromiley, IV, part 4:30; Congar, *Theologians Today*, 32.
3. Laurence Wood, *Pentecostal Grace* (Grand Rapids: Zondervan/Francis Asbury Press, 1980), 21.
4. Kittel's *Theological Dictionary of the New Testament*, VII (Grand Rapids: Eerdmans, 1971), 216, 241–43.
5. Kittel, *Theological Dictionary*, IV (1967), 335–77.
6. See Wood, *Pentecostal Grace*, 61–100; von Rad, *The Problem of the Hexateuch*, 79–102; Frank Moore Cross, *Canaanite Myth and Hebrew Epic* (Cambridge, Mass.: Harvard University Press, 1973), 83–90.
7. Durrwell, *The Resurrection*, 315.
8. G. Ernest Wright, *God Who Acts* (London: SCM Press, 1962), 63.
9. Barth, *Church Dogmatics*, IV, part IV, 30.
10. Wesley, *Standard Sermons*, II:162–63.
11. Ibid., I:162; Harald Lindström, *Wesley and Sanctification* (Nashville: Abingdon, 1946), 135, interprets Wesley to mean "full sanctification" in this context; also Lycurgus M. Starkey, *The Work of the Holy Spirit*, 21, 33.
12. Karl Rahner, *Theological Investigations*, trans. David Bourke (New York: Herder and Herder, 1971), VII:189, 197.
13. Pannenberg, *Jesus—God and Man*, 190. See also Abraham Kuyper, *The Work of the Holy Spirit*, trans. Henri De Vries (New York: Funk and Wagnalls, 1900), 15.
14. See Wesley's sermon "On Faith" where he charts out the various stages of faith beginning with the faith of those who do not even know the God of Abraham but are walking in all the light they have received and continuing through the stage of those who know God under the dispensation of the Old Testament, the dispensation of the Son before Pentecost, and up through the stage of those who have experienced a perfection of love through the Spirit. *Sermons on Several Occasions*, II:383.
15. Bultmann, *Theology of the New Testament*, I:160.
16. *Harper Study Bible*, (New York: Harper and Row, 1964), 1:702.
17. See Lindström, *Wesley and Sanctification*, 131, 155.
18. For a discussion of the language of Canaan, see Wood, *Pentecostal Grace*, 61–100.
19. Hermann Cremer, *Biblico-Theological Lexicon of New Testament Greek*, trans. William Urwick (4th ed. rev.: Edinburgh: T. and T. Clark, 1962), I:357; Arndt and Gingrich, *A Greek-English Lexicon of the New Testament* (Chicago: University Press, 1957), 506.

20. Kittel, *Theological Dictionary,* III:763; Cremer, *Biblico-Theological Lexicon,* I:357.

21. A. Skevington Wood, *Paul's Pentecost* (Exeter, Devon: The Paternoster Press, 1963), 22f.

22. Lloyd John Ogilvie, *Drumbeat of Love* (Waco, Tex.: Word, 1976), 13.

Chapter 4

1. Bultmann exaggerates the consequence of Israel's failure to be faithful to God by calling it "a miscarriage of history." *History and Eschatology* (Edinburgh: The University Press, 1957), 36, 121. More appropriately, Durrwell has shown that their failure meant a greater opportunity: "Israel had already known the Spirit. But the Prophets had foretold that in the last age the outpouring of the Spirit would exceed anything known before; that the Spirit would do greater things than ever, establishing a more sublime creation than the one he had produced when the world began. 'In that day,' he was to sanctify the messianic community and cleanse it of all defilement (Isa. iv.4)." *The Resurrection,* 255.

2. Emil Brunner, *The Misunderstanding of the Church,* trans. Harold Knight (Philadelphia: Westminster, 1953); Oscar Cullmann, *Salvation in History,* trans. Sidney G. Sowers (London: SCM, 1967), 173ff., 236–47, 278ff.; Cullmann, *The Early Church,* ed. A. J. B. Higgins (London: SCM Press, 1966), 105–37.

3. Karl Rahner, *Theological Investigations,* VII:189; Congar, *Theologians Today,* 28.

4. John Wesley writes, "The title Holy, applied to the Spirit of God, does not only denote that he is holy in his own nature, but that he makes us so," *Sermons on Several Occasions,* II:515.

5. Barth writes of God's free grace, "If we wish to state who Jesus Christ is, in every separate statement we must also state . . . that we are speaking of the Lord of heaven and earth, who neither has nor did have any need of heaven or earth or man, who created them out of free love and according to His very good pleasure, who adopts man, not according to the latter's merit, but according to His own mercy, not in virtue of the latter's capacity, but in virtue of His own miraculous power, *Church Dogmatics,* I:2, 133.

6. Hume writes, "Terror is the primary principle of religion." *Hume on Religion,* selected and introduced by Richard Wollheim (London: Collins, 1963), 202; cf. Ernst Cassirer, *The Philosophy of the Enlightenment,* trans. Fritz C. A. Koelln and James P. Pettegrove (Princeton: University Press, 1979), 179–80.

7. Kierkegaard, *Sickness Unto Death,* ed. and trans. Howard V. Hong and Edna H. Hong (Princeton: University Press, 1980), 147.

8. G. F. Oehler, *Theology of the Old Testament,* trans. George E. Day (New York: Funk and Wagnalls, 1883), 194; von Rad, *Genesis, A Commentary,* trans. John H. Marks (Philadelphia: Westminster, 1972), 201.
9. Bultmann, *Theology of the New Testament,* I:232–46.
10. Barth, *Church Dogmatics,* IV, part 4:8.
11. Bultmann, *Theology of the New Testament,* I:245ff.
12. Wood, *Pentecostal Grace,* 161–68.
13. Wesley, *Standard Sermons,* II:157.
14. Bultmann, *Theology of the New Testament,* I:158.

Chapter 5

1. Sigmund Freud, *Civilization and Its Discontents,* trans. W. D. Robson-Scott (Garden City, N.Y.: Doubleday, 1957), 56–57.
2. See Wolfhart Pannenberg, *What Is Man?* trans. Duane A. Priebe (Philadelphia: Fortress, 1970), 11–13, 90, 137–49; Pannenberg, *Anthropology in Theological Perspective,* trans. Matthew J. O'Connell (Philadelphia: Westminster, 1985), 45, 487, 525. Reinhold Niebuhr offers a careful and thorough discussion of the biblical concept of personal individuality and concludes, "Thus only Christianity (and Judaism . . .) sees and establishes the human spirit in its total depth and uniqueness," *The Nature and Destiny of Man,* I:58. The Marxist philosopher Vitezslav Gardavsky also says that the idea of transcendence and a corresponding awareness of the personal emerged for "the first time" with the book of Genesis, *God Is Not Yet Dead,* 28.
3. Fromm, *The Art of Loving,* 53–63.
4. Frankfort, et al., *Before Philosophy,* 237–62.
5. For a forceful expression of this uniqueness, see Kierkegaard, *Philosophical Fragments* (Princeton: University Press, 1974), 137–38.
6. Kuyper, *The Work of the Holy Spirit,* 15; Heidelberg Catechism (Cleveland: Central Publishing House, 1907), rev. ed., 37.
7. Søren Kierkegaard, *A Concluding Unscientific Postscript,* trans. David Swanson and Walter Lowrie (Princeton: University Press, 1974), 122.
8. *Symposium,* 207:a.
9. *Basic Writings of Nietzsche,* trans. and ed. Walter Kaufmann (New York: Modern Library, 1968), 469, 472–73.

Chapter 6

1. Ernst Bloch, *Das Prinzip Hoffnung* (2d ed.; Frankfurt am Main: Suhrkamp Verlag, 1959), II:1360f., cited by Pannenberg, *Jesus—God and Man,* 84.

2. Albert Camus, *The Myth of Sisyphus and Other Essays*, trans. Justin O'Brien (New York: Knopf, 1955).

3. Charles Hartshorne has said, "Perhaps I have a blind spot in this region, but I see no need for post-terrestrial rewards or punishments." *A Natural Theology for Our Time* (La Salle, Ill: Open Court, 1973), 108. See also 55, 106–25.

4. Fromm, *The Art of Loving*, p. 70. Fromm writes, "People capable of love, under the present system, are necessarily the exceptions: love is by necessity a marginal phenomenon in present-day Western society" (p. 111).

5. Ibid., 37.

6. Frank Lake, *Clinical Theology, A Theological and Psychiatric Basis to Clinical Pastoral Care* (London: Darton Longman and Todd, 1966), 179.

7. Ibid., 188; Fromm, *The Art of Loving*, 35, 36.

8. Fromm, *The Art of Loving*, 36, 68.

9. Ibid., 59.

10. Ibid., 53–61.

11. Thomas C. Oden, *Pastoral Theology* (New York: Harper, 1983), 9.

12. Lake, *Clinical Theology*, 180.

13. Ibid., 477–78.

14. Ibid., 477–78, 491.

Chapter 7

1. Philip Rieff, *The Triumph of the Therapeutic: Uses of Faith after Freud* (New York: Harper, 1965).

2. *Basic Writings of Friedrich Nietzsche*, 394–98.

3. Ibid., 526–27.

4. Paul Tillich, *Systematic Theology*, vol. I, *Life and the Spirit* (Chicago: University Press, 1963).

5. Alasdair MacIntyre, *After Virtue* (Notre Dame, Ind.: University Press, 1984), 30–31.

6. Abraham Maslow, *Self-Actualizing People: A Study of Psychological Health* (New York: Grune and Stratton, 1950).

7. "Religion and Peak-Experiences," *Philosophy of Religion*, ed. Norbert O. Schedler (New York: Macmillan, 1974), 531.

8. Ibid., 534.

9. Ibid., 533.

10. Rudolf Bultmann, "New Testament and Mythology," *Kerygma and Myth*, ed. Hans Werner Bartsch, trans. Reginald H. Fuller (New York: Harper, 1961), I:10, 19–34, 41.

11. Ibid., 4–5. See Cullmann, *Salvation in History*, 22; see also Karl Jaspers' rebuttal to Bultmann's claims about the possibility of believing in miracles today, "Myth and Religion," *Kerygma and Myth*, II:134ff.

12. "A Reply to Theses of J. Schniewind," *Kerygma and Myth*, I:117.

13. "New Testament and Mythology," *Kerygma and Myth*, I:26.

14. Tillich has shown how Martin Luther failed to appropriate the emphasis in Paul upon the life of the Spirit. Luther embraced Paul's doctrine of justification by faith, "but Luther did not take in Paul's doctrine of the Spirit." *History of Christianity*, ed. Carl Braaten (New York: Simon and Schuster, 1968), 230. However, Paul's concern was more focused on the need for freedom from sin rather than forgiveness of sins. See Krister Stendahl, *Paul Among Jews and Gentiles* (Philadelphia: Fortress, 1976), 82. This emphasis upon sanctification is the center of John Wesley's theology. See Tillich's perceptive discussion on how sanctification and the doctrine of the Holy Spirit were central in Paul's thinking, *A History of Christian Thought*, 317.

15. Rieff, *Triumph of the Therapeutic*, 41ff.

16. The classical formulation of the problem between faith and history is given by Ernst Troeltsch, *The Absoluteness of Christianity*, trans. David Reid (London: SCM Press, 1972).

17. See Kierkegaard's unique insights on this point, *Philosophical Fragments*, 16–27.

18. For a helpful but non-technical discussion, see Lesslie Newbigin, *Honest Religion for Secular Man* (Philadelphia: Westminster, 1966), 47–56.

Chapter 8

1. There is a tendency for some writers to play down the real importance of miraculous signs and supernatural gifts of the Spirit as evidence of the coming kingdom of God. Yet the Gospels certainly presented miracles as supporting evidence of the messiahship of Jesus. Typical of this tendency to suppress the importance of physical miracles in the Gospels is an otherwise helpful book by Gunther Bornkamm, *Jesus of Nazareth*, trans. by Irene and Fraser McLuskey with James M. Robinson (New York: Harper, 1960). For a recent and balanced discussion on the importance of miracles for faith, see Colin Brown, *Miracles and the Critical Mind* (Grand Rapids: Eerdmans, 1984).

2. Martin Kahler, *The So-Called Historical Jesus and the Historic Biblical Christ*, trans. Carl Braaten (Philadelphia: Fortress, 1964), 73.

3. Wesley, *Standard Sermons*, I:92–93.

4. Ibid.

5. A. E. Taylor believed that Socrates possessed the gift of tongues. See *Socrates* (New York: Doubleday, 1953), 45–46

Chapter 9

1. Michael Polanyi, *Personal Knowledge* (Chicago: University Press, 1958). See especially Polanyi, *The Tacit Dimension* (New York: Doubleday, 1967), 3–25.

2. Alfred North Whitehead, *Science and the Modern World* (New York: Macmillan, 1954), 18–19.

3. Pannenberg, *Jesus—God and Man*, 88–114.

4. For the best discussion of this problem which I have ever read, see Pannenberg, "Redemptive Event and History," *Basic Questions in Theology*, trans. George H. Kehm (London: SCM Press, 1970), I:15–80.

5. Pannenberg, *Jesus—God and Man*, 88–105.

6. Cassirer, *The Philosophy of the Enlightenment*, 182–96.

7. See Karl Jaspers' comments on this in his rebuttal of Bultmann's claim that the New Testament writers were myth-makers, in *Kerygma and Myth*, II:134ff.

8. A difference between the Orthodox and Pietist movements in the seventeenth century focused on the question of whether one has to be regenerated through the Spirit in order to interpret the Bible reliably. The Pietists said yes. See Tillich, *A History of Christian Thought*, 312–13. Wesley inherited his emphasis on experience in part from the Pietists.

9. Cullmann, *Salvation in History*, especially 84–135; Alan Richardson, *History Sacred and Profane* (London: SCM Press, 1964); Herbert Butterfield, *Christianity and History* (London: Collins, 1967).

10. Pannenberg's discussion of the meaning of the future as the key to understanding Jesus' teaching and life is superb. See especially his book *Theology and the Kingdom of God* (Philadelphia: Westminster, 1969); also see his essay, "What is Truth?" *Basic Questions in Theology*, II:1–27.

11. Pannenberg, *Theology and the Kingdom of God*, 52–67, 127–43; Alan Richardson, "Salvation, Savior," *The Interpreter's Dictionary of the Bible*, R–Z (1962), 171–73.

12. The classical exposition of the traditional view of God is best discussed in Mascall, *He Who Is* (Hamden, Conn.: Archon Books, reprinted 1970), 95–112.

13. Wilder Penfield, *The Mystery of the Mind: A Critical Study of Consciousness and the Human Brain* (Princeton, N.J.: University Press, 1975). For a detailed discussion of the religious implications of recent brain research, see Laurence Wood, "Recent Brain Research and the Mind-Body Dilemma," *The Asbury Theological Journal* (Spring 1986), vol. 41, no. 1, 37–78; reprinted in *The Best in Theology*, ed. J. I. Packer and Paul Fromer (Carol Stream, Ill.: Christianity Today, Inc., 1988), II:203–41.

Chapter 10

1. Paul Tillich, *Courage to Be* (New Haven: Yale University Press, 1952), 9–17.
2. Lake, *Clinical Theology*, 698.
3. For example, a widely known psychologist whose contribution to the subject of moral development has been considerable is Lawrence Kohlberg. His so-called "Seventh Stage" is simply an adoption of Spinoza's neo-Stoicism. See Lawrence Kohlberg, *Notes Toward Stage Seven, Social Sciences*, 154. Lecture transcript from Harvard University, January 2, 1975. The original lecture in December 1970 is appended. Presented to the B. L. Fisher Library at Asbury Theological Seminary by Professor Donald M. Joy, May 24, 1978. The fact that Kohlberg has little appreciation for the role of history in understanding the stages of moral growth reflects the bias of Stoic philosophy in general. It is interesting that "history" is the real foundation for becoming personally aware of the "I" of moral development, and that is why the personal first emerged from within the context of a historical revelation. It is ironic that psychologists emphasize the particularity of the "I" of human self-consciousness but reject the particularity of God's historical revelation which first made the "I" of personal development possible! There can be no "I" without the stages of a real history of the self. Moral reasoning, as Kohlberg proposes, cannot take place in a historical vacuum. We always reason from our own historical situation and development in life.
4. I am thinking particularly of John Cobb from Claremont School of Theology and Schubert Ogden from Perkins School of Theology.
5. A key to Whitehead's *Process and Reality*, ed. Donald W. Sherburne (Chicago: University Press, 1966), 190.
6. A summary of this information is given in John P. Newport, *Paul Tillich*, "Makers of Modern Theological Mind" Series, ed. Bob E. Patterson (Waco, Tex.: Word, 1984), 197–205. His wife gives a frank and unflattering account of Tillich's personal life, especially her revelations about his extramarital affairs. See Hannah Tillich, *From Time to Time* (New York: Stein and Day, 1973).
7. Tillich, *Systematic Theology*, I:244–46; II:5–7; III:422; *Courage to Be*, 184. Tillich praises Nietzsche because he refuted the idea of a personal God who possessed an independent reality of his own apart from the world, *Courage to Be*, 185. Tillich's concept of God as "personal" involves highly symbolic statements which make it questionable whether or not God for Tillich is personal at all. Tillich's god creates as we create him (*ST*, II:147); his god loves himself as we love him (*ST*, I:282); his god talks to himself as we talk to him (*ST*, III:120). Since his god has no independent reality apart from the natural world, it seems to be a meaningless statement for Tillich to say God includes the personal (*ST*, I:244).

8. Tillich, *Systematic Theology*, I:245. Hardly any writer has had more to say about the importance of the "personal" meaning of life than Tillich. Nor is he willing to omit the personal in his concept of God. Yet because God is clearly not an independent being in his own right and has no self-consciousness of his own so far as Tillich is concerned, Tillich says the idea of the personal is symbolic as it is used in reference to God. Tillich's concept of God is more of a Christianized Stoicism. One of Tillich's peers and fellow seminary professors was Nels Ferré who pointedly said that Tillich's god was impersonal because he lacked the quality of being "a self," as Tillich says (see *Systematic Theology*, I:244). See Ferré's critique, "Three Critical Issues in Tillich's Philosophical Theology," *The Scottish Journal of Theology* X (1957), 225–38. Ferré also makes the same critique in his essay, "Tillich's View of the Church," *The Theology of Paul Tillich*, ed. Charles W. Kegley and Robert W. Bretall (New York: Macmillan, 1964), 248–65. Tillich replied, "Mr. Ferré is aware that I have fought supranaturalism from my early writings on. . . . I still hold emphatically to this position which could be called self-transcending or ecstatic naturalism. Mr. Ferré is afraid that this attitude makes my idea of God transcendental instead of transcendent, that it prevents a genuine doctrine of incarnation, that it implies the negation of personal immortality, that it evaporates the independent character of the Church, that it denies a realistic eschatology. He is right. . . . All this is a supranaturalism against which my theology stands." Cited in Tillich, "Reply to Interpretation and Criticism," *A Theology of Paul Tillich*, 341.

9. Tillich, *Courage to Be*, 186ff.

10. Ibid., 189.

11. Ibid., 61–63, 113–90.

12. L. Mavis Hetherington and Jan L. Deur, *Young Children* (March 1971), 233–45. (I am indebted to Professor Donald Joy for providing me with this information.)

13. *Calvin Commentaries on the Epistle of Paul the Apostle to the Hebrews*, 92–101; Barth, *Church Dogmatics*, IV, part 4:39.

Chapter 11

1. The importance of a personal relationship with others in the process of learning is clearly demonstrated in Jesus' method of teaching his disciples; it was also effectively used by Socrates as a method of pursuing the philosophic life. That is why this conversational and dialogical method is referred to as the Socratic Method. For a brilliant discussion of this conversational method of learning, see Kierkegaard's *Philosophical Fragments*. This is not to minimize the importance of inductive and deductive logic, but thinking about the meaning of life is not something which can

be squeezed into a rationalistic methodology. Truth is more than just analysis; it is a synthesis arrived at largely through the filter of human experience. Of course this dialogical process includes deductive and inductive reasoning.

2. Wesley, *Standard Sermons*, II:343–59.

3. Tillich, *Systematic Theology*, I:3; II:84–85; *A History of Christian Thought*, 418–19, 430, 454.

4. Tillich, *Systematic Theology*, III:11–110.

5. Ibid., 147, 276; III:420–21.

6. Tillich presents God in a dynamic process of being actualized in the world out of his eternal and indeterminate Being-itself (*Systematic Theology*, I:241–82). God has no specific self as such (I:242). Hence, God loves himself as we love him (I:282); God creates himself through creating the world (II:147); and God talks to himself through us (III:120). Tillich's exposition of Hegel's thoughts express his own convictions as well: "God does not find himself in himself, but he comes to himself, to what he essentially is, through the world process, and finally through man and through man's consciousness of God. Here we have the old mystical idea that in man's knowledge of God, God knows himself and in man's love of God, God loves himself" (*A History of Christian Thought*, 417). Indeed if God "is not a person" (I:245) and if he is not a "thou" with self-consciousness, how else could he be known? Without being facetious, we could say that a cat doesn't know itself except as we know it. A cat then becomes "personal" because we have personalized it. That seems to be the case with the position of pantheism and process theology—except that somehow God is the basis of our being persons. This is the point which Nels Ferré makes when he contrasts religions like Hinduism and Buddhism with biblical religion, and he places Tillich squarely in their impersonal category in his interpretation of the reality of God (*The Scottish Journal of Theology*, 226ff.). Ferré puts it succinctly when he says that Tillich "actually did not believe in the Christian God who raises the dead and who works personally in human history" (Ferré, "Tillich and the Nature of Transcendence," *Paul Tillich: Retrospect and Future*, ed. T. A. Kantonen (Nashville: Abingdon, 1966), 8. Leonard F. Wheat argues persuasively that Tillich is more appropriately called a humanist because he really doesn't believe in a personal and transcendent God. Tillich's god, Wheat argues, is really humanity conceived as a whole. See Wheat, *Paul Tillich's Dialectical Humanism: Unmasking the God Above God* (Baltimore: Johns Hopkins University Press, 1970), 20.

7. Tillich agrees with the "protest of atheism" against the idea of a personal God who possesses a "self" of his own. "Ordinary theism has made God a heavenly, completely perfect person who resides above the world and mankind. The protest of atheism against such a highest person is correct" (I:245). Tillich agrees with Nietzsche's rejection of a personal God before

whom we should be "submissive" (*Courage to Be*, 29). Tillich thinks such a personal God would be emotionally crippling (ibid.).

8. Tillich, *Systematic Theology*, III:107–10.

9. Tillich, *Courage to Be*, 186f.

10. C. G. Jung, *Memories, Dreams, Reflections*, recorded and edited by Aniela Jaffe, trans. Richard and Clara Winston (New York: Pantheon, 1961), 90. In addition, Jung also mentions that his mother's inconsistency as a professing Christian had caused him at the age of six to experience a "growing religious skepticism" (p. 50). Only on the surface was she Christian, Jung says (p. 90). Jung also reports that the frequent angry scenes between his parents were emotionally damaging to him and subsequently also "shattered [his] father's faith" (p. 92).

11. Tillich, *Systematic Theology*, I:3–4.

12. Tillich, "Autobiographical Reflections," *The Theology of Paul Tillich*, 8. Wilhelm Pauck says of Tillich, "He felt deeply indebted to his father, a minister and high official of the Evangelical Church of Prussia. He never quite outlived the burden of authoritarianism he had encountered in his parent." See Pauck, "To Be or Not To Be," *The Thought of Paul Tillich* (New York: Harper, 1985), 32.

13. Ibid.

14. Ibid.

15. Ibid.

16. Mark Kline Taylor, *Paul Tillich* (San Francisco: Collins, 1987), 15.

17. Kegley and Bretall, eds., *The Theology of Paul Tillich*, 9–10.

18. Tillich, *A History of Christian Thought*, 332.

19. Tillich, *Courage to Be*, 29.

20. C. S. Lewis, *Surprised by Joy* (New York: Harcourt, 1955), 172, 228.

21. Ibid., 139.

22. Ibid., 21.

23. Ibid., 228–29.

24. C. S. Lewis, *Christian Reflections* (Grand Rapids: Eerdmans, 1967), 43.

25. Lewis, *Surprised by Joy*, 64f.

26. Ibid., 173, 228–29.

27. Tillich, *A History of Christian Thought*, 458.

28. Kierkegaard defines dread in reference to sin because dread is the feeling of the loss of any ultimate relationship and with this loss comes the feeling of "nothingness." Sin is the loss of relationship to a personal God; only through revelation do we therefore know that we are sinners. But with the awareness of the origin of dread in revelation comes the offer of faith and the establishment of a relationship to God. To be sure, paganism (which refers to anyone who does not know about or does not believe in a personal God who is distinct from the world of nature) lives in sin, but the consciousness of sin is developed through revelation. *The Concept of Dread*, trans. Walter Lowrie (Princeton: University Press, 1946), 23–46, 84, 86. See Lake, *Clinical Theology*, 704.

29. Kierkegaard, *Concept of Dread*, 32–46.

30. Kierkegaard, *Sickness Unto Death*, 96–97; *Philosophical Fragments*, 56ff.

31. Kierkegaard, *Concluding Unscientific Postscript*, 111ff. Kierkegaard emphasized the "difference" between God and man and our "unlikeness" to God because he wanted to preserve the personal character of God as an independent reality from the world of nature. Paganism confuses God with nature; only in revelation do we become aware of our difference from nature and of the distinctive meaning of the personal. This distinctiveness is the meaning of "spirit." See *Philosophical Fragments*, especially 46–67.

32. Lake, *Clinical Theology*, 721.

33. See Walter Lowrie, *A Short Life of Kierkegaard* (Princeton: University Press, 1951), for an interesting account of the formative events in Kierkegaard's life. For a stirring account of Kierkegaard's reconciliation with his father and the corresponding reconciliation with his heavenly Father, see pp. 118ff. Following his father's confession of love for his son and that his intentions to be a good father were often thwarted through his overly anxious desire to protect his son from the sensuality which had engulfed him, Kierkegaard wrote in his journal, "I learnt from him what father-love is, and thereby I got a conception of the divine father-love, the one unshakable thing in life, the true Archimedean point" (cited by Lowrie, p. 119). See Lake, *Clinical Theology*, 595, for his comments on the relation between Kierkegaard's life and thought.

34. Kierkegaard, *Philosophical Fragments*, 108.

35. Lake, *Clinical Theology*, 697.

36. Ibid., 478, 739–41, 935ff.

37. Some of the results of his tests were discussed in chapter 9.

38. Kierkegaard, *The Concept of Dread*, 37–41; Lake, *Clinical Theology*, 721.

39. Kierkegaard, *Concluding Unscientific Postscript*, 217–24, 329, 203.

40. Kierkegaard shows that only in revelation can we know that we are sinners and are not in proper relationship with a personal God. Real peace as release from dread comes in the forgiveness of sins. Forgiveness of sins means that we are related to God, but pantheism denies sin and attempts to construct a oneness with a God who is impersonal and thus no forgiveness of sins is possible. Pantheism seeks to construct a synthesis between God and the self immediately out of rational understanding. By denying the personal character of God, pantheism denies the meaning of personal existence. See *Sickness Unto Death*, 96–100, 117; *Concluding Unscientific Postscript*, 111, 202–03. Kierkegaard shows that apart from this relationship, we are not truly personal: "Essentially it is the God-relationship that makes a man a man" (*Concluding Unscientific Postscript*, 219).

41. Frank Lake sees a close relationship between Tillich's theology and the emotional state of mind which he calls the "schizoid position" (not to be confused with schizophrenia). The schizoid position is the life-orientation of those who are plagued with dread and compensate for it by retreating

from a personal view of the world into an intellectualized and pantheistic idea of the world. See *Clinical Theology*, 599, 555, 590, 608.

42. Lake, *Clinical Theology*, 179–81, 188–89, 418, 447, 555.

43. See Walter Lowrie's report on the stages of Kierkegaard's pilgrimage to God which culminated in a moving reconciliation with his father, *A Short Life of Kierkegaard*, 118–27.

44. Tillich, *Courage to Be*, 39.

45. Wilhelm and Marion Pauck, *Paul Tillich: His Life and Thought*, vol. I: *Life* (New York: Harper, 1976), 49–50.

46. Tillich, *Systematic Theology*, I:3–6.

47. Tillich, *Systematic Theology*, II:28; *Courage to Be*, 34ff. Tillich's writings contain numerous insights derived from psychoanalytical theory. See William R. Rogers, "Tillich and Depth Psychology," *The Thought of Paul Tillich*, 102–18.

48. Tillich, *My Search for Absolutes*, ed. Ruth Nanda Anshen (New York: Simon and Shuster, 1967), 74ff. See also John B. Cobb, Jr., "Past, Present, and Future," *Theology as History*, ed. James M. Robinson and John B. Cobb, Jr. (New York: Harper, 1967), 216.

49. Erik Erikson, *Young Man Luther* (New York: Norton, 1962).

50. Nehemiah Curnock, ed., *The Journal of John Wesley*, Standard Edition, (London: Epworth, 1909), I:476.

51. Ibid., 144.

52. John Telford, ed., *The Letters of John Wesley* (London: Epworth, 1931), V:16.

53. Umphrey Lee, *The Lord's Horseman* (Nashville: Abingdon, 1964), 212–13.

Chapter 12

1. A review of the literature in New Testament scholarship fails to show any significant writer who distinguishes among these various phrases, such as "filled with the Spirit" and "receive the Spirit." I have examined the writings of John Calvin, Rudolf Bultmann, F. X. Durrwell, Karl Barth, Alan Richardson, Ernst Kasemann, Oscar Cullmann, Joachim Jeremias, Markus Barth, and William Barclay. I have also researched the widely recognized New Testament commentaries. James G. Dunn says that there are no differences in the meaning of these different phrases, *Baptism with the Holy Spirit* (London: SCM, 1970), 56ff.

2. J. Baines Atkinson, *The Beauty of Holiness* (London: Epworth, 1953), 151ff.

3. Billy Graham, *The Holy Spirit* (Waco, Tex.: Word, 1978), 62–73.

4. F. F. Bruce, "The Holy Spirit in the Acts of the Apostles," *Interpretation*, 27:2 (April 1973), 176.

5. "A Discourse on Confirmation," *The Whole Works of the Right Reverend Jeremy Taylor* (London: Henry G. Bohn, 1867), III:14.

6. Ibid., 6.

7. Ibid.

8. John Wesley, *Works*, XI:306.

9. Ibid.

10. Fletcher, *Works*, III:171.

11. Ibid., III:177–78.

12. Ibid., I:575

13. Telford, ed., *Letters*, VI:137.

14. Luke Tyerman, *Wesley's Designated Successor: The Life, Letters, and Literary Labours of the Rev. John William Fletcher* (London: Hodder and Stoughton, 1882), 468–69.

15. Telford, ed., *Letters*, IV:300.

16. Fletcher, *Checks*, II:617.

17. Telford, ed., *Letters*, VI:137.

18. Wood, *Pentecostal Grace*, 182.

19. Ibid., 210ff.

20. Wesley, *Works*, VI:174–75.

21. Fletcher, *Checks*, II:617.

22. Karl Rahner, *A New Baptism in the Spirit: Confirmation Today* (Denville, N.J.: Dimension Books, 1965).

23. Wesley, *Works*, XI:306.

24. V. Raymond Edman, *They Found the Secret: Twenty Transformed Lives That Reveal a Touch of Eternity* (Grand Rapids: Zondervan, 1971).

25. Daniel Steele, *Half-Hours with St. Paul* (Boston: The Christian Witness Company, 1895), 305–06. I mentioned above that Fletcher's writings were standard reading for American Methodists even before the rise of the holiness denominations. Steele is an example of an American Methodist who was influenced by the writings of Fletcher (p. 3) and who at the same time tried to distance himself from the newly emerging holiness movement because it represented a split from the Methodist Episcopal Church. He implied that the revivalistic movement of "Palmerism in the East, and of Nazariteism in the West" might hinder the acceptance of Wesley's doctrine of entire sanctification among Methodists in general (Ibid., 287). Steele's larger concern was that "American Methodism has come near losing the doctrine of the fullness of the Holy Spirit as a blessing distinct from regeneration" (Ibid.). It is interesting that the Wesleyan-holiness movement adopted Steele as one of their greatest exponents even though he dissociated himself from the movement as it was emerging. I mention this fact because of a widespread notion that it was the Wesleyan-holiness movement apart from the mainline church which initiated a new style of holiness theology with an emphasis on the fullness of the Spirit.

26. Cited in Edman, 95–96.

27. Ibid.

28. E. Stanley Jones, *A Song of Ascents* (Nashville: Abingdon, 1979), 194–207.
29. Ibid., 52.
30. Ibid., 52–53.
31. Ibid.
32. Ibid.
33. Rahner, *New Baptism,* 7.
34. See an exposition of Barth's view of the baptism with the Holy Spirit in *Pentecostal Grace,* 50–54.
35. Barth, *Church Dogmatics,* IV, part 4:40, 42ff.
36. Ibid., 78.
37. Edman, *They Found the Secret, 86.*
38. Ibid., 153–54.